Sketches of Thought

Sketches of Thought

Vinod Goel

A Bradford Book

The MIT Press
Cambridge, Massachusetts
London, England

This book was set in Sabon by Compset Inc. and was printed and bound in the United States of America.

Library of Congress Cataloging-in-Publication Data

Goel, Vinod.
    Sketches of thought / Vinod Goel.
    p.   cm.
    "A Bradford book."
    Revision of the author's thesis (doctoral), University of
    California, Berkeley, 1991.
    Includes bibliographical references (p.   ) and index.
    ISBN 0-262-07163-0 (hc : alk. paper)
    I. Title.
BF316.6.G64   1995   95-3318
153—dc20   CIP

To the memory of my father,
R. G. Goel
and for my mentor,
J. R. Searle

Contents

Preface and Acknowledgments

This monograph chronicles the clash of a widely accepted theory of mind with some deeply seated intuitions that I hold about the richness and diversity of human symbolic functioning. The theory of mind under consideration is cognitive science's computational account of mental processes; the claim is that the mind is in part a computer and as such requires a representational medium—a language of thought—in which to represent information and to carry out computations. As Fodor (1975) notes: no representations, no computations; no computations, no theory of mind. But the Computational Theory of Mind is much more than a bland commitment to internal representations. It requires that the system of mental representation have some very stringent properties, properties that render thought processes precise, unambiguous, discrete, determinate, rigid, and so on.

The intuitions under consideration are that (i) thoughts often are imprecise, ambiguous, fluid, amorphous, indeterminate, and so on, and in fact, sometimes *need* to be so; and (ii) there is a close relationship between the structure of our thoughts and the structure of our symbol systems. If there is anything to these intuitions, then it follows that any system of internal representation must have the properties necessary to accommodate imprecise, ambiguous, fluid, amorphous, indeterminate thoughts. These intuitions are not freely voiced in the cognitive science community and betray my early training in, and empathy for, the visual and literary arts and architecture.

The clash arises because this seemingly innocuous intuition is incompatible with the Computational Theory of Mind. The whole explanatory apparatus of cognitive science literally breaks down if we try to accommodate the possibility of such symbol systems. This is an issue that, surprisingly, has escaped the notice of much of the community.

My resolution is to go as far as possible with the Computational Theory of Mind but no further. I think there is something right about the theory. I also believe that, at the moment, "it is the only game in town." However, this is no excuse for clinging to it blindly. We need to be aware of the source of its strengths and limitations and be prepared to modify and reformulate it as it becomes necessary. The general conclusion I reach is that our current notions of computation and representation will not do as much work for us as needs to be done. We need to reconstruct them in such a way that they can do justice to the full range of human symbolic activity.

The title of the volume is triply apt. First, the work claims that mental states have certain properties (those of being imprecise, ambiguous, fluid, amorphous, indeterminate, etc.) shared by the symbol system of sketching. However, it says nothing about pictorial and linguistic representations as these are generally construed in the cognitive literature. In particular, I am *not* interested in the depictional properties of sketches. I am interested in the fact that sketches are imprecise, ambiguous, fluid, amorphous, indeterminate, and so on, not in the fact that they may "resemble" what they refer to. Thus the claims made with respect to sketches apply equally to the linguistic forms found in poetry, song, and much of everyday discourse. Second, the work itself is sketchy and incomplete insofar as no alternative framework is offered, although the issues we need to confront to move ahead are identified. Third, the title alludes to Jerry Fodor's seminal monograph, *The Language of Thought*. It is this conception of mind that the volume addresses.

The character and style of the work is metatheoretical and interdisciplinary. I use both logical analysis and empirical methods as necessary and trespass on relevant areas of psychology, philosophy, design theory, and computer science. I view this as a strength of the work. Readers will undoubtedly draw their own conclusions. My intended audience is primarily the cognitive science community, but I hope that members of the design and artificial intelligence communities will also find something of value here.

The body of this work was completed in 1990–91 and constituted my doctoral dissertation in cognitive science at University of California, Berkeley (1991). It takes a very special place and some very special people to encourage and foster genuine interdisciplinary work. UC-Berkeley is such a place, and John R. Searle, Peter Pirolli, Brian C. Smith, Steve Palmer, Andrea diSessa, Alison Gopnik and J. P. Protzen are some of the people who make it so.

Each of these individuals played an important role in my program of study, but my greatest intellectual debt is to John R. Searle. From Professor Searle I learned that to engage in scholarship was not to be able to quote chapter and verse but rather to question, probe, and think for oneself. What's more, by example, he showed me what it was to think critically and clearly. Two of my greatest joys in life during my Berkeley years were strolling across the Berkeley campus and attending John Searle's lectures.

I am indebted to Brian C. Smith for bringing me to Xerox PARC and CSLI at Stanford University and supporting me for four summers. During this period I enjoyed a tremendous intellectual environment, excellent facilities, and, most important, complete freedom to pursue my interests in representation and computation as I saw fit. Brian made me aware of the complex and subtle intellectual issues surrounding the deceptively simple phenomenon of computation, and forced me to differentiate between cognitive science's characterization of computation and "computation in the large." I am concerned with only the former here and leave him to grapple with the latter. Brian also gets credit for the title of the volume. While at Xerox PARC, I benefited greatly from discussing the work of Nelson Goodman with Ken Olson and David Levy.

J. P. Protzen arranged for me to come to Berkeley. Peter Pirolli provided the administrative and financial support that enabled me to pursue an interdisciplinary program in the first place. From Peter I learned how to do empirical work. His unflagging support was crucial to the success of the project. In Steve Palmer I found a psychologist unafraid and aware of the deep philosophical issues surrounding cognitive psychology. Steve was the first to see a book in the dissertation and bring it to the attention of The MIT Press. I also benefited from the advice and support of Andy diSessa and Alison Gopnik.

These individuals, along with Gabriela Goldschmidt, Mark Rollins, and Mark Gross, read the original dissertation manuscript and offered encouraging words and valuable suggestions for improvement. I am indebted to each one. Now, if only I could hold them responsible for its shortcomings!

I am also indebted for an invitation to attend the Meaning Holism Seminar at Rutgers University, June 29–August 15, 1992, hosted by Jerry Fodor and Ernie LePore, and sponsored by the National Endowment for the Humanities. This gave me an opportunity not only to hear Jerry Fodor lecture on the language of thought but also to discuss it with him over the course of the summer. I hope my characterization does him justice.

On a more personal note, I am indebted to Susan Newman and Mimi Recker for the years of intellectual criticism, companionship, and friendship; and to my wife, Kalpna, for shielding me from many of the mundanities of human existence and making life more pleasurable than it otherwise would have been.

The dissertation was reworked into the present form during the summer and fall of 1993 while I was a Fogarty Fellow at the Cognitive Neuroscience Section, Medical Neurology Branch of the National Institute for Neurological Disorders and Strokes, at the National Institutes of Health, in Bethesda, Maryland.

Over the years I have been fortunate to receive financial support for this work from a number of sources, including the Myrtle L. Judkins Memorial Fellowship (UC-Berkeley, 1987–88), a Canada Mortgage and Housing Corporation Scholarship (Government of Canada, 1987–91), the Gale Fellowship (UC-Berkeley, 1990–91), an Office of Naval Research Cognitive Science Program grant (N00014-88-K-0233) to Peter Pirolli, and research internships at the Cognitive Science Institute at UC-Berkeley, the System Sciences Lab at Xerox PARC and CSLI at Stanford University (1989–92). It is a pleasure to acknowledge each source.

Some of the material in chapter 3 appeared in *Minds and Machines* (Goel, 1991); parts of chapters 4 and 5 appeared in *Cognitive Science* (Goel and Pirolli, 1992) and *Artificial Intelligence in Engineering* (Goel, 1994). Papers based on these three chapters were also presented at the Fourteenth Annual Conference of the Cognitive Science Society in Bloomington, Indiana (Goel, 1992a, b, c). I am grateful to Kluwer Press, Ablex Publishing, Elsevier Science Ltd., and Lawrence Erlbaum Associates, Inc. for permission to reproduce these materials. I would also like to thank Ablex Publishing for permission to reproduce figure 1 and tables 2 and 3 and to quote approximately a hundred words from page 70 of "Why a Diagram Is (Sometimes) Worth Ten Thousand Words" (Larkin and Simon, 1987) and Van Nostrand Reinhold for permission to reproduce figures 1-6, 1-18, 1-26, 2-30, 5-6 (a through d), 7-17, and part of 9-15 from *Graphic Thinking for Architects and Designers* (Laseau, 1989).

1

Introduction

If our psychological theories commit us to a language of thought, we had better take the commitment seriously and find out what the language of thought is like.

—Jerry Fodor

Much of cognitive science is based on the Computational Theory of Mind (CTM) hypothesis.[1] Loosely, the claim is that cognitive processes are computational processes and require a representational medium—*a language of thought*—in which to represent information and to carry out computations. There are several ways of arriving at this conclusion. One strategy, pursued by Fodor (1975), is to postulate computation on independent grounds and infer a system of mental representation. An alternate strategy, pursued by Fodor (1987) and Pylyshyn (1984), is to postulate mental representations on independent grounds and argue for computation.

Fodor (1975) argues that our best psychological theories of cognitive processes (such as decision making, learning, and perception) presuppose computation, and computation presupposes a system of internal representation. With respect to learning, for example, Fodor summarizes his argument as follows:

[A]s far as anyone knows, concept learning is essentially inductive extrapolation, so a theory of concept learning will have to exhibit the characteristic features of theories of induction. In particular, concept learning presupposes a format for representing the experiential data, a source of hypotheses for predicting future data, and a metric which determines the level of confirmation that a given body of data bestows upon a given hypothesis . . . . But to accept that learning which 'goes beyond the data' involves inductive inference is to commit oneself to a language in which the inductions are carried out. (p. 42)

The structure of this line of argument is this: no representations, no computations; no computations, no theory of mind (Fodor, 1975).

An alternative strategy for arriving at the same conclusion is to presuppose a system of mental representation and to argue that this necessitates a commitment to computation. Mental representations can be motivated and justified in one of several ways. One route, pursued in Fodor (1987), is to take seriously folk psychology's ontological commitments to mental representations and argue that a scientific psychology needs to preserve and explain this commitment. This line of argument has much to recommend it, and I employ it in the second chapter.

Another route to the same end, pursued by Pylyshyn (1984), is simply to ignore folk psychology and argue that only psychological theories that appeal to mental representations capture the right empirical generalizations. Strictly behavioral accounts—in terms of stimulus-response contingencies—are simply inadequate. This latter position differs from the former in terms of its metaphysical assumptions. Either way, once mental representations have been introduced, the idea is to postulate computational mechanisms and processes to explain certain recalcitrant properties of such entities. Rephrasing Fodor, we might summarize these forms of arguments in the following way: no computations, no representations; no representations, no theory of mind.

By either route, we end up with a commitment to representation and computation. One leads to the other. If this is indeed the case, then one of the major preoccupations of cognitive science needs to be articulating the structure of mental representations. As Fodor (1975) writes, "If our psychological theories commit us to a language of thought, we had better take the commitment seriously and find out what the language of thought is like" (p. 52).

Fodor's use of the locution "language of thought" (LOT) to refer to the system of internal representation is not just a metaphorical way of speaking. It is meant to be taken literally. The commitment is not to a natural language but to some sort of universal *languagelike* system of representation possessing many of the properties of not only natural languages but also formal languages, such as the predicate calculus.[2]

Most thinkers concerned with understanding human thought and actions think it perfectly reasonable, even necessary, to postulate a system of mental representations. The existence of symbol systems and the indispensable role they play in our cognitive functioning is a fact apparent to all. Imagine a life without natural language, mathematical systems, the various forms of painting, sketching, drawing, musical notation, and so on. It would not be life in our present sense of the word.

If one is impressed by human symbolic activity, one can not be oblivious of the fact that there exist many different types of symbol systems. For example, natural language seems to be a different type of symbol system than algebra or first-order logic, and each of these seems quite different from sketching and painting—though, of course, we may not be able to say how they differ. Furthermore, it is not unreasonable to suggest that these different symbol systems may serve different cognitive functions. So, the question arises: It is well and fine, perhaps even necessary, to postulate a system of mental representation, but why does the language of thought have to be a *language* (Kolers and Smythe, 1984; Kosslyn, 1983; Paivio, 1977; Shwartz and Kosslyn, 1982; Smythe, 1984)?

The general argument made in this monograph is that, not only does the Computational Theory of Mind require that the language of thought be a language, it also requires that it be a language with some very stringent properties—what I will call the *CTM-properties,* because they are entailed by the Computational Theory of Mind. The CTM-properties are introduced below and formally specified in chapter 3. For the moment let me simply say that they are properties that enable symbol systems to be rigid, precise, unambiguous, and determinate. I will argue that the Computational Theory of Mind is necessarily committed to these properties, and this in turn places much of human cognitive/symbolic activity beyond the explanatory grasp of cognitive science. We will find ourselves in the position of having to either drastically reduce the explanatory scope of the discipline or rework our notions of computation and representation so that they are not dependent on the CTM-properties. All this will take some doing. Before beginning, I need to acknowledge the successes of cognitive science, more fully articulate my concerns and driving intuitions, and establish a common vocabulary for talking about representations.

1.1   The Successes of Cognitive Science

Cognitive science has been an active and productive field of research for over thirty years. On many counts it has been a great success. It may now well be the predominate mode of inquiry into human cognition. During this period, progress has been made in a number of cognitive and perceptual domains, including linguistic competence (Chomsky, 1957, 1965, 1981), language processing (Schank, 1972; Winograd, 1973, 1983), vision (Marr, 1982), object recognition (Biederman, 1987; Warrington, 1982), visual imagery (Kosslyn, 1980, 1981; Metzler and Shepard, 1974), attentional mechanisms (Posner, 1989; Treisman, 1988) structure of memory (Anderson and Bower, 1973; Collins and Quillian, 1969; Baddeley, 1992; Craik and Lockhart, 1972; Tulving and Donaldson, 1972), organization of spatial concepts (Jackendoff, 1983, 1988; Lakoff, 1987; Olson and Bialystok, 1983; Talmy, 1983, 1988), learning and developmental mechanisms (Anderson, 1986; McClelland and Rumelhart, 1986a; Newell, 1990; Smith and Franklin, 1979), reasoning (Braine, 1978; Johnson-Laird, 1983), decision making (Tversky and Kahneman, 1974, 1981), and problem solving (Newell and Simon, 1972). I explicitly discuss only the problem-solving domain, although my conclusions are meant to apply more generally.

Problem solving—our ability to recognize dissatisfactory states of affairs and transform them into satisfactory states—is a fundamental human cognitive capacity. On most definitions, it requires at least the following conditions: (i) that there be two distinct states of affairs, (ii) that the agent be in one state and want to be in the other state, (iii) that it not be apparent to the agent how the gap is to be bridged, and (iv) that bridging the gap be a rational, consciously guided (at least at the top executive level), multistep process. Any theory of cognition will have to give a robust account of this process.

Cognitive scientists, working within the framework of Newell and Simon's (1972) Information Processing Theory, have accumulated an impressive body of data and theoretical constructs on human problem solving over the past three decades (Ernst and Newell, 1969; Evans, 1983; Newell, 1990; Newell and Simon, 1972; Reitman, 1965; Simon and Newell, 1958). The domains of investigation have included puzzle games, such as cryptarithmetic, the Moore-Anderson task, Tower of Hanoi, and chess (Newell and Simon, 1972; Simon, 1975; Simon and Simon, 1962); physics problems (diSessa, 1993; Larkin, 1981); mathematical problems (Ginsburg, Kossan, Schwartz, and Swanson, 1983; Heller and Hungate, 1985; Mayer, 1985; Schoenfeld, 1985); design and engineering problems (Akin, 1986b; Brown and Chandrasekaran, 1989; Eastman, 1969; Goel and Pirolli, 1989; Guindon, Krasner, and Curtis, 1987; Kant and Newell, 1984; Ullman, Stauffer, and Dietterich, 1987); computer programming tasks (Anderson, 1990; Anderson, Farrell, and Sauers, 1984; Jeffries, Turner, Polson, and Atwood, 1981; Kant, 1985; Pirolli, 1986); and even scientific discovery tasks (Kulkarni and Simon, 1986; Langley, 1979).

Within these domains researchers have explored a number of aspects of problem solving, including how problems are structured and prepared for solving (Akin, 1986a; Simon, 1973b), general-purpose strategies to search for solutions (Ernst and Newell, 1969; Laird and Newell, 1983; Newell and Simon, 1972; Simon, 1983), use of specialized knowledge to guide the search for a solution (Newell, 1969; Simon, 1967; Simon and Newell, 1958), problem representation (Hayes and Simon, 1974; Larkin, 1985; Larkin and Simon, 1987; Simon, 1978), structure of concepts (diSessa, 1988; Gentner and Stevens, 1983; Metz, 1985), learning mechanisms and processes (Anzai and Simon, 1979; Feigenbaum and Simon, 1984; Laird, Rosenbloom, and Newell, 1986b; Larkin and Simon, 1981; Rosenbloom and Newell, 1986), analogical mappings across domains (Anderson and Thompson, 1989; Carbonell, 1983, 1986; Clement, 1982; Vosniadou and Ortony, 1989), and cognitive differences between experts and novices (Larkin, 1985; Pentland, 1987). The overall achievement is quite impressive and a fitting tribute to the pioneering work of Newell and Simon.

I want to make it clear from the beginning that I think there is something *right* about much of this work. However, I also think that the wide-ranging applicability and success of cognitive science's theoretical apparatus, which one might infer from the above diverse list of cognitive domains, is largely illusory. The computational model of problem solving was developed in the context of "well-structured" puzzle problems and works best in these domains. In cases where it is applied to "ill-structured" open-ended, real-world problems, such as design, planning, and scientific discovery, the problems have been prestructured by the researchers to such an extent that it is not clear that anything substantive has been explained (Anderson et al., 1984; Kulkarni and Simon, 1986).[3] I articulate some of my concerns below.

1.2   The Worry

The general worry I have is that as we move away from circumscribed puzzle-game domains, like cryptarithmetic, into more open-ended cognitive domains, like planning and design, and continue in the direction of the arts (literature, poetry, painting, music, etc.), cognitive science's ability to explain the relevant cognitive processes approaches zero. It is not that the problems are simply more difficult, so there is a steeper incline, and we simply have to work harder and longer; we seem to be facing a vertical wall, suggesting that perhaps something qualitatively very different is going on here. My concern is that our failures to make headway in these domains have some very deep roots. I believe they follow from some structural properties of the language of thought, more specifically, the CTM-properties that I referred to earlier; the very same properties that provide the Computational Theory of Mind with its explanatory power, or so I argue.

This is not a worry commonly raised in the literature. In fact, the issue of the structural properties of the language of thought is rarely mentioned except for some notable foundational papers (Fodor and McLaughlin, 1990; Fodor and Pylyshyn, 1988; Smolensky, 1987a, 1987b). Many empirically minded psychologists and linguists would not even recognize this issue as a legitimate concern. Their attitude would be, who cares about the structure of the language of thought? We are interested in the structure of concepts, not the structure of the symbol systems in which they happen to be contained.

If pushed, most cognitive scientists would probably maintain one of the following positions:

1. There is no internal *symbol* system. There are only concepts. We can directly specify the structure and content of mental concepts.
2. One needs to recognize that there are different "storage formats" for different forms of information. Hence we need to postulate a dual coding scheme, one for propositional information and one for pictorial information.
3. There is a powerful, general-purpose language or symbol system that will allow us to represent all cognitively significant concepts.

The first view is very recent (Lakoff, 1993) and put forward to be incompatible with the Computational Theory of Mind, in which, on the classical reading, the motto is still "No computation without representation." This may change as our understanding of computation evolves. At the moment, however, it is unclear how the position is to be understood. I have nothing to say about it.

The second position, on the surface, seems to address the concerns I am raising and claims to be compatible with the Computational Theory of Mind (Kosslyn, 1980, 1981, 1983; Kosslyn, Pinker, Smith, and Shwartz, 1981; Kosslyn and Pomerantz, 1981; Kosslyn and Shwartz, 1977, 1978; Kroll and Potter, 1984; Paivio, 1977, 1986; Potter, 1976; Shepard, 1975; Shepard and Cooper, 1982; Shepard and Metzler, 1971; Snodgrass, 1980). As we progress, it will become clear that the issues addressed by this literature are largely independent of those that concern us here. We return to this literature in chapter 8.

By far the most pervasive position among cognitive scientists is the third, that there is some languagelike symbol system sufficient to encode all that is cognitively significant. This is actually quite an old view, traceable, at least, to Leibniz's dream of a *characteristica universalis* (Leibniz, 1684/1965):

If we had some exact *language* . . . in which the ideas were reduced to a kind of *alphabet of human thought,* then all that follows rationally from what is given could be found by a *kind of calculus,* just as arithmetical or geometrical problems are solved. . . . I think that controversies will never end . . . unless complicated reasonings can be reduced to simple calculations, and words of vague and uncertain meaning to determinate *characters.* (pp. 12–14)

This sentiment has been echoed this century by some of our most distinguished philosophers of language and logic, including Frege, Russell, Carnap, and Tarski. There is also consensus as to some of the properties this language needs to have. Two sets of properties are generally considered necessary. One set has to do with the expressive scope of the language, with capturing the structure of the world, the other with the mechanization of reasoning.

In terms of expressive scope, the primary requirements are that the language be discursive and have a subject-predicate structure. A discursive language is one in which atomic symbols are strung out sequentially.[4] It is needed because "only thoughts which can be arranged in this peculiar order can be spoken at all; any idea which does not lend itself to this 'projection' is ineffable, incommunicable by means of words" (Langer, 1942, p. 77).

The subject-predicate structure is thought to mirror the object-property structure of the world and is considered both necessary and sufficient to capture it. Russell can perhaps be taken as a spokesman for the group when he explains why all articulate symbolic activity must be of this form:

It may well be that there are facts which do not lend themselves to this very simple schema; if so, they cannot be expressed in language. Our confidence in language is due to the fact that it . . . shares the structure of the physical world, and therefore can express that structure. But if there be a world which is not physical, or not in space-time, it may have a structure which we can never hope to express or know. Perhaps that is why we know so much physics and so little of anything else. (quoted in Langer, 1942, p. 82)

The subject-predicate structure also subserves the semantic relation between language and the world, at least insofar as this relation is restricted to truth. It allows us to predicate properties to objects and state propositions that can be true or false.

The second set of properties, required for the mechanization of reasoning, constitute a subset of the CTM-properties and are of primary interest to us. Some of the candidate properties for this category are the following:

• Each symbol token must belong to at most one symbol type.
• It must be possible to tell which symbol type a token belongs to.

• Every symbol type must have the same referent in every context in which it appears.
• The classes of referents must be disjoint; that is, each object referred to must belong to at most one reference class.
• It must be possible to tell which class a particular object belongs to.
• The rules of transformation of the system must be well specified.
• The legal transformations of the system must be such that these properties are preserved at every state.

Why these properties are necessary for the language of thought will become clear by chapter 3, when we meet them again.

I accept that in certain cases these are useful, even desirable, properties of symbol systems. Some thought contents have this character and could be captured in symbol systems with these properties. A convenient example is provided by the game of chess. In chess, no tokens of the type 'rook' belong to the type 'queen'. Given the types 'queen' and 'rook' and a token of the type 'rook', it is possible to tell which type it does and does not belong to. No 'bishop' refers to a knight regardless of context and no pawn belongs to the class of rooks.[5] Given a king and two classes of objects, one can determine which class, if any, the king belongs to. Finally, the rules of transformation, or moves, are well specified. For example, there is no question as to what does and does not constitute a legal move for a bishop. So it would not be unreasonable to represent the thought processes involved in playing chess in a symbol system with the above properties.

I argue later, however, that these are not universally desirable properties of symbol systems, as the Computational Theory of Mind *must* claim. The resulting notion of symbol systems is too restrictive. The distinguished company notwithstanding, the implication of this line of thought is that thoughts/contents that can not be embodied in a language with such properties are *unthinkable*. This position relegates all human symbolic activity that lacks these properties to the "emotive cries of animals." It simply excludes too much. Most of everyday discourse, literature, poetry, mythology, music, painting, sculpture, and so on, must simply be dismissed as having no cognitive content. Do we relegate such works as Shelley's *Prometheus Unbound*, Debussy's *La Mer*, and Michelangelo's *Pieta* to the noncognitive dustbin or accept (contra the Computational Theory of Mind) that many symbol systems derive their power and usefulness by virtue of being vague, fluid, ambiguous, and amorphous?

1.3 The Intuitions

The basic intuition is that there is a close relationship between the structure of our thoughts and the structure of our symbol systems. If there is a system of internal representation—a language of thought—then thoughts with certain properties will require symbol systems with certain properties, and, more strongly, the properties of symbol systems will affect the properties of thoughts. As the structure of our thoughts changes, the structure of our symbol systems will need to change. Conversely, as the structure of our symbol systems change, the structure of our thoughts will change. Symbol systems are not passive/transparent structures on which to hang arbitrary concepts. They can vary quite radically in their structural properties. These properties, in turn, constrain and filter the character of our thoughts and concepts. There are no reasons to believe that there could be a privileged symbol system capable of expressing every possible human thought content, and many reasons to doubt it.[6]

The most obvious refutation of the prevailing claim—that a discursive symbol system with the CTM-properties is both necessary and sufficient to encode all human thought contents—is to assume that it is true and examine the absurd conclusions that follow. For example, if it were true, then we should, for example, be able to substitute a music critic's discursive description of Beethoven's Ninth Symphony, for the symphony itself, without loss of cognitive significance. The two should be interchangeable in the sense that after reading a complete, accurate description of the work one would know all there was to know about the symphony. We would not gain any additional *knowledge* by listening to the actual symphony. This is clearly absurd.

A similar point can be made with a less fanciful mathematical example. For two thousand years it seemed that Euclid was the final word in geometry. One of the great intellectual upheavals of the nineteenth century was the discovery that this was not the case. Euclidean geometry was but one of a large number of possible geometries, mathematically no more or less distinguished than any other. About midway through the century, Felix Klein proposed an elegant and novel way of thinking about and classifying geometries (Flegg, 1974; Medawar, 1974). Klein noted that a geometry—any geometry—can be thought of as an ensemble of geometrical properties that remain unchanged under a specific set of geometric transformations. Given this insight, it is possible to construct hierarchies of geometries, such as the following:

Oriented geometry
  Equivalence class   • Congruence and identical orientation
  Permitted transformations   • Translation
  Example invariant properties • Angle values, line lengths, number of
                                 sides, separation of plane surface into in-
                                 terior and exterior, perimeter length, area
                                 enclosed by perimeter, orientation with
                                 respect to some axis

Euclidean geometry
  Equivalence class   • Congruence classes
  Permitted transformations   • Translation, rotation and reflection
  Example invariant properties • Angle values, line lengths, number of
                                 sides, separation of plane surface into in-
                                 terior and exterior, perimeter length, area
                                 enclosed by perimeter

Similarity geometry
  Equivalence class   • Euclidean minus magnitude
  Permitted transformations   • Euclidean plus magnification/contraction
  Example invariant properties • Angle values, line lengths, number of
                                 sides, separation of plane surface into in-
                                 terior and exterior

Affine geometry
  Equivalence class   • Similarity minus angle and shapes
  Permitted transformations   • Similarity plus shear and strain
  Example invariant properties • Parallelism of lines, ratios at which
                                 points divide straight line segments,
                                 finiteness of configurations (no distinc-
                                 tion between squares and parallelograms,
                                 and between circles and ellipses at this
                                 point)

Projective geometry
  Equivalence class   · Affine minus parallelism of lines
  Permitted transformations   · Perspective and parallel projections
  Example invariant properties   · Straightness of lines, collinearity of
                                     points, concurrence of lines, finiteness
                                     of configurations, and cross ratios

Topology
  Equivalence class   · Projective minus straight lines
  Permitted transformations   · Projective plus elastic deformations
  Example invariant properties   · Neighborhood, interior/exterior, hole/no
                                     hole

While there are a number of interesting things to note here, the relevant point for our purpose is that it is possible to make and represent distinctions at the lower levels that the higher levels do not support. Similarly, it is possible to make and represent distinctions at the higher, more abstract levels that can be made at the lower levels only in a hidden or obscure fashion. For example, metric distinctions are preserved in Euclidean geometry but not in topology. And whereas every proposition of topology is trivially true in Euclidean geometry, topology does not come into its own until the system of representation abstracts away from metric and other details.

A third and more pertinent example for our purposes is provided by the domains of architectural, engineering, and graphic design, which fall somewhere in the middle of the spectrum between geometry and art. It is from design domains that I draw many of my empirical results and insights.

Design is an excellent forum for studying human symbolic activity in much of its richness and diversity. As we will see in part II, it involves a complex array of cognitive processes and a number of distinct symbol systems. We will also see that these different symbol systems are used in a particular sequence. That is, different symbol systems correlate with different cognitive phases (see figure 1.1), which in turn are associated with different cognitive processes. More specifically, natural language will be most prominent during the problem-structuring phase, whereas sketching dominates the preliminary-design phase. As one moves from preliminary design to refinement, the forms of sketching become more constrained, until they become a full-fledged drafting system during the detailing phase.

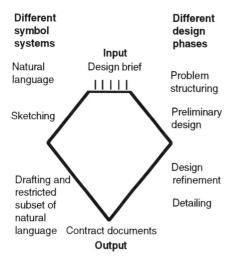

Figure 1.1
Correlation of different symbol systems and design phases

I will make the argument that these symbol systems have different properties that affect their expressive capacities and cognitive functions. We need to take seriously the structure of the symbol systems in which we construct, use, and communicate our concepts, and our theoretical framework must allow for the possibility that different thought contents may require different symbols systems for their expression.

In the foreword to his *Ways of Worldmaking,* Nelson Goodman (1978) expressed a similar intuition as follows:

I think of this book belonging in that mainstream of modern philosophy that began when Kant exchanged the structure of the world for the structure of the mind, continued when C. I. Lewis exchanged the structure of the mind for the structure of concepts, and that now proceeds to exchange the structure of concepts for the structure of the several symbol systems of the sciences, philosophy, the arts, perception, and everyday discourse. (p. x)

I am not proposing that cognitive science abandon its interest in the structure of concepts. Rather, my contention is that we can not understand human conceptual structure without seriously considering the structure of our various symbol systems. Having laid out my worries and intuitions, let me be more explicit about the form and structure of the argument.

1.4   Overview and Structure of Argument

Cognitive science is in the business of explaining intelligent human behavior. More specifically, it wants to explain cognition as symbol manipulation or information processing. But this will work only if we can first explain or discharge the notion of symbol manipulation (which, after all, is itself an Intentional notion). The cognitive science proposal is to consider symbol manipulation explained via computation, and once so discharged, use it to explain the rest of cognition. This discharge is dependent on certain properties of computational symbol systems that I call the CTM-properties. The general argument is that although this notion of symbol manipulation may be adequate to explain symbolic functioning in well-structured puzzle domains like cryptarithmetic and the Tower of Hanoi, it does not do justice to the data on symbol use in open-ended, ill-structured problem domains, which constitute the majority of human symbol processing. Many, perhaps most, of the problem-solving tasks we engage in require symbol systems with properties very different from the CTM-properties. I argue that human symbolic activity, in fact, ranges over a wide variety of symbol systems and that different symbol systems serve different cognitive functions. The main thesis can be stated as follows: While it may be true that traversal of a well-structured problem space[7] can be explained by postulating mental representations exhibiting the CTM-properties—as entailed by the Computational Theory of Mind—there are many ill-structured problem spaces where mental representations need to exhibit very un–CTM-type properties, in particular, properties associated with symbol systems of sketching.

This thesis makes several claims, some logical, others empirical. First, it makes the logical claim that the Computational Theory of Mind entails mental representations with the CTM-properties. Second, it claims that there is a principled distinction to be made between well-structured and ill-structured problems. This second claim turns out to have both a logical and an empirical component. Third, it accepts as an empirical fact that cognitive processes in certain problem spaces can indeed be explained by postulating mental representations with CTM-properties. Fourth, it claims—also as an empirical fact—that the cognitive processes in at least some ill-structured problem spaces can not be so explained. Fifth, it makes the empirical claim that these ill-structured problem spaces require postulating symbol systems with the formal/structural properties of sketching. And sixth, there is a logical claim that symbol systems like sketching do not have the CTM-properties and thus are incompatible with the Computational Theory of Mind. Each claim is problematic in its own right and will be argued for in the appropriate way during the course of the argument.

The monograph is organized into three parts, each with different subtheses and methods. Part I motivates and explicates the Computational Theory of Mind and shows that it is necessarily committed to mental representations with very stringent properties (the CTM-properties). It is suggested that while one may be able to explain the solution of well-structured puzzle problems by postulating such a stringent representational system,[8] there are many ill-structured problems whose solution requires mental representations that lack the CTM-properties.

Part II shows that there is a logical and psychological distinction to be made between ill-structured and well-structured problems and confines the subsequent investigation to ill-structured problems. An empirical study identifies some of the cognitive processes involved in one type of ill-structured problem solving (design) and points out that different cognitive processes are correlated with different external symbol systems. In particular, it is noted that the symbol system of sketching is correlated with preliminary design. The symbol system of sketching is classified with respect to the CTM-properties and is found to lack each one. Some predictions are made as to how this failure to satisfy the CTM-properties facilitates certain cognitive processes associated with preliminary design. In a second empirical study, the external symbol systems that subjects are allowed to use during preliminary design are manipulated along the dimensions of the CTM-properties. A number of predicted breakdowns occur. This leads to the conclusion that external symbol systems that lack the CTM-properties play an important cognitive role in the solution of some ill-structured problems.

Part III extends these results about external symbol systems to internal representations, by logical argument. It leads to the conclusion that accepting a cognitive role for external symbol systems lacking the CTM-properties requires postulating internal symbol systems lacking the CTM-properties. The Computational Theory of Mind can not however, accommodate such symbol systems. This leads to a general conclusion about the inadequacy of the theory (though not of computationalism in general) and a discussion of some promising avenues of research.

1.5   Historical Context

Like any intellectual endeavor, this work has not arisen in a vacuum. My intuitions and sympathies are clearly in line with the train of thought stemming from Peirce, Cassirer, Langer, through to Goodman, which recognizes both the importance of symbolic activity and the multiplicity of symbol systems. Indeed, much of the theoretical apparatus I introduce and use to explicate computation and sort out symbol systems is borrowed from the work of Nelson Goodman. It is perhaps worth retracing the main distinctive features of this stream of thought, noting its entry into psychology and explicitly pointing out what my approach adds to it.

This school of thought is distinguished by a number of themes. The first is simply the recognition of the cognitive significance of symbol systems. The second is the idea that symbol systems shape our concepts. A third theme is the recognition of the multiplicity of symbol systems and attempts at classification. However, the theme that sets this work apart from other work in the Anglo-American analytic tradition is a sensitivity to, and appreciation of, the fine arts and the recognition that they constitute genuine cognitive activity.

A number of these themes were exhibited in the work of Ernst Cassirer. Cassirer, drawing on the work of Uexkull, wrote:

Every organism, even the lowest, is not only in a vague sense adapted to (*angepasst*) but entirely fitted into (*eingepasst*) its environment. According to its anatomical structure it possesses a certain *Merknetz* and a certain *Wirknetz*—a receptor system and an effector system. . . . The receptor system by which a biological species receives outward stimuli and the effector system by which it reacts to them are in all cases interwoven. They are links in one and the same chain. (1944, p. 24)

Cassirer went on to acknowledge that the human world

> forms no exception to those biological rules which govern the life of all the other organisms. Yet in the human world we find a new characteristic which appears to be the distinctive mark of human life. The functional circle in man is not only quantitatively enlarged; it has undergone a qualitative change. Man has, as it were, discovered a new method for adapting himself to his environment. Between the receptor system and the effector system, which are to be found in all animal species, we find in man a third link which we may describe as the *symbolic system*. This new acquisition transforms the whole of human life. As compared with the other animals man lives not merely in a broader reality; he lives, so to speak, in a new *dimension* of reality. . . . No longer in a merely physical universe, man lives in a symbolic universe. Language, myth, art and religion are parts of this universe. They are the varied threads which weave the symbolic net, the tangled web of human experience.

Cassirer argued for a symbolic medium to mediate between the sensors and effectors on the insight that man does not respond to the environment per se, but to some complex interaction between the environment and the contents of his internal knowledge states. He painted a very rich, colorful, and compelling—but intuitive—picture of symbolic activity and went on to define man as an *animal symbolicum*. Although Cassirer acknowledged the rich diversity of human symbolic activity, he did not try to classify various symbol systems. This was left for Susan Langer and Nelson Goodman.

Langer (1942), a student of Whitehead, wrote a wonderful book entitled *Philosophy in a New Key,* in which, drawing from many disciplines, including philosophy, psychology, logic, linguistics, and music, she reaffirmed and illuminated the mind's incessant, insatiable need to symbolize, to find meaning in a meaningless world. But in addition to synthesizing and enlivening much of the work on symbolic form, she took a step that few with her training in the logical-analytical tradition dared to conceive. She argued that "there is an unexplored possibility of genuine semantic beyond the limits of discursive language. . . . Clearly, poetry means more than a cry; it has reason for being articulate; and metaphysics is more than the croon with which we might cuddle up to the world in a comfortable attitude. We are dealing with symbolisms here, and what they express is often highly intellectual. . . . The field of semantics is wider than that of language" (p. 81). Her own treatment of this unexplored semantic territory beyond language is wanting and has not survived the test of time.

Nelson Goodman, a logician and analytical philosopher with a keen, sympathetic eye for the arts, took up the challenge in his *Languages of Art* and raised the level of discussion by several orders of magnitude. His analysis of the structure, relationship, and semantic functioning of the various symbol systems of the arts is still the most sophisticated in the literature. We will have an opportunity to examine the theoretical apparatus at some length and use it in later chapters.

As cognitive scientists, our interest in this literature is twofold. First, we need to know whether the distinctions picked out by the theoretical framework—in particular the Goodman (1976) apparatus—have psychological reality, such that we can use them to inform and shape our inquiry into the structure of mental representations. Second, if the distinctions do have psychological plausibility, we need to know what follows for the Computational Theory of Mind.

The first question was the focus of several investigations, led by Howard Gardner, at Project Zero, Harvard University. Gardner and his colleagues applied the Goodmanian ideas to understanding symbolic functioning in both brain-damaged and normal children and adult populations (Gardner, 1982, 1983; Perkins, 1981; Perkins and Leondar, 1977; Wapner and Gardner, 1981). The results of their studies are suggestive but inconclusive. The second question does not seem to be addressed in the literature except for Kolers and Smythe (1984) and Goel (1991).

Unfortunately, both the philosophical work of Cassirer, Langer, and Goodman and the psychological investigations of Gardner and his colleagues have failed to attain the recognition they merit within cognitive science circles. I suspect there are various reasons for this. First, these researchers had no particular commitment to cognitive science and were not writing for this audience. Second, and more importantly, there is a degree of blasphemy involved in undertaking this line of research. The ideas involved are not only contrary to conventional cognitive science theory (i.e., the Computational Theory of Mind), they are downright hostile to it. So, it is not surprising that cognitive science remains blissfully oblivious of them. A third reason is the failure of researchers to specify the relationship between Goodman's theoretical apparatus and the Computational Theory of Mind. The specification of this mapping is a necessary precondition for establishing a communicative link between the two views of symbolic functioning.

I hope to further progress in this area by explicitly addressing the cognitive science community, making the connection between the Goodman theoretical apparatus and the Computational Theory of Mind, and arguing that although the results turn out to be incompatible with the Computational Theory of Mind, they need not be incompatible with computation per se. That is, we should view them not as a condemnation of computation in general, but only of some specific current notions, and seize the opportunity to explore alternative notions of computation and representation.

1.6   Representations: Establishing a Common Ground

The interaction that results when diverse disciplines struggle to understand a common phenomenon can be an exciting, heady affair. It is also fraught with danger. Different disciplines use different methodologies and vocabularies, which limits genuine cross-disciplinary communication. Worse yet, they often use the same vocabularies in slightly different ways and to mean slightly different things. This gives the illusion of communication and understanding. The vocabulary of representation clearly falls into this category. Every intellectual discipline dealing with cognitive agents has a legitimate claim on it. It is therefore worthwhile to take a few moments to introduce and discuss the vocabulary I use to talk about representations.

To begin with, 'representation' is a relational, two-place, asymmetric predicate, which we might write as follows: *R(s,w)*, where *s* and *w* are distinct entities and *s* stands in the relation *R* to *w* (but *w* does not stand in the relation *R* to *s*). So, in this respect, 'is a representation of' is similar to 'is a father of' but not to 'is red' or 'is a sibling of.'[9] This, of course, no more explains what it is to be a representation than it explains what it is to be a father or to be red, but it does serve to place certain important constraints on the relation.

To stand in a representational relation, or to be a representation, is, in the first instance, to be semantically evaluable. To be semantically evaluable, is to be *about* or to be *directed at* something. The world happens to be such that most things—rocks, trees, chairs, cars, mountains, galaxies, and so on—are not semantically evaluable. To ask the question "what does the Milky Way mean or refer to?" is simply to misunderstand the nature of galaxies. A few things are semantically evaluable; perhaps the most clear-cut candidates are certain human mental states characterized by Intentionality.[10]

Intentionality is that property of some of our mental states that allows them to refer to, or be directed at, states of affairs beyond themselves. Beliefs and desires are prototypical Intentional states. A belief is always a belief *about* something. A desire is always a desire *for* something. If someone has a belief or desire, there is always an answer to the question "what is it that you believe or desire?" The same holds for hope, fear, wishes, love, and so on. There is always a state of affairs at which these mental states are directed.

Although every Intentional state is a mental state, not every mental state is an Intentional state. Pain is an example of a bona fide mental state that is not an Intentional state. It lacks the aboutness feature. There is no distinction between the qualitative experience of pain and the pain itself. The qualitative experience *is* the pain. Nonetheless, since Brentano (1874/1970), Intentionality has been widely regarded as the "hallmark of the mental."

I will adopt the somewhat controversial position that the Intentionality of human mental states constitutes the core or prototypical case of representation.[11] All other semantic phenomena—speech acts, sentences, words, pictures, red traffic lights, a knock on the door, and so on—are presumably derivative from it in ways we have yet to fully understand. However, I will not assume that this is the exact or sole notion of representation at work in the theories of cognitive scientists. In chapter 2, I distinguish between several representational theories of mind. But I do believe that the Intentionality of mental states is the right place to start.

If we look to Intentional states to understand representation, we find a structure with two components, a "psychological mode," or "attitude," and the object or representational content of the attitude, typically depicted as *S(r)*. Philosophers variously characterize the structure as a "representational content under a psychological mode" (Searle, 1983) or a relation between an organism and the Intentional object (Fodor, 1981c).[12] Each Intentional state has what Searle (1983) calls a direction of fit and conditions of satisfaction.

The direction of fit is determined by the psychological mode and specifies primary responsibility for change in the case of a mismatch between the representation and the world. Beliefs have a mind-to-world direction of fit, so if there is a mismatch between a belief and the world, then the onus is on the belief to change to fit the world. Desires have a world-to-mind direction of fit. Here if there is a mismatch, then it is the world that must change. A desire can not be satisfied by changing your mind.

The conditions of satisfaction specify the conditions under which a belief or desire will be satisfied. They are determined by the representational content. Truth, although it plays an inordinately large role in semantic theory, is but a special instance of the satisfaction relation when the direction of fit is mind to world (i.e., for beliefs). But it is clearly not the only relation; desires are *fulfilled,* commands are *complied with,* questions are *answered,* and so on. Amidst their preoccupation with declarative sentences, and hence with the truth relation, twentieth-century philosophers and logicians of language have tended to forget this truism and needed to be reminded by Austin (1962) and Searle (1969). I think we should take this truism one step further and, following Goodman (1976, 1978), generalize the notion of satisfaction to the notion of "rightness" or "appropriateness."

I understand questions about the structure of Intentional states to be questions about the structure of *S(r)*. Questions about the structure of mental representations I take to be questions about the structure of *(r)*, where *(r)* is a token of a symbol belonging to some system. More accurately, they are questions about the structure and properties of the symbol system(s) to which the symbol tokens belong. Most computational cognitive theories make claims about the structure of *(r)*, so it is the structure of *(r)* that I am concerned with here.[13] Accordingly, I will introduce some vocabulary for talking about symbol systems.

The notion of a symbol system is at once a simple intuitive idea and a deep philosophical puzzle. Much of twentieth-century philosophy has been devoted to its explication. I offer a few orientating remarks.

To be a symbol is to belong to a system of representation. A system of representation, or symbol system, consists of a scheme, a realm, and a relation.[14] These basic components are diagrammed in figure 1.2.

A scheme is a purely syntactic notion. It can be characterized as a set of tokens organized into types, where the tokens are the individual marks or inscriptions and the types are character-indifferent marks or inscriptions, typically referred to as symbols, characters, or expressions. The terms 'marks', 'inscriptions', and 'tokens' are used interchangeably and are meant to encompass any physical occurrence that instantiates a symbol (e.g., the letter 'e', a stone, a dead fish, a grunt, and the weather pattern over San Francisco at time *t*). Depending on one's metaphysics, a relationship of instantiation or membership exists between marks and symbols (tokens and types). We can speak of marks, inscriptions, or tokens as instantiating a type (symbol, character, or expression), or we can speak in terms of symbols or types as equivalence classes of marks or inscriptions. In the latter case, the relation of membership holds. I employ the two vocabularies interchangeably.

The terms 'character', 'symbol', and 'expression' are used interchangeably. In particular, the term 'character' is not restricted to an element of the alphabet. It can be any symbolic expression from any symbol system, including language, music, and painting. Furthermore, the expression can be of any complexity, ranging from a single letter or

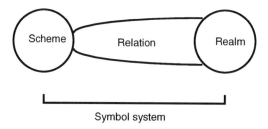

Figure 1.2
Basic components and relations of a symbol system

line to a complete novel or painting. Some—but not all—schemes differentiate between simple and complex expressions and allow for rules of composition that transform simple expressions into complex expressions. When this distinction is necessary for the discussion, we will speak of complex characters, symbols, or expressions.

Although the notion of a symbol (as a purely syntactic element) plays a central role in characterizing a symbol system, it remains an unexplained primitive. In particular, no guidelines are provided for individuating symbols, for recognizing and differentiating parts of the world that are symbols from parts that are not. All that can be said is that the symbols are given by the symbol system in effect. To know the symbol system is to know the symbols (and what they refer to). Although this characterization is less than satisfactory,[15] it will have to do for our present purposes. There are no completely satisfactory alternatives.

The realm is the part of the world structured and picked out by a scheme. If one is endorsing a purely external account of reference—which would be rather odd from a cognitive science perspective—the realm would be the world exclusive of mental contents. If one is endorsing a mixed account of reference (as most current theories do), then the realm could consist of either mental contents (or ideas) and/or the external world. As most symbols in a system are general terms, rather than proper names, they usually pick out or comply with classes of elements in the realm.

The relation or "connection" between the symbols and the realm varies depending on whether an extensional or intensional account is being advocated. In the extensional case, we refer to this connection as denotation or reference. In the intensional case, we talk about a symbol as having a content. I will use the term *compliance* to talk about this relation when I wish to be neutral with respect to the extensional/intensional issue.[16] I will refer to classes of elements picked out by a reference link as reference classes and classes of contents as content classes. When I wish to be neutral with respect to reference classes and content classes, I will speak of compliance classes.

The system as a whole, the scheme of symbols "connected to" or "correlated with" classes of elements in some realm (i.e., the syntax plus the semantics), constitutes a symbol system. These additional components and relations are depicted in figure 1.3.

This apparatus can be used to talk about both external and internal symbol systems, and we will have occasion to use it for both. However, notice that the apparatus objectifies the notion of a symbol system. This is perhaps appropriate when discussing internal symbol systems. However, in the case of external symbol systems, one must keep in mind that they do not exist independently of us. External symbol systems are parasitic on human Intentionality. They are generally given by precedent practices and always exist and function in societal contexts.[17] To talk of them as if they have an independent existence is not to deny any of this. It is simply not to inquire into the factors that shape and sustain them, but rather to focus on the resulting structures and relations of the systems.

Lastly, this is, of course, not a theory of representation. It is a minimalist view that can be made compatible with a number of different theories of representation. To actually have a theory of representation

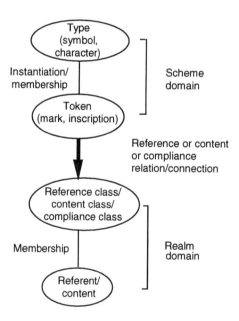

Figure 1.3
Additional components and relations of a symbol system

is to have answers to many of the following questions: (1) What types of entities occupy the scheme domain? (2) What are the various ways characters can be combined and manipulated in a particular scheme? (3) What types of entities occupy the realm domain? (4) What is it for a member of the scheme domain to refer to (or be true of) a member of the realm domain? (5) How does the manipulation of characters in the scheme affect the correspondence between the scheme and realm? (6) What types of reference relations can/should exist between the scheme and the realm? (7) How does metaphor work? (8) What do fictive labels (e.g., 'unicorn') refer to? (9) Why are some contexts referentially opaque? (10) In virtue of what is reference fixed? (That is, what are the roots of reference?) We return to several of these questions throughout the course of the monograph.

I

The Computational Theory of Mind: Metatheoretical Underpinnings

Mighty is the charm
Of these abstractions to a mind beset
With images, and haunted by herself,
And specially delightful unto me
Was that clear synthesis built up aloft
So gracefully; even then when it appeared
Not more than a mere plaything, or a toy
To sense embodied: not the thing it is
In verity, an independent world,
Created out of pure intelligence.

—Wordsworth

2

From Mental Representations to Computation

Truly the fabric of mental fleece
Resembles a weaver's masterpiece,
Where a thousand threads one treadle throws,
Where fly the shuttles hither and thither,
Unseen the threads are knit together,
And an infinite combination grows.
—Goethe (translation by Bayard Taylor)

2.1 Motivating a Representational Theory of Mind

Folk psychology has always known that the way to predict and understand human thoughts and actions is to assign to the agent certain beliefs about the world, certain goals or desires, and some measure of rationality. To assign beliefs and desires to an organism is to attribute mental representations to that organism. Such attributions are indispensable to our day-to-day functioning in the world. They allow us to accurately predict, with limited knowledge and resources, the thoughts and actions of our fellow creatures and to adjust our behavior accordingly.

The "folk" are not the only ones who freely make attributions of Intentionality. Intellectual disciplines, such as sociology and history, also make such attributions to agents and do so as part of their theoretical explanations. So, for example, Malcolm Gladwell, writing in the *Washington Post*[1] offered the following tongue-in-cheek explanation, from a Canadian/British perspective, of the cause of the American Revolution. I summarize a subset of his argument:

• The British desired to keep an army of 7,500 men in the colonies, believing it was necessary to ensure that the French and Spanish (whom they had just gone to such trouble to kick out of North America in the Seven Years' War) stay out. They also wanted to protect the settlers from the native Indians.

• The British, overextended from the Seven Years' War, thought it fair that the colonists contribute a very small fraction for the upkeep of the army—which after all was there for the colonists' benefit—and asked them to do so.

• The colonists—being peevish, ungrateful tax evaders—refused to contribute toward the defense and upkeep of the colonies.

• Most of the instigators of the revolution ("Founding Fathers") owed huge debts to British merchants. So in addition to evading taxes, they also hoped to avoid repaying these debts. ("If we now have to pay debts due to British merchants, what have we been fighting for all this while?"—George Madison)

• The colonists believed they could achieve both of these goals by breaking away from Britain. They also believed they could effect a break by declaring war, and they believed they could win such a war.

• Hence they declared war.

There are a number of important things to note about this explanation. The foremost for our purposes is that it utilizes Intentional vocabulary. The use of such vocabulary makes an ontological commitment to four distinct and independent factors:[2]

1. Persons or agents
2. A set of attitudes or psychological states (e.g., beliefs, desires, hopes, fears)
3. The propositional content of the psychological states (e.g., that we not be taxed)
4. An etiological appeal to the psychological state and its propositional content

The principal unit of analysis for folk psychology is thus the individual agent or person. There is a relatively small set of psychological states (e.g., believe, desire, hope, fear, shame) that are attributed to the agent, and there are an infinite number of propositional contents that these states can be directed at. The state and the content are etiologically implicated (against background assumptions of rationality) in the explanation of the behavior. So we say that x did y because x feared that p, hoped that p, believed that p, desired that p, and so on.

Until recently we used to apply Intentional vocabulary indiscriminately to the world by anthropomorphizing natural forces and appealing to the loves, joys, jealousies, and the like, of gods and goddesses. Even in Aristotelian physics, a falling object descended downward because it was *seeking* the center of the earth. Our great advances in the physical sciences followed when we learned that such attributions are factually incorrect. The world is simply such that rocks and trees do not have beliefs and desires.

Despite this, we do consider the above explanation of the American Revolution to be a genuine explanation of the phenomenon. Whether we agree or disagree with the specific content, the *form* of the explanation—particularly its utilization of Intentional vocabulary—is not in question. In fact, most of us would find an account that lacked such vocabulary uninformative. For example, a detailed description of the pattern of neuron firings inside the skull of every New World colonist may explain much, but it would simply not *explain* why the colonists revolted against the British.

This form of explanation is not problematic for the social sciences, because in explaining the behavior of social organizations they can accept Intentional states of agents as primitive, just as geology can accept water as a primitive notion and chemistry can accept atomic structure as a primitive building block. However, for a number of reasons, a scientific psychology does not have this option.

First, psychology needs to explain the mental states of individual agents. Intentional vocabulary has little or no explanatory value, because it simply replaces the mysterious notion of cognition with the equally mysterious notion of mental representation. A theoretically satisfying psychological explanation—like most scientific explanations—must reach down to the level below and *construct* the notion of mental representation by appealing to the entities and laws existent at that lower level; entities and laws that will presumably not themselves be Intentional.

Second, the scope of a scientific psychology is greater than that of folk psychology, and it is not clear how deep the folk psychology apparatus will go. That is, while folk psychology claims to account for the conscious rational behavior of cognitive agents, a scientific psychology must also account for irrational behavior of cognitive agents (such as that treated by psychoanalysts) and unconscious, automatic processes (such as those involved in perception, attention, and natural language processing) attributable to cognitive subsystems (as opposed to the agent).

The history of psychology over the past one hundred years can be viewed as an attempt to either vindicate or abolish the folk psychology ontology. One radical position is that, just as the attribution of Intentional vocabulary was found to be factually incorrect for the physical world, it is equally incorrect for human mental life and should simply be eliminated (P. M. Churchland, 1984; P. S. Churchland, 1986). A conclusion with similar consequences was reached by the behaviorists, but for different reasons.

Skinner (1953), for example, granted that there may be such entities as mental states, but since they were not available for third-party observation and direct manipulation, they did not constitute a suitable basis for a scientific psychology. Furthermore, if there were such things, they could be manipulated indirectly by manipulating the environment (for example, we can make an animal thirsty by depriving it of water for an extended period of time or by bleeding it) and measured in terms of behavioral response. So an appeal to mysterious mental entities is scientifically unnecessary and undesirable.

Yet another position, championed by Dennett (1987; 1978), is that in certain cases the attribution of Intentional states may have heuristic value in predicting behavior and, as such, is a perfectly appropriate thing to do; but when it comes right down to it, there are no facts of the matter as to the ontology of such attributions.

Cognitivists, on the other hand, have always argued that it is factually correct and necessary to ascribe Intentional states to agents (human or otherwise). Tolman (1932), for example, put the case thus:

But surely any "tough-minded" reader will by now be up in arms. For it is clear that thus to identify behaviors in terms of goal-objects, and patterns of commerces with means-objects as selected short ways to get to or from the goal-objects, is to imply something perilously like purposes and cognitions. And this surely will be offensive to any hard-headed, well-brought-up psychologist of the present day. And yet, there seems to be no other way out. Behavior as behavior, that is, as molar, *is* purposive and *is* cognitive. These purposes and cognitions are of its immediate descriptive warp and woof. It, no doubt, is strictly and completely dependent upon an underlying manifold of physics and chemistry, but initially and as a matter of first identification, behavior as behavior reeks of purpose and of cognition. (p. 12)

He went on to note that these purposes and cognitions play an important causal role in behavior: "We have sought to show that immanent in any behavior there are certain immediate 'in-lying' purposes and cognitions. These are functionally defined variables which are the last step in the causal equation determining behavior. . . . They are the last and most immediate causes of behavior" (p. 19).

I think it is reasonable to interpret folk psychology and many of the traditional cognitivists as endorsing what we might call the *Intentional Theory of Mind* (ITM).[3] The Intentional Theory of Mind places at least the following three constraints on a theory of mind:

ITM-Constraints on A Theory of Mind:
1. It should quantify over the attitudes and semantic contents of mental states.
2. It should causally implicate both the attitudes and semantic contents in the explanation of behavior.
3. The specified mechanisms and processes should be physically realizable.

These constraints ascribe psychological states or attitudes with a semantic content to the cognitive organism and require that these contents, along with the attitudes, be causally efficacious in the production of behavior. On this view, one might claim that genuine *cognitive* processes are just those processes involving Intentional states and their contents.

I think the Intentional Theory of Mind has much to recommend it, especially if one is dealing with conscious rational behavior. In fact, since Freud (1933/1965) it has also been marshaled to explain conscious irrational behavior. Seemingly irrational or unintended behavior can be rendered rational and transparent by postulating unconscious mental (Intentional) states, which are just like conscious Intentional states minus the consciousness, and causally implicating them in the agent's behavior.[4] It is the psychotherapist's job to bring these deeply repressed states to the surface so the agent can confront and deal with them.

Much current cognitive psychology studies unconscious, automatic processes—perception, language, attention, and so on—associated with subagents/subsystems. As discussed above, there is no introspective/phenomenological evidence for beliefs and desires and semantic contents, thus the need for the full folk psychology ontology, particularly the attitudes, is less clear. This results in two moves. First, the representations are postulated to be unconscious, but unlike Freud's unconscious states, which can be brought to consciousness with the therapist's help, they are, as a matter of fact, not accessible to consciousness. "As I am using the term, knowledge may be unconscious and not accessible to consciousness" (Chomsky, 1980, p. 12).

Second, if there are unconscious mental representations, it is not clear what types of attitudes would be associated with them. For example, it seems bizarre to think that the representation that the rule 'move alpha' operates over will be anything like a *belief*. Fodor (1987), for one, responds to this by noting that it would be a miracle if the folk psychology inventory of the attitudes was complete. So although it is unlikely that such representations will have any of the known attitudes associated with them, they will nonetheless have some—as yet undiscovered—associated attitudes.

However, most modern cognitive psychologists dealing with unconscious, subagent processes do not make a theoretical commitment to the attitudes. That is, in their day-to-day practice, they do not use psychological states, such as beliefs and desires, as theoretical constructs. By the same token, they do feel perfectly justified in appealing to the representational content of psychological states and implicating that content in the explanation of behavior. The position is that it is incoherent to assign attitudes to subagent processes and that one can get a perfectly good notion of representation by focusing in on the propositional content.

Here is an excerpt, selected from a prominent researcher in the field of visual perception, to illustrate the point:

In summary, my argument is that the 2.5-D sketch is useful because it makes explicit information about the image in a form that is closely matched to what early visual processes can deliver. We can formulate the goals of intermediate visual processing as being primarily the construction of this representation, discovering for example what are the surface orientations in a scene, which of the contours in the primal sketch correspond to surface discontinuities and should therefore be represented in the 2.5-D sketch, and which contours are missing in the primal sketch and need to be inserted into the 2.5-D sketch in order to bring it into a state that is consistent with the structure of three-dimensional space. (Marr, 1979, pp. 53–54)

There are several things to note here. First, the unit of analysis is the visual system, not the organism qua agent. Thus the primal and 2.5-D sketches are constructed by, and are useful to, the visual system, not the organism as a whole. They are actually quite inaccessible to the conscious, thinking organism. Second, both the primal sketch and the 2.5-D sketch are genuine representations with reference. For instance, "contours in the primal sketch correspond to surface discontinuities" out in the world. They can be semantically evaluated and be veridical or unveridical or true or false with respect to the world. Third, the representational content is attributed to the states of the system independent of any ascription of belief-desire psychological states. There is some mention of the "goal" of the system, but it is a device used by the theorist to communicate the explanation, rather than being part of the explanation. Fourth and finally, the system proceeds through the steps it does because it has a certain representational content and certain rules and procedures defined over that content. Thus the content is implicated in the behavior of the system.

This position leads to a modified, weaker version of the Intentional Theory of Mind widely known as the *Representational Theory of Mind* (RTM). The Representational Theory of Mind differs from the Intentional Theory of Mind in that it makes a commitment to the semantic content of mental states but not to the attitudes. The Representational Theory of Mind places the following three constraints on a theory of mind:

RTM-Constraints on a Theory of Mind:
C1. It should quantify over the semantic content of mental states.
C2. It should causally implicate semantic content in the explanation of behavior.
C3. The specified mechanism and processes should be physically realizable.

I will refer to these constraints as the ITM-constraints and RTM-constraints respectively. A theory that satisfies either of these sets of constraints I will call a theory of cognitive information processing.

I take both the Intentional Theory of Mind and the Representational Theory of Mind to be instances of representational theories of mind. Furthermore, I do not take the Representational Theory of Mind to be incompatible with the Intentional Theory of Mind, just weaker. The Intentional Theory of Mind will satisfy the RTM-constraints, but the Representational Theory of Mind will only be necessary, but not sufficient, to satisfy the ITM-constraints. When I write 'representational theory of mind' in lower case, I am referring to either or both instantiations. When I capitalize, I am referring to the version that satisfies only the RTM-constraints.

Outside of Fodor, who is perhaps the Intentional Theory of Mind's most eloquent proponent, the Representational Theory of Mind is the most widely held position in cognitive science. To maintain the generality of my arguments, I will assume the weaker Representational Theory of Mind and confine my claims to the structure of mental representations as opposed to complete mental states. The discussion thus far is summarized in figure 2.1. I will add to the figure (in figures 2.3 and 3.1) as the argument develops.

All this talk of representations and cognitive information processing, with or without the attitudes, is just loose talk so far. To render it useful for purposes of scientific explanations, one needs answers to a number of difficult questions. Among the more pressing questions are the following:

1. What type of entity is an Intentional object?
2. What is the relationship between a psychological state and its Intentional object?
3. What are semantic properties?
4. How is reference or content fixed or established?
5. How can state changes of a physical system preserve semantic properties?
6. How can a thought cause another thought or the movement of my body?

The Intentional Theory of Mind will have to answer all six questions while the Representational Theory of Mind need only worry about the last four.

It is at this point that modern cognitive science and the Computational Theory of Mind enter the picture. In the late 1950s several psychologists, linguists, and computer scientists (Chomsky, 1957; McCarthy, 1960; Miller, Galanter, and Pribram, 1960; Newell, Shaw, and Simon, 1957; Newell and Simon, 1956; Simon, 1956, 1961; Simon and Newell, 1958), working with computational ideas and mechanisms, noted that digital computers seemed to traffic in symbols just like cognitive systems. There is nothing mysterious about digital computers. After all, we build them and understand how they work. Perhaps they can provide some leverage in understanding the representational capacities of the mind. That is, maybe we can understand the information processing that cognitive agents do in terms of the information processing that computational systems do. In brief, the claim underwriting cognitive science is that we can discharge the notion of mental representation in terms of computation—which we presumably understand—and then proceed to legitimately use it as an explanatory construct without begging the question. This intuition lies at the heart of the Computational Theory of Mind. It is a wonderfully seductive idea if it can be made to work.

Much of mainstream cognitive science rests on the claim that the computer is not just another metaphor for cognition. And if it is a metaphor at all, it is the last metaphor (Johnson-Laird, 1983); more strongly, cognition *is,* in some literal sense, computation (Pylyshyn, 1984). On this account computation is a *necessary* condition of cognition. That is, cognition may be much more than computation, but it is at least computation.[5]

Actually, as the account is diagrammed in figure 2.1, there is not one but several overlapping versions of the Computational Theory of Mind. There is general agreement that the success of the enterprise depends on answering the above questions. There is even agreement on the form these answers will take. But there are differences in the importance placed on individual questions and a major difference of opinion as to whether computation does provide answers to questions 3 and 4. I will review and

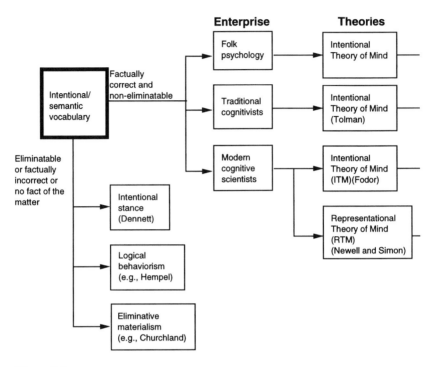

Figure 2.1
Motivating and explicating a representational theory of mind (see text)

compare the two major positions in the literature, Fodor's (1975, 1978, 1981a, 1981b, 1981c, 1987) LOT and Newell and Simon's (Newell, 1980, 1990; Newell and Simon, 1981) Physical Symbol System Hypothesis, and then introduce an alternate interpretation of the Computational Theory of Mind that I think is more reasonable and revealing. The reader should keep in mind that in sections 2.2 and 2.3, I am not necessarily endorsing the stated positions, but trying to accurately report them. I will offer my view of the Computational Theory of Mind in section 2.5.

2.2   Jerry Fodor: The Language of Thought

Jerry Fodor—perhaps the ultimate cognitivist—takes the whole apparatus of folk psychology very seriously and expects it to be substantially

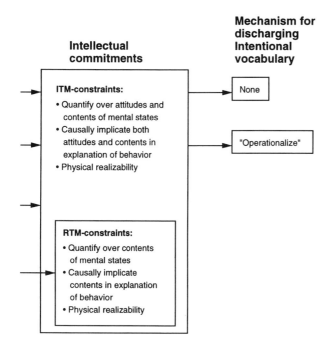

vindicated by a scientific psychology, and he sees cognitive science with its computational vocabulary as offering us just this possibility. His answers to the above questions take the following form (Fodor, 1975, 1981b, 1981c, 1985, 1987):

(1) *What type of entity is an Intentional object?* It is a formula in an internal language.

(2) *What is the relationship between a psychological state and its Intentional object?* Propositional attitudes are relations between organisms and formulas in an internal language, such that

For any organism O, and any attitude A toward the proposition P, there is a ('computational'/'functional') relation R and a mental representation MP such that MP means that P, and
O has A iff O bears R to MP (Fodor, 1987, p. 17).

Informally, to believe that p is to have tokened in your head (in your belief box) a mental symbol that means *p*.

(3) *What are semantic properties?* Computation does not explain what semantic properties are.

(4) *How is reference or content fixed or established?* Computation does not explain how the reference or content of a mental state is established.

(5) *How can state changes of a physical system preserve semantic properties?* The development of formal systems gives us insight into how the state changes of a physical system can preserve semantic properties. The significance of formal systems for our purpose is that symbols in such systems are formal syntactic structures. Their "content" is strictly a function of their syntax. Since syntax is an arbitrary property of the world that we use to individuate elements to which we will assign a semantical interpretation, it can be instantiated as some physical property (such as shape, size, or color). Now, as is well known, in a formal system, given an interpretation of that system in which the axioms are true, the purely syntactic rules of inference will guarantee the truth of the theorems under the same interpretation.[6] If the physical properties that instantiate the syntactic properties are preserved and propagated in the state changes of a dynamical system, then the semantic properties will also be preserved and propagated. This is generally expressed by saying that the operation of the system is sensitive to the syntax, or that "the semantics follows the syntax," or "if you take care of the syntax, *the semantics will take care of itself*" (Haugeland, 1981).

(6) *How can a thought cause another thought or the movement of my body?* If we have a physical system whose state changes can preserve and propagate semantic properties, we are on our way to explaining semantic causation. All we need to do is build a physical system whose operations/state changes are sensitive to the very physical properties instantiating the syntactic properties. In such a case, the symbols can said to be causally efficacious in the operation of the machine (see figure 2.2).

The claim here is that the explanation for the transformation or state changes of computational states (i.e., that the transformation process is sensitive to the syntactic properties of the states) also provides an explanation for the puzzle of semantic causation (Fodor, 1975, 1981, 1987). In fact the computational story seems to be the only one we have for connecting the semantic and causal properties of symbols.

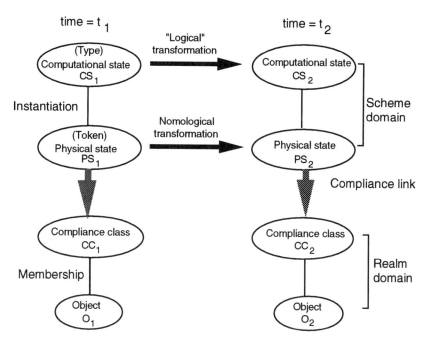

Figure 2.2
Information processing in computational systems

Computers show us how to connect semantical with causal properties for *symbols*. . . . [t]he machine is so devised that it will transform one symbol into another iff the propositions expressed by the symbols that are so transformed stand in certain semantic relations—e.g. the relation that the premises bear to the conclusion in a valid argument. (Fodor, 1987, pp. 18–19)

2.3   Newell and Simon: Physical Symbol Systems

Unlike Fodor, Newell and Simon are not explicitly concerned about vindicating folk psychology. They are, however, concerned with explaining the rational, conscious problem-solving behavior of human agents. They take two factors—*universality* and *symbolic behavior*—to be the key to human rationality. By universality they mean the wide variety of response functions people are capable of exhibiting in the face of changing environmental factors. By symbolic behavior they mean our ability to represent "states of affairs" and "goals." They argue that both universality and symbolic behavior are necessary for rationality, because

1. A rational agent must have some means of representing goals, and "[s]ymbols that designate the situation to be attained (including that it is to be attained, under what conditions, etc.) appear to be the only candidate for doing this." (Newell, 1980, p. 172)

2. A rational agent must have some means of representing candidate states of affairs that partially or fully satisfy the goals. Again, symbols seem to be the only viable candidate.

3. A rational agent must adjust its response to the demands of the environment. "As the diversity of tasks expand, i.e., as the intelligence becomes general, there would seem to be no way to avoid a flexibility sufficient to imply universality and hence symbols." (Newell, 1980, p. 172)

In sum, "(1) rationality demands designation of potential situations; (2) symbol systems provide it; (3) only symbol systems can provide it when sufficient novelty and diversity of task are permitted." (p. 172)

Over the past thirty years, Newell and Simon have developed the notion of a physical symbol system—a class of machines identical with general-purpose computing machines, such as virtual LISP machines—that they argue can simultaneously satisfy the constraints of both universality and symbolic behavior. They hypothesize that "humans are instances of physical symbol systems, and, by virtue of this, mind enters into the physical universe" (Newell, 1980, p. 136). Newell states the Physical Symbol System Hypothesis as follows:

Physical Symbol System Hypothesis: The necessary and sufficient condition for a physical system to exhibit general intelligent action is that it be a physical symbol system.

Necessary   means that any physical system that exhibits general intelligence will be an instance of a physical symbol system.

Sufficient   means that any physical symbol system can be organized further to exhibit general intelligent action.

General intelligent action   means the same scope of intelligence seen in human action: that in real situations behavior appropriate to the ends of the system and adaptive to the demands of the environment can occur, within some physical limits. (1980, p. 170)

Newell goes on to state, "The hypothesis takes as given the identity of symbol systems and universal systems, and asserts their connection to rationality, a concept which did not enter into their formulation. . . .

It can be taken as also asserting the essential role of human symbols in human rational behavior, if that cannot be taken for granted." (p. 170)

Their answers to our six questions take the following form: (1) *What type of entity is an Intentional object?* (2) *What is the relationship between a psychological state and its Intentional object?* While Newell and Simon do ascribe "knowledge" and "goals" to agents, their use of these terms is a little different than that found in the philosophical literature. For them, knowledge is just the representation of any "state of affairs" (not the philosopher's "justified true belief" notion), and goals are representations (or knowledge states) distinguished by the fact that they guide the computational search process. Given this, it is difficult to infer their position on the attitudes. On the most charitable interpretation, I think one would say that they do not make a commitment to the attitudes—certainly not to the relational view—and thus are not required to answer questions 1 and 2.

(3) *What are semantic properties?* (4) *How is reference or content fixed or established?* The major difference between Newell and Simon's position and Fodor's position regards how computation explains semantic properties. Fodor does not think that computation provides an answer to the questions of what semantic properties are and how they are fixed, only to how they can be preserved in the state changes of a physical system. Newell and Simon think computation does explain what semantic properties are and how reference and content are fixed. On their account, this is the single most important thing that computation explains. Perhaps more accurately, they think it is obvious what semantic properties are and that physical symbol systems show us how they can exist in the world.

They argue that physical symbol systems provide us with a general notion of symbol systems and a general account of information processing. In discussing physical symbol systems, Newell is careful to distinguish his notion of symbol from the various other notions in the literature, particularly those that depart from the logical tradition:

So far I have been careful always to refer to *physical* symbol system, in order to emphasize two facts. First, such a system is realizable in our physical universe. Second, its notion of symbol is *a priori* distinct from the notion of symbol that has arisen in describing directly human linguistic, artistic and social activities. (1980, p. 141)

But he also makes it clear that all human symbolic activity is to be encompassed by the type of symbolic processing engaged in by physical symbol systems: "[S]ystems that satisfy the constraint of universality also are capable of a form of symbolic behavior. The Physical Symbol System Hypothesis states in essence that this form of symbolic behavior is all there is; in particular, that it includes human symbolic behavior" (p. 141).

In the first chapter, I introduced some vocabulary for talking about symbol systems and a number of questions that one would need to answer to have a theory of representation. I think Newell and Simon's position would be that their notion of physical symbol systems provides an answer to the following five questions:

a. What types of entities occupy the scheme domain?
b. What types of entities occupy the realm domain?
c. What types of reference relations exist between the scheme and the realm?
d. By virtue of what is reference fixed?
e. By virtue of what is content fixed?

Scheme Domain   The scheme domain consists of equivalence classes of physical states to which computational states are assigned.

Realm Domain   The realm domain consists of sets or classes of (i) tokens, replicas, or instantiations of other computational states; (ii) "hard-wired" actions (such as read, write, assign, copy, delete); (iii) mathematical entities (such as numbers, functions, sets); and (iv) objects, states of affairs, actions, events, in the world external to the system.

Structure of Reference Link   In the case of atomic symbols, the reference link consists of computational pointers. In compound symbols or expressions, reference is a function of the reference of the constitutive atomic symbols plus the rules of composition of the system.

Fixing of Reference   The reference links in the cases of computational states and hard-wired actions are underwritten by genuine causal correlation. The reference links in the cases of mathematical entities and states of affairs external to the system are generally fixed by the programmer and thus left unexplained by this story. However, I suspect Newell and Simon would extend the story in the following way to accommodate the latter: Understanding what a symbol denotes in the external world is a matter of matching up, or setting up associations between, symbols in the "language of thought" and the symbols produced by the sensory systems in the "presence of the denoted things." That is, our sensory apparatus is a transducer system. It takes as input physical stimuli impinging on the surface extremities of the organism and produces "corresponding" or "associated" symbolic structures. These symbols are then linked to each other and to the other symbols in the "language of thought" via computational pointers. To the extent that reference to states of affairs external to the system can be explained by this story, it needs to be underwritten by causal correlation, as in the case of computational states and hard-wired actions. Finally, it is not clear how reference in the case of mathematical objects is to be explained by this story.

Fixing of Content   The content of a computational state is fixed by the network of causal reference links in which it participates.

This gives us a story about reference and content in a "static" symbol system (or a single time slice of an evolving system), as depicted in figure 1.2 in the previous chapter. We can extend it to a story of a system that dynamically evolves through time, as in figure 2.2 above, and get a notion of a computational information processing system. The difference between the two systems is the addition of the "logical" and nomological transformation links between the instantaneous descriptions of the systems.[7] The nomological transformation connects physical states that stand to each other in the lawful relation of cause and effect. The "logical" transformation connects computational states that are systematically related to each other. Although it is inappropriate to talk of causation at this level, it is appropriate to talk about some form of logical necessity, where the exact type of transformation varies with the type of system. For example, in the predicate calculus, this relationship would be derivation; in LISP, it would be evaluation.

(5) *How can state changes of a physical system preserve semantic properties?* (6) *How can a thought cause another thought or the movement of my body?* Newell and Simon's answers to these questions can be somewhat different than Fodor's above. The reader will recall that on Fodor's account, it was the syntactic properties of computational states that were causally efficacious (because computational states do not have semantic properties). However, since Newell and Simon are prepared to claim that computational states actually do have semantic properties, underwritten by causal relations, they can directly implicate the semantic content of these states in the production of behavior.

The Computational Theory of Mind   Sections 2.2 and 2.3 constitute a summary of how two prominent schools of thought in cognitive science think computation discharges some recalcitrant problems confronting a representational theory of mind. The cognitive science claim that cognition is computation is to be understood as the claim that the mechanisms that underwrite computational information processing are the very mechanisms that underwrite cognitive information processing. Given that there are differences in what computation does and does not explain, there are differences in the particulars of the claims, but as we will see below, they do appeal to identical mechanisms.

2.4   Critique of Language of Thought and Physical Symbol Systems

Having outlined two versions of the Computational Theory of Mind, the question arises, do they cash out the notions of reference/content and mental causation and make good on a representational theory of mind (the Intentional Theory of Mind or the Representational Theory of Mind)? There are a number of worries one should have in responding positively to this question. They all arise from one source: the status of the semantic properties of computational systems. On Newell and Simon's account, computational systems actually possess semantic properties and thus can explain reference and semantic causation. On Fodor's account, computational systems neither possess nor explain semantic properties but nonetheless give us an account of mental causation.

The fact that computation is being endorsed as a candidate to satisfy the RTM-constraints—on the one hand because it has semantic properties, on the other hand because it lacks such properties—should give us cause to worry. Both of these positions are problematic. I here offer a brief critique of them and propose what I take to be a more reasonable interpretation of the computational theory of mind. I will begin with the Newell and Simon position.

There seem to be important differences in the notions of reference and content as they are used in the case of physical symbol systems and in the human case. Reference, insofar as it is explained by physical symbol systems, is correlated with causation. But reference in general seems to outstrip causation. (I confess I do not know what this might mean). Certainly causal correlation is not sufficient for reference. For example, I can refer to the first human to walk on Mars without any obvious causal connections to him or her. Furthermore, there are some traditional problems with reference, such as context dependence, opacity, fictional discourse, and metaphor, that seem to have no counterpart in computational systems.[8]

There is also a difference between how the notion of semantic content is used in the computational information processing story and how it is used in the case of human mental states. In the case of human mental states, there is always, from the first-person point of view—independent of any third-person observer/interpreter—a fact of the matter as to what the content of a given mental state is. There is no such fact for computational states. The attribution of content is always dependent on, or derived from, human mental states. Furthermore, if the attribution of a content is withheld from the system, its dynamical trajectory remains unaffected, strongly suggesting that, unlike the case of human mental states, the "content" of computational states is causally inert or epiphenomenal.

There are several brave souls, in addition to Newell and Simon, who, for different reasons, choose to reject this distinction between human mental states and computational states (Dennett, 1987; Dietrich, 1994). However, this is not a serious option. I take the distinction to be self-evident and prior to argument.[9] I am not alone in adopting this position. I do not think most cognitive scientists believe that the notions of reference and content that we apply to human mental states apply *literally* to computational states. Most do believe that computation gives us something that—in some unspecified way—is *like* reference/content. So the question of interest is, if one accepts this distinction between the genuine reference/content of mental states and the derivative reference/content of computational states, then what exactly is the explanatory leverage provided by the Computational Theory of Mind? Before answering this question, let us have a quick look at Fodor's position.

The alert reader may have noticed an apparent inconsistency in Fodor's position. Both the Intentional Theory of Mind and the Representational Theory of Mind are supposed to give us laws (counterfactual supporting generalizations) that quantify over semantic properties. The computational solution to mental causation quantifies over syntactic (i.e., nonsemantic) properties. Stich (1983) and Devitt (1991), at least, have found this puzzling.

Fodor (1991) explains away the puzzle by clarifying that the Intentional Theory of Mind and the Computational Theory of Mind apply at different levels. The Intentional level of folk-psychology ascription is *implemented* at the purely syntactic/nonsemantical computational level, which in turn is implemented at the hardware level. The implementation relation itself is explained as follows:

[C]onsider a psychological causal law of the form *A-states cause B-states* where "A" and "B" expresses intentional properties. For present purposes, the implementation principle says: for each individual that falls under the antecedent of this law there will be some syntactic property AS, such that for each individual that falls under the consequent of the law there will be some syntactic property BS such that *AS-states cause BS-states* is a law. (Fodor, 1991, p. 284)

The Computational Theory of Mind is presumably offering us a mechanism that instantiates a particular solution. But the solution is for states that *lack* semantic properties. I suggest in chapter 3 that it is a very peculiar solution and there is no reason to believe that it is required for states that have genuine semantic properties.

2.5   An Alternative Interpretation of the Computational Theory of Mind

Returning to the question raised a few paragraphs ago, if one accepts that the semantic properties of computational states are derivative, what exactly is the explanatory status of the computational theory of mind? What work does it do? What intuition does it satisfy? I think that the classical cognitive science story rests on the intuition that certain types of computational systems can satisfy the RTM-constraints if the RTM-constraints are interpreted in the following way:

RTM'-Constraints on a Theory of Mind:

C1′. Interpret C1 as requiring (i) the ability to *assign* (at the initial state of the system, $t = 0$) a subset of the physical states of the system to computational states; (ii) the ability to *correlate* a subset of the computational states with compliance classes; and (iii) that once the assignments and correlations have been set up, one be able to look at the physical states of the system and systematically recover the computational states and compliance classes. To recover computational states means, minimally, that it is possible to identify equivalence classes of physical states and "read off" their values. In certain cases this value will be a pointer to another computational state or device. To recover compliance classes means, minimally, to trace through these pointers to the actual computational state or device being referred to.[10]

C2′. Interpret C2 as requiring (i) the ability to *maintain* the assignment and interpretation of the system as it evolves through time (i.e., given any instantaneous description of the system, one should be able to recover the computational states, the compliance classes, as above, and a pointer to the next instantaneous description in the sequence); (ii) that given a temporal sequence of instantaneous descriptions, certain physical states of the instantaneous description at t *cause* certain physical states or device activations at instantaneous description $t+1$; and (iii) that the computational story one tells of the system parallels the causal story.

C3′. Computation guarantees C3. (In fact it guarantees something much stronger than physical realizability; it guarantees *mechanistic* realizability.)

I will refer to these as the "RTM'-constraints." On the account I am advocating, they constitute *necessary* constraints on computational information processing systems. All my references to computation and computational information processing—unless I specify to the contrary—should be interpreted as references to systems that satisfy these constraints. These added complexities to the structure of our argument are summarized in figure 2.3.

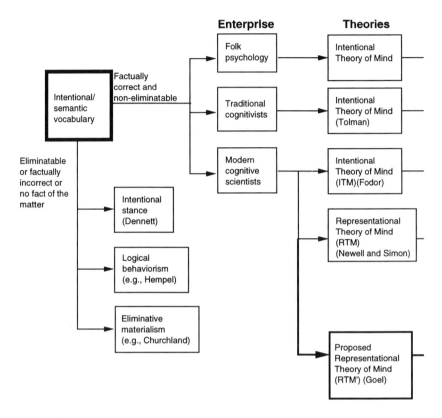

Figure 2.3
Alternative interpretation of the Computational Theory of Mind (see text)

The mapping between the RTM-constraints and the RTM'-constraints is not arbitrary. The connection is the following: In C1 (the case of human mental states) there is, from the first-person point of view, a fact of the matter as to the content of a mental state, independent of any third-person assignability and interpretability. There can be no such fact in the computational case. So C1' replaces this fact with another fact, that the system be such that a content can be systematically assigned to, and recovered from, a state of the system from a third-person point of view. C2 requires that the content of mental states be causally implicated in behavior. I take it that there is a fact correspond-

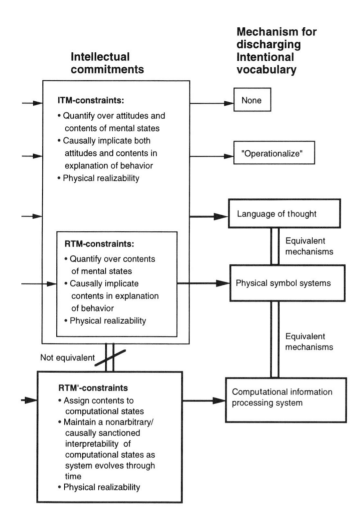

ing to this constraint in the case of human mental states. But there seems to be no such fact in the computational case. Again, C2' replaces this fact with the fact that the systematic assignability and interpretability of the instantaneous descriptions be maintained and that there be a parallelism between the causal and the logical levels as one traces the trajectory of the system. One might (loosely) view the move from the RTM-constraints to the RTM'-constraints as an attempt to trade in some troublesome first-person ontology for third-person epistemology. Such a move is not without precedent in psychology.

The satisfaction of the RTM'-constraints by certain computational systems is supposed to provide us with some explanatory leverage in understanding how the RTM-constraints might be satisfied. Very briefly, the claim is that the mechanisms that enable the satisfaction of the RTM'-constraints are also *necessary* (but not sufficient) for the satisfaction of the RTM-constraints. In the next chapter, I attempt to deduce some of the constraints that such a mechanism must satisfy and consider their implications for the structure of mental representations.

3

Entailments of the Computational Theory of Mind

First, the *collegium logicum*.
There will your mind be drilled and braced,
As if in Spanish boots 'twere laced,
And thus, to graver paces brought,
'Twill plod along the path of thought,
Instead of shooting here and there,
A will-o'-the-wisp in murky air.

—Goethe (translation by Bayard Taylor)

In the previous chapter, I introduced two versions of a representational theory of mind, the Intentional Theory of Mind and the Representational Theory of Mind, and suggested that cognitive science's unique contribution to the study of mind lay in its promise to deliver a theory of cognitive processes that satisfy the constraints associated with the latter (and perhaps the former). The reader will recall that these constraints involved quantifying over and explaining semantic content/reference and semantic causation. I then argued that it is simply a serious confusion to think that computation satisfies these constraints. I concluded by suggesting that the Computational Theory of Mind's notion of computational information processing satisfies only the epistemic counterpart of these constraints, what I called the RTM'-constraints. I now want to explore some of the consequences of this conclusion for the structure of mental representations.

3.1 Computational Information Processing Entails CTM-Properties

The RTM'-constraints entail some very severe consequences for the structure of the symbol system, and the mechanism in which the scheme is instantiated, which a computational information processing theory can postulate. Some requirements that *must* be met are the following:

CTM-properties:

CTM1. *Causally efficacious syntax:* Equivalence classes of physical states (i.e., computational states) must be specified in terms of some function of causally efficacious characteristics, such as shape or size.

CTM2. *Syntactic disjointness:* The equivalence classes of physical states that constitute computational states must be disjoint.

CTM3. *Syntactic differentiation:* Membership of physical states in equivalence classes that constitute computational states must be effectively differentiable, where differentiability is ultimately limited by physical possibilities and, more immediately, by our ability to devise sensory instrumentation. That is, for every physical state *ps* that does not actually belong to two computational states *cs* and *cs'*, it is perceptually possible (for the relevant mechanism) to determine that *ps* does not belong to *cs* or that *ps* does not belong to *cs'*.

CTM4. *Right causal connections:* Each state in the evolution of the system must be "causally connected in the right way." Although the specification of "causally connected in the right way" is obviously problematic, the intuition is reasonably clear. Certain physical states in the instantaneous description at t_n must be (directly) causally connected under the relevant aspect—where the relevant aspect is determined by the causal property used to individuate computational states (CTM1)—to certain physical states in instantaneous descriptions at t_{n-1} and t_{n+1}. The connection must be such that certain physical states at t_{n-1} cause or bring about (under the relevant aspect) certain physical states at t_n, which in turn bring about (under the relevant aspect) certain states at t_{n+1}, and so on. Furthermore, the transformation of the computational state cs_n at t_n into cs_{n+1} at t_{n+1} must be *realized as* the causal transformation of physical state ps_n at t_n into ps_{n+1} at t_{n+1}, where ps_n at t_n and ps_{n+1} at t_{n+1} are a subset of physical states of the system that are mapped onto computational states.

CTM5. *Unambiguity:* The correlation of equivalence classes of physical states (i.e., computational states) with compliance classes—within each instantaneous description of the process—must be unambiguous in the sense that each member of an equivalence class of physical states must be correlated with the same single compliance class in every occurrence of that instantaneous description.

CTM6. *Semantic differentiation:* The membership of entities in compliance classes must be effectively differentiable. That is, given any two computational states *cs* and *cs'* whose compliance classes are not identical and an object *o* that does not actually belong to both, it is perceptually possible (for the relevant mechanism) to determine that *o* does not belong to the class referred to by *cs* or that *o* does not belong to the class referred to by *cs'*.

CTM7. *Maintenance criterion:* The transformation of the system from one instantaneous description to the next must be such that the above six criteria are preserved.

I will refer to these as the "CTM-constraints" or "CTM-properties." The reader will recall that the term was informally introduced in chapter 1. Any system that satisfies all of these constraints will be referred to as a "CTM-system." References to "CTM-schemes" will be references to systems that meet constraints CTM1, CTM2, CTM3, CTM4, and CTM7', where CTM7' reads "the transformation of the system from one instantaneous description to the next must be such that constraints CTM1, CTM2, CTM3, and CTM4 are preserved."

Four of these seven constraints (CTM2, CTM3, CTM5, and CTM6) are derived from Goodman's (1976) theory of notationality. A summary of Goodman's original discussion and an explanation of the borrowed mapping is offered in chapter 7 when we reuse these constraints to sort out symbol systems.

CTM-systems play a very special role in cognitive science, because they are *necessary* for the satisfaction of RTM'-constraints on computational information processing systems. That is, if any of the CTM-constraints are violated, then some RTM'-constraint will be violated. For example:

A. If the individuation of equivalence classes of physical states is not disjoint (CTM2), there will not be a fact of the matter as to which computational state some physical state belongs to, thus thwarting the assignment of computational states to physical states. This would be a violation of C1' and C2'(i).

B. If the membership of physical states in equivalence classes of computational states is not effectively differentiable (CTM3)—regardless of whether the classes are disjoint—no procedure will be able to effectively make the assignment of physical states to computational states. For example, if the individuation of computational states is dense, then in the assignment of physical states to computational states, there will always be two computational states such that membership of the physical state to either computational state cannot be ruled out. This would also violate C1' and C2'(i).

C. If the correlation of computational states with compliance classes is ambiguous (CTM5), then there will be no fact of the matter as to the referent of any given computational state, and the systematic interpretability of the system will be impaired. This would violate C1'(iii) and C2'(i).

D. If membership in compliance classes is not effectively differentiable (CTM6), then no effective procedure will be able to specify which object any given computational state refers to. For example, if the compliance classes are densely ordered, then in the assignment of objects to classes there will be two classes for any object o, such that it is not effectively possible to say that o does not belong to one. This would violate C1'(ii, iii) and C2'(i).

E. If the computational states are not individuated causally (CTM1), then qua computational states they cannot cause other computational states or device activations. This is a violation of C2'(ii).

F. If the causal constraint is violated (CTM4), then C2'(ii, iii) will also be violated. This will lead to the absurd results that time-slice sequences of arbitrary, unconnected patterns (e.g., the conjunction of the physical states consisting of craters on the moon at t_1, the meteor shower on Neptune at t_2, the food on my plate at t_3, the traffic pattern on the Golden Gate Bridge at t_4,) qualify as computational systems. We will return to this point in section 3.6.

G. If at any instantaneous description of the system any of the above constraints are violated (CTM7), then at that point some RTM'-constraint will be violated.

Thus we see that a commitment to the Computational Theory of Mind is a commitment to a system that satisfies the RTM'-constraints, and that a commitment to the RTM'-constraints in turn is a commitment to a system that satisfies the CTM-constraints. This is the final step in the structure of our argument motivating and characterizing the Computational Theory of Mind. The complete argument is summarized in figure 3.1.

It is worth taking a moment to appreciate fully the consequences of this conclusion. The Computational Theory of Mind in effect is *necessarily* committing us to a system of mental representations (and mental states if one is endorsing the Intentional Theory of Mind) with the CTM-properties. The CTM-properties constitute a claim about the structure of mental states and representations. Among other things, all thoughts must be distinct, determinate, and unambiguous. There can be no room here for vague, ambiguous, amorphous, and diffuse thought contents and processes. Much of part II is devoted to showing that this is an undesirable restriction because many of our thought processes may need to be of this latter kind.

However, before moving on to this phase of the discussion, I would like to show that the Computational Theory of Mind's commitment to the CTM-properties is independent of the particular interpretation I have given it. So even if you accept Newell and Simon's (1980) Physical Symbol System Hypothesis, the resulting systems will still have to satisfy each of the seven CTM-constraints. Fodor's (1975) language of thought and Cummins's (1989) interpretational semantics (which we have yet to meet) *must* also satisfy a majority of these constraints.

3.2   Physical Symbol Systems Are CTM-Systems

We have already seen that the class of mechanisms that Newell and Simon appeal to when talking about computational information processing are physical symbol systems (Newell, 1980; Newell and Simon, 1981). In this section I argue that physical symbol systems do indeed meet the CTM-constraints.

In a physical symbol system, the physical states of the machine correspond to tokens and the computational states correspond to types. A function (which Pylyshyn [1984] calls an instantiation function) maps physical states onto computational states such that computational states are disjoint equivalence classes of machine states.

The mapping from the physical states to the computational states is determinate. That is, for any computational states, cs_1 and cs_2, and any single physical state, ps_1, if ps_1 does not genuinely belong to both cs_1 and cs_2, it is perceptually possible (for the relevant mechanical process) to determine that ps_1 either does not belong to cs_1 or does not belong to cs_2.

The causal constraint is also met. Certain physical states in the instantaneous description at t_n have "the right kind of causal connection"

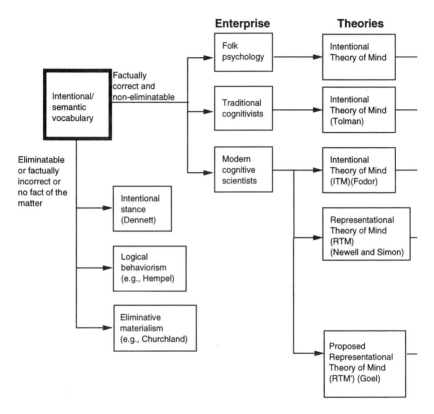

Figure 3.1
Entailments of the Computational Theory of Mind (see text)

to certain physical states in instantaneous descriptions at t_{n-1} and t_{n+1}. The transformation of the computational state cs_n at t_n into cs_{n+1} at t_{n+1} is realized as the causal transformation of physical state ps_n at t_n into ps_{n+1} at t_{n+1}, where ps_n at t_n and ps_{n+1} at t_{n+1} are a subset of physical states of the system that are to be mapped onto computational states.

The compliance link (computational pointer) in physical symbol systems is unambiguous. Every symbol has the same single compliance class in every instance, regardless of context. However, this is not an uncontentious claim. Some prominent computer scientists (Smith, 1996, forthcoming) insist that computation is fraught with context

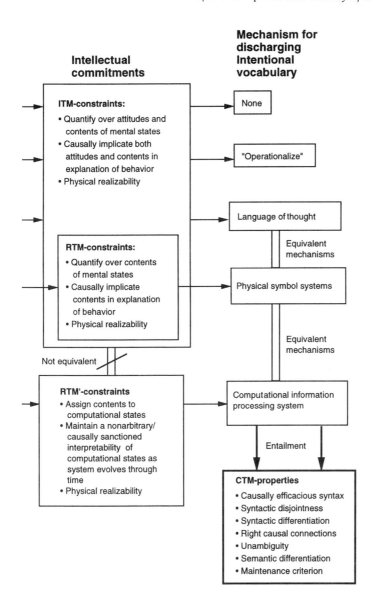

dependency and hence ambiguity. They point to the following types of phenomena to substantiate their claims: (1) When a function *f1* is called from inside another function *f2,* the two functions can use the same variables but give them different referents. For example, in function *f1* the variable *deviceJ* might be initialized to *printer1.* In function *f2,* the variable *deviceJ* might be reused but in this case be initialized to *plotter3.* So we would seem to have a case in which at the same point in time we have the variable *deviceJ* referring to either *printer1* or *plotter3.* (2) When you type 'mail' to your Unix system, it retrieves the messages that are *currently* on the queue, specifically, *m7, m8,* and *m9.* But when you gave the command yesterday, it retrieved the messages that were there *then,* specifically, *m3, m4, m5,* and *m6.* So we would seem to have a case of the same symbol having different referents depending on temporal context.

I do not think either of these cases is problematic. In the first case, the system is structured in such a way that it only has access to the variables associated with the function just called. The calling function is pushed lower onto the stack and momentarily inactivated. Thus there is no ambiguity. The second example is not a case of semantic ambiguity either, because all that the CTM-constraints required was unambiguity internal to each instantaneous description. This is all that is necessary because the interpreter evaluates the states at each instantaneous description; past and future ones are not considered. The mail example clearly reaches across instantaneous descriptions.

The membership of entities in compliance classes is effectively differentiable. Since the correlated objects are other states that have already passed the requirement of syntactic finite differentiation, semantic finite differentiation comes for free.

The transformation of the system from one instantaneous description to the next is such that the above five criteria are preserved.

Thus we see that physical symbol systems do indeed meet the seven constraints on CTM-systems. Indeed, it is CTM-properties that make physical symbol systems possible. The syntactic criteria (CTM2 and CTM3) allow us to assign computational states to physical states and collapse the distinction between the two. This means that we can manipulate the computational states by manipulating the physical states of the machine. The semantic criteria of unambiguity ensures that syntactic equivalence will entail semantic equivalence. Collectively, the two semantic criteria (CTM5 and CTM6) ensure that the system can always be systematically interpreted. When these criteria are preserved in the dynamical evolution of the system (CTM7), we can interpret the intermediate steps. When the two causal constraints are satisfied (CTM1 and CTM4), we can causally implicate the semantic content of the computational states in the explanation of behavior. It is by virtue of being CTM-systems that physical symbol systems satisfy the RTM'-constraints on computational information processing. As I indicated earlier, I do not believe they satisfy the RTM-constraints.

3.3   Fodor's LOT Is Substantially a CTM-System

I now want to show that the CTM-properties are a prerequisite for the LOT architecture that Fodor has in mind. Fodor and Pylyshyn (1988) focus on several crucial properties of cognitive systems, namely, the causal efficacy of mental states and the structure of mental states. In chapter 2 we discussed Fodor's solution to the problem of mental causation and saw how the syntactic solution it offered was dependent on the property of structure sensitivity. We will now look at the structure of mental states.

Fodor and Pylyshyn (1988) pick out four properties that the structure of mental states must satisfy—productivity, systematicity, compositionality, and inferential coherence—and argue that only a system with a combinatorial syntax and semantics can meet these constraints, hence LOT must have a combinatorial syntax and semantics.

The *productivity argument* says that the generative/understanding capacity of the human cognitive system is unbounded—but is achieved by finite mechanisms. One way of achieving this is with the recursive application of a finite set of rules to a finite set of primitive symbols, which results in an unbounded set of expressions.

The *systematicity argument* is that the human cognitive system's ability to "produce/understand some sentences is *intrinsically* connected to the ability to produce/understand certain others" (Fodor and Pylyshyn, 1988, p. 37). That is, learning a language is not the same as memorizing lists of words or phrases. (If it were, then it would be possible to understand "John loves Mary" without understanding "Mary loves John.") If you have mastered a language, there is a remarkable degree of systematicity in your ability to understand sentences in that language. Such systematicity is a mystery unless one assumes constituent structure.

The *compositionality argument* is related to systematicity. The argument is that a word "makes approximately the same semantic contribution to each expression in which it occurs" (Fodor and Pylyshyn, 1988, p. 42); thus the meaning of a complex expression is a function of the reference of the atomic symbols and the rules of composition of the language.

Finally, the *inferential coherence argument* requires that similar logical form be handled with similar inference machinery and entail similar consequences. For example, if we are prepared to infer P from P&Q&R, we must also be prepared to infer P from P&Q. Again, such a result naturally falls out of the classical architecture because "[t]he premises of both inferences are expressed by mental representations that satisfy the same syntactic analysis (viz., $S_1 \& S_2 \& S_3 \ldots \& S_n$); and the process of drawing the inference corresponds, in both cases, to the same formal operation of detaching the constituent that expresses the conclusion" (p. 47).

The claim in each case is that these are properties of mental states and are also properties exhibited by certain computational mechanisms by virtue of their combinatorial syntax and semantics, thus giving us reason to believe that LOT also has a combinatorial syntax and semantics.[1]

So a commitment to LOT is a commitment to a system with a combinatorial syntax and semantics and structure sensitivity of process. The task then is to specify the relationship between the seven CTM-constraints on computational information processing systems and the combinatorial syntax and semantics and structure sensitivity of process requirements.

An effective combinatorial syntax requires partitioning symbol tokens into nonoverlapping, differentiated symbol types; that is, it requires an alphabet. Without syntactic disjointness and finite differentiation (CTM2, CTM3) there can be no such alphabet, and without such an alphabet it would be senseless to talk about combinatorial syntax. However, it is quite possible to have a disjoint and finitely differentiated alphabet without further committing oneself to a combinatorial syntax. Without a combinatorial syntax it is senseless to talk about a combinatorial semantics. But it is possible to have a combinatorial syntax without committing to a combinatorial semantics.

The structure sensitivity of process requires that (i) character indifference (symbol equivalence) be a function of some causally efficacious property of physical states (CTM1); (ii) equivalence classes of computational states be disjoint (CTM2); (iii) computational states be effectively differentiable (CTM3); (iv) the causal constraints specified in CTM4 be met; and (v) the correlation of compliance classes with computational states be unambiguous (CTM5). Finally, if the combinatorial syntax, the semantics, and the structure sensitivity of process are to be maintained, then each of the above constraints must be maintained (CTM7).[2]

Requirements (i), (ii), and (iii) permit the collapse of the distinction between physical states and computational states. If we add requirement (v), we get a guarantee that syntactic equivalence will entail semantic equivalence. If we further add requirement (iv), we get an isomorphism between the computational states and physical states. Each of these is necessary for structure sensitivity of process.

So the conclusion is that CTM-systems constitute a necessary condition for LOT. But LOT only constitutes a sufficient condition for CTM-systems. Thus LOT is a CTM-system, but not every CTM-system is a realization of LOT. (This same relationship holds between physical symbol systems and CTM-systems.)

Thus both LOT and physical symbol systems are CTM-systems and, by virtue of being CTM-systems, qualify as computational information processing systems. But interestingly, they are not coextensive with CTM-systems. They are both subsets of the set of CTM-systems. This means that the CTM-properties are a more basic and less restrictive commitment for cognitive science than physical symbol systems or LOT. It also means we can coherently be committed to some form of computational information processing without being committed to physical symbol systems or LOT.

3.4   Cummins's Interpretational Semantics Requires a CTM-Scheme

I have introduced and elaborated a story of computational information processing that I think captures the intuitions and practices of much of the community. I have also shown that the system this story appeals to, indeed must appeal to, is a CTM-system. Cummins (1989) has a related notion of computational information processing that is similar in some respects and different in others. The task of this section is to show that Cummins's construal requires a commitment to a subset of the CTM-constraints.

Rather than speaking in terms of information processing, Cummins prefers to talk about computing functions. On his account, the claim that a certain cognitive capacity is a computational capacity is a claim that the cognitive capacity in question is a cognitive function from certain inputs to certain outputs and that the cognitive system computes this function. There are two obvious problems here. The first problem is simply, how does one individuate *cognitive* functions? The second problem is, what is it to *compute* a function? Cummins does not seem concerned about the first but does try to deal with the second.

Cummins distinguishes between function computation and function satisfaction. He recognizes that any physical system can satisfy functions (e.g., "set mouse traps satisfy a function from trippings to snappings without computing it" [Cummins, 1989, p. 91]) but wants to argue that not just any physical system can compute a function. Computing is to be explained as "program execution." Program execution reduces to "disciplined step satisfaction": "The obvious strategy is to exploit the idea that program execution involves steps, and to treat each elementary step as a function that the executing system simply *satisfies*. To execute a program is to satisfy the steps" (p. 92).

The steps must of course be satisfied in the right order, hence the need for the "discipline." But the discipline comes for free: "Functions satisfied by d specify causal connections between events in d, so if d satisfies f and g and if the current value of f is an argument for g, then an execution of the f step will produce an execution of the g step" (p. 92).

He suggests thinking of program execution in the following way:

Imagine the program expressed as a flow chart. Each box in the chart represents a step. To execute a step is to satisfy its characteristic function, i.e., the function specified by the input/output properties of the box. If you think of the arrows between the boxes as causal arrows, the result is a causal network with steps (i.e., functions to be satisfied) at the nodes. A system executes the program if that causal network gives the (or a) causal structure of the system. (p. 92)

What Cummins's account amounts to is the claim that there is some function and some device and that certain states and state transformations of the device can be *interpreted* as the variables and logical transformations called for in the program that executes the function. While I believe there are some serious problems in talking about computing functions,[3] the picture that emerges here is not unlike the picture in figure 2.2 in that there is an isomorphism between the states of the machine and the steps in some algorithm. But there is one important difference betweem the two stories. On Cummins's account there is no accompanying story of reference, either internal or external to the system. Thus the picture is actually more like the one in figure 3.2.

Cummins does not go far enough, however, in specifying the constraints on such a system. What are some of the properties that a system must have if it is to be interpretable in this way? What is it that makes "disciplined step satisfaction" possible and allows us to distinguish function computation from function satisfaction?

I want to suggest that any system that qualifies as computing a function on Cummins's account will have to meet a subset of the CTM-constraints. In particular it must be a CTM-scheme and satisfy constraints CTM1, CTM2, CTM3, CTM4, and CTM7′.

If the system fails CTM2 such that equivalence classes of physical states that are mapped onto computational states are not disjoint, there will be no fact of the matter as to which computational state some physical state instantiates. If there is no such fact, then there can be no mapping of that physical state onto a computational state. If the system fails CTM3 such that it is not possible to determine which equivalence

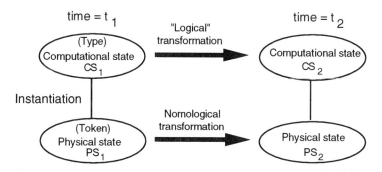

Figure 3.2
Cummins's picture of function computation

class a given physical state belongs to, then no procedure will be able to effectively make the assignment. If the system fails CTM1 and CTM4, then we will not get the "discipline" Cummins requires. If the system fails CTM7', then one or more of the above four constraints will be violated.

Notice that if Cummins were to incorporate a notion of reference into his story, then it would be identical to the physical symbol system story of computational information processing articulated in the previous sections and would then have to satisfy all seven of the CTM-constraints.

3.5   Recapitulation and Summary of Argument

I have argued that the Computational Theory of Mind is committed to mental representations that satisfy the CTM-properties. I have also mentioned in passing that this is often undesirable and have promised to address this latter issue in part II. The structure of the argument thus far is as follows (see also figure 3.1):

• To fulfill its promise, cognitive science needs to make good on a representational theory of mind.

• This means having a theory that can at least satisfy the RTM-constraints (and the ITM-constraints, on some accounts).

• Satisfying the RTM-constraints requires answering a number of difficult questions, including questions about semantic content and mental causation.

• The Computational Theory of Mind proposes to answer these questions by noting that certain computational systems traffic in representations, and there is no mystery about how they work. Perhaps the same principles/mechanisms underlie the mind's cognitive information processing capabilities. The substance of the claim associated with the slogan "cognition is computation" needs to be something like the following: The mechanisms that allow computers to traffic in symbols or to do computational information processing are the very mechanisms that underwrite the mind's representational or cognitive information processing capabilities.

• Computation cannot explain semantic properties and give convincing answers to questions about reference and content. Therefore, it cannot satisfy the RTM-constraints.

• Certain computational systems can, however, satisfy the RTM′-constraints, which are but a pale epistemic reflection of the original RTM-constraints.

• Computational systems that satisfy the RTM′-constraints do so by virtue of having CTM-properties or being CTM-systems.

• Therefore, the Computational Theory of Mind is committed to mental states or representations with the CTM-properties.

I have buttressed the conclusion by showing that it is independent of my particular interpretation of the Computational Theory of Mind. The standard stories in the literature, including Fodor (Fodor and Pylyshyn, 1988), Newell and Simon (Newell, 1980, 1990; Newell and Simon, 1981), and Cummins (1989), are also committed to the CTM-properties. This is not an accident. Computational accounts derive their explanatory power from the CTM-properties.

Before continuing, I want to consider one more argument in support of the CTM-properties. This line of argument suggests that vacuity may well be the price that computational theories have to pay for *not* conforming to the CTM-properties.

3.6   CTM-Properties Save Computational Explanations from Vacuousness

As we have seen, cognitive science theories quantify over the notion of computational information processing and use this notion in the explanation of cognition. I have suggested that on most accounts computational information processing is "as if." It is a matter of ascription. This results in a worrisome problem. Anything can be described *as if* it is doing computational information processing. If anything can be described as if it is doing computational information processing, then to explain cognition as computational information processing is not to advance a substantive thesis.

Searle has recently made the case as follows: Computation is defined syntactically. But syntax is not intrinsic to the physics. It is *assigned* to the physics by an outside observer. In fact, it can be assigned to any physical system. This is disastrous, because we want "to know how the brain works." It is no help to be told that "the brain is a digital computer in the sense in which the stomach, liver, heart, solar system, and the state of Kansas are all digital computers." We want to know what fact about brains makes them digital computers. "It does not answer that question to be told, yes, brains are digital computers because everything is a digital computer" (Searle, 1990b, p. 26).

The logical structure of Searle's argument is the following:

P1. Computation is defined syntactically.
P2. Syntax can be assigned to any system.
C.   Therefore, any system can be described as a computational system.

A number of other researchers have acknowledged the problem (Cummins, 1989; Dietrich, 1990; Fodor, 1975) but have not been overly concerned by it. In fact, much of the community seems to adopt the attitude that sometimes it is useful to describe a system as doing computational information processing and at other times it is not. When it is useful to do so, one should. When it is not useful, one should not. One might call this the utility reply.

A few researchers have appreciated the force of the objection. Chomsky (1980) for one accepts that if everything can be described as knowing and following certain rules (in our sense of doing computational information processing), then rule following is not a very interesting concept. But he thinks that not every behavior is, or can be described as, rule-governed behavior and that there is a fact of the matter as to whether something falls (or does not fall) into this category. He raises the objection and responds to it in the following way:[4]

True, there would be little point to a concept of "cognizing" that did not distinguish "cognizing the rules of grammar" from the bicycle rider's knowing that he should push the pedals or lean into a curve, given what we assume to be the facts of the matter. But it seems easy enough to make the relevant distinction. In the case of riding a bicycle, there is no reason to suppose that the rules in question are represented in a cognitive structure of anything like the sort I have described. Rather, we take bicycle riding to be a skill . . . based on certain reflex systems, in which case it would be incorrect to attribute a cognitive structure . . . to the person who exercises the skill. . . . [N]othing seems to be explained by attributing to the bicycle rider a cognitive structure incorporating the rules with which his practice accords. But suppose we are wrong, and in fact the bicycle rider does have a representation of certain physical principles in his mind and uses them to plan or compute his next act. In this case we should attribute to him a cognitive structure, and in fact, it would be quite appropriate to say that he cognizes these principles as he does the rules of his language. The question, I take it, is basically one of fact.

To help clarify the issue, consider two missile systems, each of which is designed to send a rocket to the moon. One of them operates along lines once proposed by B. F. Skinner; it has several pigeons looking at a screen that depicts what lies directly ahead, trained to peck when the rocket veers off course, their pecking restoring the image of the moon to a focused position on the screen. Consider, in contrast, a system that incorporates an explicit theory of the motions of the heavenly bodies and information about its initial position and velocity and that carries out measurements and computations using its internalized theory to adjust its course as it proceeds. . . . [Although the two systems may be behaviorally equivalent] [i]n the second case, but not in the first, inquiry might lead us to attribute to the missile something like a "mental state." . . . In the first case, such an account would be factually wrong. I think that the two cases fall on opposite sides of an important divide. (Chomsky, 1980, pp. 10–11)

Although Chomsky has some suggestive intuitions here, he does not really provide us with explicit criteria to distinguish between the two cases. Many questions remain. What facts about the second case differentiate it from the first case such that we can claim it is doing computational information processing (or "cognizing" or "rule following," in Chomsky's vocabulary) and attribute "something like a 'mental state' " to it? Is there a principled "divide" between systems that do computational information processing (and satisfy the RTM′-constraints) and systems that do not? If so, what is the basis of the divide? If not, what is the explanatory force of the notion?

I think the concerns raised by Searle (1984; 1990b) are legitimate and should worry us. The ideal response would be to claim that computational information processing traffics in genuine Intentionality and satisfies the RTM-constraints, and is thus immune to the difficulty. Unfortunately, this option does not exist. The next best move is to claim that computational information processing is based on the RTM′-constraints, which in turn entail the CTM-constraints, and respond to Searle as follows: We can grant the intuitions about the free assignment of syntax. But we need to insist that, contrary to (P1), the notion of syntax, while necessary, is not sufficient for the notion of computation that we use in classical cognitive science. The CTM-constraints also require notions of causation and interpretability, and these notions in turn place stringent restrictions on the assignment of syntax to physical systems for purposes of describing them as computational systems. If there is more to computation than syntax, then from the fact that syntax can be assigned to any system (P2), little of interest about computation follows.

Are the CTM-constraints adequate for this purpose? Do they provide the principled divide that is needed to differentiate between dynamical systems to which we can attribute "something like a mental state" and dynamical systems to which we cannot? Are they adequate to ensure that not every physical system is a computational information processing system and that there is indeed a fact of the matter as to whether some system is or is not a computational information processing system?

I think (in the absence of genuine Intentionality) they are certainly *necessary* for this purpose; whether they are *sufficient* depends on how unique a fact one requires. There is a case to be made that the class of CTM-systems is not coextensive with the class of dynamical systems. Whereas every CTM-scheme or CTM-system is a dynamical system, not every dynamical system, under the relevant analysis, is a CTM-scheme or CTM-system. CTM-schemes and CTM-systems are proper subsets of dynamical systems.

What would it mean for the class of CTM-systems to be a subset of dynamical systems? It means, at least in part, that the physical/causal story one tells of some dynamical systems meets the CTM-constraints and that there are dynamical systems whose physical/causal story violates one or more of the CTM-constraints. So the question becomes, is there a fact of the matter as to whether a given dynamical system meets the constraints for CTM-schemes or CTM-systems? I will argue that in the case of CTM-schemes there is such a fact relative to an individuation of computational states. In the case of CTM-systems, there is such a fact relative to an interpretation of the computational states. Such facts exist because both the individuation and the interpretation of computational states are constrained by the physical/causal structure of the system.

Let us take a particular dynamical system—for example, the solar system—and ask whether it is a computational information processing system. If we accept the physical/causal story given by Newtonian mechanics—which recognizes things like planets, gravitational force, and the shape of orbits—and use it to individuate the states and transformations of the systems (which are mapped onto computational states and transformations), our question becomes something like, do the orbits of the planets around the sun constitute a computational information processing system? I think one can unproblematically say they do not. For one thing, the instantaneous descriptions of the system will be densely ordered and thus violate the effective-differentiability constraints.

Of course it is possible to take the solar system and individuate components and relations in such a way that the CTM-constraints are met. For example, a colleague suggested the following individuation: "We can divide up the orbit into quadrants, assign them numbers, think of them as states, and observe that each is followed by the next with law-like regularity."[5] Although this is logically coherent, the point is that there is nothing in our physics (i.e., our science of the solar system) that requires, necessitates, or sanctions such an individuation. There are two reasons why such individuations are not generally sanctioned. First, they do not pick out higher-level regularities that deepen our understanding of the system. (If they did pick out such regularities, we would incorporate them into our scientific story.) Second, they may not even coincide with our scientific story. For example, where a planet is located in a quadrant at time t_n does not matter for this particular individuation, but it may matter very much to the physical/causal story. It may be that particular locations in the quadrant are associated with varying degrees and types of causal interactions with other heavenly bodies. If this is the case, this individuation does not coincide with our physics and can be dismissed on that basis.

Let us ask the same question about digital-state computers. In such systems voltage levels constitute states of the machine. The actual voltage levels are of course continuous and variable, as depicted in figure 3.3, and every point and fluctuation of the current is (for some purpose or under some analysis) causally efficacious in the world. But not every point and fluctuation is causally efficacious in the operation of the system as a digital state computer.

The system is structured in such a way that a function like that in figure 3.4 can be used to map the continuous, variable voltage levels onto

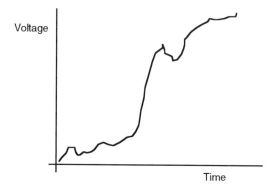

Figure 3.3
Actual voltage levels over time

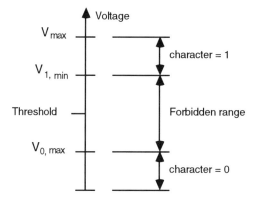

Figure 3.4
Function to map voltage levels onto computational states (adopted from Hamacher et al., 1978)

a notational scheme having two elementary characters (0/1, true/false, on/off) by[6] (1) demarcating two ranges of voltage levels (character inscriptions) such that they are "perceptually" discernible to the relevant mechanical process; (2) setting up the system so that every voltage level within a range has identical causal consequences (i.e., is character indifferent); (3) making sure there is a gap (discernible by the relevant mechanical process) between ranges that is not causally efficacious in the operation of the system (i.e., is not an inscription or character in the system).

The result is a notational scheme like that graphed in figure 3.5. It is figure 3.5 rather than figure 3.3 that captures the correct causal account of the dynamics of the system qua digital computer. This account both captures interesting regularities that deepen our understanding of the system and coincides with the scientific/physical story of the system.

Can we make the same claims about the semantic constraints? Given an arbitrary dynamical system, can there be a fact of the matter as to whether it does or does not satisfy the semantic constraints on CTM-systems? If one chooses not to interpret the system semantically, clearly there can be no such fact. The question will never arise. The important point is that if one does choose to interpret the system, then relative to a specific individuation of states and transformations (i.e., a particular syntactic individuation) and a specific semantic interpretation, there is a matter of fact as to whether the system is a computational information processing system. To get this matter of fact, proceed as follows:

1. Decide on the system and phenomenon you are interested in and the level at which it occurs.

2. Understand the system/phenomenon on its own physical/causal terms; that is, explicate the structure and dynamics of the system that are causally relevant in the production of the phenomenon under investigation.

3. Use the physical/causal structure to individuate equivalence classes of physical states and transformations that are to be assigned to computational states and transformations (i.e., the syntactic interpretation).

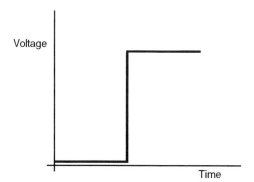

Figure 3.5
Voltage levels under the relevant causal aspect

4. Specify the program the system is supposed to be running (i.e., the semantic interpretation) and again use the causal structure and dynamics of the system to interpret the computational states and transformations.

5. Ask whether this individuation and interpretation meets the constraints on CTM-systems.

The system under investigation may or may not meet the CTM-constraints. It may fail in the first instance because the causal structure and dynamics of the system result in an individuation of (computational) states and transformations that do not meet the syntactic constraints. It may fail in the second instance because—since reference is correlated with causation—the causal network of the system may not support the interpretation of computational states and transformations required by the program the system is supposed to be running (i.e., the semantic constraints).

Is our stomach—as a processor of food—a computational information processing system with respect to a certain individuation and interpretation of computational states and transformations? It is an empirical question. There is no a priori answer independent of the causal structure and dynamics of the system and a specific semantic interpretation. One needs to proceed as above and discover the answer. Is our brain a computational information processing system under the relevant individuation and interpretation of computational states and transformations? That is, do the structure and dynamics of the brain that are causally relevant in the production of mental life satisfy the CTM-constraints? Maybe they do; maybe they do not. It is, as cognitive science claims, an empirical question.

Since the facts about computational information processing systems are relative to some individuation and interpretation of computational states and transformations, they will not be unique facts. A system may turn out to be a computational information processing system with respect to several individuations and interpretations. But there is no reason to believe that it will turn out to be a computational information processing system with respect to every individuation and interpretation, because the CTM-constraints tie the individuation and interpretation into the physical/causal structure of the system.

Note the important difference between this construal and the utility reply. The utility reply says that given any physical dynamical system one can choose to describe it in either physical or information processing vocabulary. The phenomenon stays constant; only the description changes depending on which is more useful. On the account here, what I am suggesting is that before one has the option of switching vocabulary (i), the actual physical system and the individuation and interpretation of computational states and transformations have to meet certain stringent constraints; and (ii) by making the switch, the theorist is making the very strong empirical claim that those aspects of the structure and dynamics of the system captured by the CTM-constraints are causally relevant in the production of the phenomenon under investigation.

So one desirable consequence of the CTM-constraints is that not every dynamical system under every description is a computational information processing system. Technically, this is sufficient to offset the charge of vacuousness. But it still leaves us with too many computational systems and this should give us continuing cause for concern.

3.7   Conclusion

It should be clear by now that the explanatory power of the Computational Theory of Mind comes from the CTM-properties. These properties are necessary to license the interpretation of a system in the manner required by the RTM'-constraints and to save the resulting explanation from charges of vacuousness. Cognitive science's commitment to the Computational Theory of Mind is really a commitment to CTM-systems. That is, in appealing to computation and claiming it is a necessary condition for cognition, we are claiming that the system that underwrites computational information processing (i.e., a CTM-system) is also necessary (but not sufficient) for cognitive information processing.

Thus the Computational Theory of Mind *necessarily* commits us to an internal symbol system with some very restrictive properties—the CTM-constraints—and the three most popular versions of the theory, the physical symbol system hypothesis, the language of thought hypothesis, and interpretational semantics meet, indeed *must* meet, all or most of these constraints. Furthermore, computational accounts that do not meet these constraints are in danger of being vacuous. This is our first substantive result and will play an important role in the overall argument.

But there is something very odd here. We started out by being interested in the Representational Theory of Mind or the Intentional Theory of Mind. Unable to satisfy the constraints associated with either of these, we settled for RTM'-constraints because they are "sort of" like the RTM-constraints. The difficulty is, given a system that can satisfy the RTM'-constraints, little of interest logically follows about its ability to satisfy the RTM-constraints. It seems that in explaining the state changes of a system with genuine semantic properties, we should not need to appeal to the CTM-properties, because the interpretation they make possible would be irrelevant. There would be a fact of the matter, independent of the interpretation. This is a worrisome point to which we will return to in chapter 10.

At this juncture it is important to acknowledge that symbol systems meeting the CTM-constraints do exist. As noted in chapter 1, one of the major contributions of cognitive science to date has been to show that there are a number of problem-solving tasks that can be understood and explained by postulating mental representations with CTM-properties. Some examples of such cognitive tasks are cryptarithmetic, the Moore-Anderson tasks, chess (Newell and Simon, 1972), Tower of Hanoi (Anzai and Simon, 1979). Each can be explained as a series of computations defined over symbol systems with the CTM-properties.

Interestingly, these are all well-structured games and puzzle problems. But most real-world problems are ill structured and open-ended. My second major conjecture is that, in order to understand cognitive functioning in ill-structured problem domains, one needs to postulate an internal symbol system that lacks at least some of the CTM-properties. Parts II and III of the monograph are devoted to substantiating this claim. The strategy will be to argue (in part II), by appeal to empirical considerations, that *external* symbol systems that lack the CTM-properties play an important cognitive role in solving a certain class of ill-structured problems. This empirical claim about external symbol systems will be extended, by a brief logical argument in part III, to a claim about *internal* symbol systems.

II

Lessons from Design Problem Solving

[T]hose people suppose, that because the smallest circle hath as many degrees as the largest, therefore the Regulation and Management of the World require no more Abilities than the handling and turning of a Globe.
—Jonathan Swift

Part I concluded by suggesting that there is an important distinction to be made between well-structured problems and ill-structured problems, and that while cognitive processes involved in well-structured problems may be accounted for by postulating mental representations with CTM-properties, one needs to postulate symbol systems lacking the CTM-properties to account for cognitive processes involved in ill-structured problems. Part II takes up these issues in earnest.

The ill-structured and well-structured distinction was introduced into the literature by Reitman (1964). In a seminal paper on ill-defined problems, Reitman (1964) suggested a categorization of problems into six types based on the distribution of information within a problem vector. A problem vector is an *n*-tuple of the form *[A, B, =>]*, where components *A* and *B* represent the start and terminal states respectively, and the component => denotes some transformation function. Problems in which each vector component is well defined are instances of well-structured problems. Most games are good examples of such problem types. For example, in tic-tac-toe the start state is a board with nine blank squares. The goal is to place marks ('x' or 'o') on three consecutive squares to form a horizontal, diagonal, or vertical line. The transformation function is to place your mark on any blank square.

Problem statements in which each of the vector components are underspecified constitute the ill-defined or ill-structured category. Some typical examples are the following: compose a fugue; design a vehicle that flies; write a short story; design a building; build a paper airplane that will stay airborne for twelve minutes. While these statements encompass widely varying activities, Reitman observed that they constitute formally similar problems, by virtue of the amount and distribution of information among the three components of the problem vector. The invariant characteristic is the lack of information. For instance, (i) the start state A is unspecified (e.g., design a vehicle with what? putty? cardboard? prefabricated parts from GM?); (ii) the goal state B is incompletely specified (e.g., how long should a story be? what should the plot be? how should it end?); (iii) the transformation function => is unspecified (e.g., how should the airplane be made? by folding the paper? by cutting and pasting?). After Reitman's analysis, design problems became identified with ill-defined problems.

However, the distinction between ill-structured and well-structured problems (and the identification of design with the ill-structured category) has not gone unquestioned. At least one prominent researcher (Simon, 1973b) has argued that the distinction is not clear-cut, and is perhaps even illusory. Thus the first thing we need to do is revisit the claim and make an explicit argument for it. It is necessary to my overall argument that a convincing distinction be made, because I do not want to claim that non–CTM-type symbol systems are required for *all* cognitive processes. It is important to acknowledge the progress cognitive science has made in explaining certain types of problem-solving activity by postulating CTM-type symbol systems. The goal is not to question, or take anything away from, this body of work. Rather, the objective is to point out that it constitutes a subset of cognitive activity and that there are problem-solving domains where one needs to postulate non–CTM-type symbol systems.

The second task is to show that the external symbol systems subjects use in solving the two problem types differ with respect to CTM-properties. More specifically, it needs to be shown that external symbol systems that do not satisfy the CTM-constraints play an important cognitive role in ill-structured domains.

The distinction between problem types will be made at both the logical level (through analysis of task environments) and the psychological level (through analysis of problem spaces). The distinction will not however be made at the fully general level of ill-structured and well-structured problems. Rather I will distinguish between design and non-design problems, where design problems are a type of ill-structured problem and the nondesign problems under consideration belong to the class of well-structured problems.

It is preferable to draw the distinction at this lower level. The ill-structured and well-structured categories may contain many heterogeneous subcategories, thus making it difficult to identify a set of homogeneous cognitive processes and associate them with each category. The design and nondesign distinction is finer grained, more constrained, and more manageable. Therefore, it is easier to identify the cognitive processes associated with each class. The design and nondesign categories provide the needed distinction with fewer commitments.

The task environment analysis identifies design problems with a cluster of twelve properties. An analysis of the task environments of certain puzzle-game problems (cryptarithmetic and the Moore-Anderson task) shows that they differ with respect to each of these twelve properties. This leads one to expect important cognitive differences at the level of the problem space.

I conduct a study to see whether this is indeed the case. It actually yields three results. First, it shows that the logical differences at the level of the task environment do result in psychological differences at the level of the problem space. Second, it identifies a number of cognitive processes specific to design problem solving. Third, it results in the observation that designers use a number of external symbol systems as they traverse the design problem space, and that different symbol systems correlate with different cognitive processes.

This observation leads to a digression on the structure and classification of symbol systems. I argue that the standard criteria that cognitive science uses to classify symbol systems—that of informational and computational equivalence—are simply inadequate to account for the richness and diversity of symbolic functioning in design domains. I describe an alternate classification scheme based on the work of Nelson Goodman and apply it to the design domain.

The value of Goodman's apparatus is two-fold. First, it does justice to the phenomena; second, there is a transparent mapping between a subset of this scheme and the CTM-properties. Some of the symbol systems used by designers meet the CTM-constraints, whereas others do not. In particular, I note that the system of sketching—which fails the CTM-constraints—is used in the early, creative, open-ended phases of design problem solving. I identify certain reasons why sketching should be correlated with this phase of problem solving and predict that if the system of sketching is replaced by a symbol system that satisfies the CTM-constraints, certain breakdowns will occur in the cognitive processes identified in the first study. This manipulation is carried out in a second experiment. It turns out that there are statistically significant differences in the predicted direction between the two cases.

The results of the two studies indicate that (a) there is a logical and psychological distinction to be made between design problems and nondesign problems, (b) there are certain cognitive processes that can be identified with design problem solving, and (c) when the external symbol systems designers are allowed to use are manipulated along the CTM dimensions, certain of these cognitive processes are hampered.

This final result is about the role of *external* symbol systems in design problem solving. But the Computational Theory of Mind is making a claim about the system of *internal* representations, and it is the structure of this internal symbol system that we are ultimately interested in explicating. The implications of these results to the structure of internal symbol systems may not be transparent at this point. They will be articulated in part III.

4

A Framework for Studying Design

Let him be educated, skillful with pencil, instructed in geometry, know much history, have followed the philosophers with attention, understand music, have some knowledge of medicine, know the opinions of the jurists, and be acquainted with astronomy and the theory of the heavens.
—Vitruvius (on the education of the architect)

4.1 Introduction

To carry out the proposed tasks, one first needs to develop a criterion for demarcating design problems and arrive at some understanding of their essential characteristics. The vocabulary for this needs to be compatible with the theoretical vocabulary in which the empirical investigation will be conducted. Information processing theory satisfies this constraint.

Newell and Simon's (1972) Information Processing Theory provides us with three major theoretical constructs: the information processing system, the task environment, and the problem space. The information processing system is a cognitive agent with a problem. The task environment is the external environment, including the problem, in which the information processing system operates. The problem space is a modeling space molded by the characteristics of the information processing system and the task environment. It is defined in terms of a state space, operators that allow the traversal of this space, evaluation functions that measure how close a given state is to the goal or some subgoal state, and control strategies that guide the search. The framework is depicted in figure 4.1 and discussed in subsequent sections.

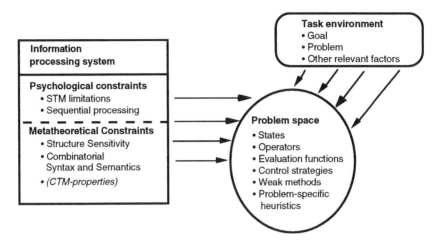

Figure 4.1
Components of information processing theory

The intuitions, hinted at in the introduction to part II, about design problems constituting a natural category amount to the claim that there must be a psychological description of problem-solving activity that both captures the similarities in the problem-solving processes across various design tasks and disciplines and recognizes certain important differences between design and nondesign problem-solving processes. It can be formulated in information processing theory as a hypothesis about the design problem space.

Design Problem Space Hypothesis   Problem spaces exhibit major invariants across all design problem-solving situations and major variants across design and nondesign problem-solving situations.

The strategy for explicating the design problem space is as follows: (a) specify some salient features in the cognitive structure of the designer; (b) specify the salient common features or invariants in the task environment of design problems; (c) show that they constitute a rather unique set of invariants not found in an arbitrary problem task environment; (d) let the problem space be shaped by these two sets of constraints; (e) note the structure of the resulting problem space and make "explanatory connections" between this structure and the invariants of the design task environment and the cognitive system; (f) show that the structure of at least some nondesign problem spaces is very different from design problem spaces; (g) make the Newell and Simon (1972) argument that, given the structure of the problem solver as a constant across all cognitive activity, any interesting differences across problem spaces of vastly different tasks will be a function of the task environment; and (h) on this basis claim that these features are invariants of design situations and collectively constitute a design problem space.

The next two sections specify the structure of the information processing system and design task environment. We will see that there are important differences in the task environments of design and nondesign problems. In section 4.4 the structures of the information processing system and design task environment are used to anticipate the structure of design problem spaces. In chapter 5, actual design problem spaces from three different design disciplines are examined and compared with the problem spaces of two nondesign tasks.

4.2 The Structure of the Information Processing System

The classic Newell and Simon (1972) theory of human problem solving defines a cognitive system as a physical symbol system, also known as an information processing system. It is useful to think of physical symbol systems as incorporating two sets of constraints (see figure 4.1). The first set, which I call the metatheoretical constraints, have already been examined in part I. These are essentially combinatorial syntax and semantics, structure sensitivity of process, and, at an even more fundamental level, the CTM-properties.

When we are talking about actually modeling cognitive processes, a second set of constraints comes into play. I refer to this second set as the "psychological" constraints. They do not logically follow from the metatheoretical constraints. They are postulated on empirical grounds. The major ones identified in Newell and Simon's (1972) original formulation are the organization of memory and the sequential nature of information processing. There are actually three distinct memories: a long-term memory, a short-term memory, and an external memory. Each is characterized by its organization and read/write times, the specifics of which are not relevant for our present purposes. The processor performs some basic elementary operations, such as reading, writing, testing, comparing, discriminating, and replacing symbols, but there is no single necessary and sufficient set. These elementary processes operate on one expression at a time and are strictly serial. The elementary operations can be combined into any arbitrarily complex computation.

There are of course several more-sophisticated accounts in the literature. The present commitment to the Newell and Simon (1972) theory is simply a way of providing a reasonable first-order approximation of human information processing that is consistent with a wide variety of more recent proposals of human cognitive architectures (Anderson, 1983; Newell, 1990). The essential constraints on human information processing proposed by Newell and Simon (1972) that are relevant to our characterization of the design problem space—the limitations on short-term memory, external memory, and the sequential nature of symbolic processing—would probably show up in many alternative architectures. Even more important for our overall argument are the metatheoretical or foundational constraints, and, as we have seen, they are, and need to be, constant across all computational architectures.[1]

4.3   The Structure of the Design Task Environment

Task environments typically consist of a goal, a problem, and other relevant external factors (Newell and Simon, 1972) (see figure 4.1).[2] In practice, the motivation or goal of the human problem solver has always been assumed, and the other relevant external factors have effectively been ignored. Studies have focused on how the structure and content of a *particular* problem gets mapped onto the problem space. The process of explicating the design task environment is, in effect, the process of looking beyond the individual problem and specifying the relevant external factors common to all design problems.

Two difficulties arise. First, before one can identify common relevant external factors across design problems, one must specify what constitutes the category or at least identify members of it. Second, in some real sense, every aspect of the task environment is a relevant external factor. But if one takes this route, one ends up with theoretically uninteresting categories. One needs criteria whereby one can say what matters and what does not. Both have proven to be notoriously difficult problems.[3] I rely on concepts from categorization theory to deal with the problem of individuation, and on intuitions, developed through immersion in the discipline of architectural design, to pick out aspects of the task environment deemed to be more relevant than others.

I think design is too complex an activity to be specified by necessary and sufficient conditions. Rather, design as a category exhibits what Rosch (1978) calls prototype effects. Furthermore, it is what Lakoff (1987) calls a radial category—a category in which there is a central, ideal, or prototypical case and then some unpredictable but motivated variations. If one shows subjects a list of professions—for example, doctor, lawyer, architect, teacher, engineer, researcher—and asks which are the best examples of design professions, they will pick out the same few cases. In the above list, the best examples are considered to be architecture and engineering. Let us call these "prototypical" examples of design professions.

This strategy results in a nonarbitrary and interesting demarcation of the design category, or at least of the prototypical cases. One can now seriously examine the task environments of these prototypical design professions and attempt to isolate some interesting common features. The presence or absence of these features can then be used to identify other members of the category. The following are features of design-task environments:[4]

1. Availability of information: As initially noted by Reitman (1964), each of the three components of design problems lacks information. The start state is incompletely specified, the goal state is specified even less, and the transformation function from the start to goal states is completely unspecified.

2. Nature of constraints: The constraints on design task environments are generally of two types: (a) nomological and (b) social/political/legal/economic, and the like. Nomological constraints are dictated by natural law. So, for example, if a beam is to support a downward thrust of x psi, it must exert an upward thrust of equal force. Nomological constraints are hard, nonnegotiable constraints. But they are not definitional or constitutive of the task. They, in fact, vastly underdetermine

design solutions (see Polanyi [1966] for a nice discussion). The second set of constraints that designers must deal with are the social, economic, cultural, and the like. There is much to be said about this category. But what is important for our purposes is that, whereas many of these constraints may be regulative, they are not constitutive or definitional.[5] They are, in fact, negotiable. For example, if you go to an architect and ask to have a four-bedroom house built, and the architect convinces you to build a three-bedroom house or to renovate your existing house instead, it would be odd to say that the architect is not playing the game of design.

3. Size and complexity of problems: Design problems are generally large and complex, requiring days to months to complete.

4. Component parts: Any problem of any size and complexity has parts. Being large and complex, design problems have many parts. But little in the *structure* of design problems dictates the lines of decomposition. Decomposition is dictated by the practice and experience of the designer.

5. Interconnectivity of parts: The components of design problems are not *logically* interconnected. There are, however, many contingent interconnections between them.

6. Right and wrong answers: Design problems do not have right or wrong answers, only better and worse ones.

7. Input/output: The input to design problems consists of information about the people who will use the artifact, the goals they want to satisfy, and the design behavior the artifact/process needs to facilitate in order to satisfy those goals. The output consists of the artifact specification. Functional information mediates between the input and the output information. This is a rather standard characterization adapted from Wade (1977) and further discussed in appendix A in the context of the coding scheme.

8. Feedback loop: There is no genuine feedback from the world during the problem-solving session. It has to be simulated by the designer in internal and external modeling spaces. Real-world feedback comes only after the design is completed and the artifact is constructed and allowed to function in its intended environment. At this point the feedback cannot influence the current project, but only the next "similar" project.

9. Costs of errors: There are costs associated with every action in the world, and the penalty for being wrong can be high (Rittel and Webber, 1974).

10. Independent functioning of artifact: The artifact is required to function independently of the designer.

11. Distinction between specification and delivery: The specification of the artifact is distinct from the construction and delivery of the artifact.
12. Temporal separation between specification and delivery: The specification and delivery/construction of the artifact are separated in time. Specification precedes delivery.

The claim is that these twelve factors are significant invariants in the task environments of prototypical design situations and can be used to identify other cases of design. To the extent that the task environment of a given problem situation conforms to this template, that problem situation is a prototypical design situation. To the extent that a task environment varies from this template—by omission of one or more of the requirements—the less it is a case of design activity.

I am not stipulating what is and is not a design activity. To do that I would have to insist that the twelve task-environment characteristics, or some subset of them, constitute necessary and sufficient conditions for design activity. All I am saying is that we have here a template of salient characteristics common to the task environment of problem situations that people consistently recognize as good examples of design activity. Problem situations in which the task environment fails to conform to this template on one or more accounts are deviations from the central case. Here I will only discuss central cases, and thus I have no interest in saying how far one can deviate from the prototype and still be "really" designing. I will use the label "design" to refer to situations that closely conform to the prototypical or central cases.

Problem-solving situations that fit well into the schema are engineering and architectural design, city planning, instructional design, interior design, some forms of software design, and music composition. Writing and painting deviate slightly, because there is usually no separation between design and delivery. The problem solver actually constructs the artifact rather than specifying it. Activities that deviate more radically are classroom teaching, spontaneous conversation, and game playing. To show that this really is the case, I will examine the task environments of two games—cryptarithmetic and the Moore-Anderson task—that have been extensively studied in the literature (Newell and Simon, 1972).

Cryptarithmetic is a puzzle consisting of an arithmetic problem in which the digits have been replaced by letters of the alphabet. The goal is to decipher the letters (i.e., map them back onto the digits) using the constraints provided by arithmetic and the additional constraint that no two letters can have the same numerical value. A well-known example is the following:

SEND
+ MORE
―――――
MONEY

The Moore-Anderson task (Newell and Simon, 1972) is a puzzle that involves the "recoding" of one set of symbolic strings into another set according to a given set of rewrite or transformation rules. A typical example is the following:

Start state: $(P \vee Q) \cdot (Q \supset R)$
Goal state: $P \vee (Q \cdot R)$
Rules of transformations: See figure 4.2.

The task is to apply the rules until the start string is transformed into the goal string. Solving the problems is isomorphic to theorem proving in the propositional calculus. However, subjects are not logicians and are unaware that they are engaged in theorem proving. It is very much a puzzle-solving situation. The claims to be made in regards to this task are not meant to generalize to expert logicians engaged in real theorem proving.

The characteristics of the Moore-Anderson task and cryptarithmetic task environments, with respect to each of the twelve "design" features, are summarized below:

1′. Availability of information: In the case of cryptarithmetic, the start state is completely specified. The goal state is not specified, but there is no ambiguity as to what it will be like and no question as to when it has been reached. The transformation function is restricted to only two operations—substitute a number between zero and nine and add—and they are specified in advance. In the Moore-Anderson task both the start and goal states are completely specified. The set of legal operators is also specified. The subject has only to figure out the ones to apply and the order of application.

2′. Nature of constraints: In both cryptarithmetic and the Moore-Anderson task, as in all games, the rules are definitional or constitutive of the task. They have a logical necessity about them. If we violate a

1. $A \lor B \to B \lor B$
    $B \cdot A \to B \cdot A$

7. $A \lor (B \cdot C) \leftrightarrow (A \lor B) \cdot (A \lor C)$

2. $A \supset B \to \sim B \supset \sim A$

8. $A \cdot B \to A$
    $A \cdot B \to A$

3. $A \lor A \leftrightarrow A$
    $A \cdot A \leftrightarrow A$

9. $A \to A \lor X$

4. $A \lor (B \lor C) \leftrightarrow (A \lor B) \lor C$
    $A \cdot (B \cdot C) \leftrightarrow (A \cdot B) \cdot C$

10. A
    B
    $\to A \cdot B$

5. $A \lor B \leftrightarrow \sim (\sim A \cdot \sim B)$

11. $A \supset B$
    A
    $\to B$

6. $A \supset B \leftrightarrow \sim A \lor B$

12. $A \supset B$
    $B \supset C$
    $\to A \supset C$

Figure 4.2
Rules of transformation for the Moore-Anderson task (Newell and Simon, 1972, p. 406). Arrows show the direction in which the recoding or transformation may take place. The expression at the tail of the arrow may be rewritten as the expression at the head of the arrow. Where the arrow is bidirectional, the expression on either side may be rewritten as the expression on the other side.

rule, we are simply not playing the game. For example, if we are playing chess and I move my rook diagonally across the board, I am simply not playing chess.

3′. Size and complexity: In both cryptarithmetic and the Moore-Anderson task, the problems are relatively small and simple. The ones we will examine in the next chapter took from ten to forty minutes to solve.

4′. Component parts: Even though the problems are relatively small, they do break down into a number of components. In cryptarithmetic each column is treated as a component. In the Moore-Anderson task each well-formed string or formula (wff) constitutes a component. However, in both cases this breakdown is enforced by the logical structure of the problem rather than the whim of the problem solver or the practice of some community.

5'. Interconnectivity of parts: In cryptarithmetic the few components (columns) that do exist are logically connected. That is, any column may sum to greater than nine and affect the next column. In the Moore-Anderson task there are some *logical* connections between the wffs, but they are not obvious. A good part of the problem is to discover these interconnections.

6'. Right and wrong answers: In the cryptarithmetic problems examined here, there was only one right answer. In the Moore-Anderson task the answer consists of the right sequence of operators. Although there may be a small set of right sequences (rather than a single one), all others are definitely wrong. It is clear when one has found a right sequence.

7'. Input/output: In cryptarithmetic the input is limited to letters, numbers, and the rules of the game. The output is a particular mapping of letters to numbers. In the Moore-Anderson task the input consists of the wffs and the operators. The output consists of the sequence of lawful operator applications sufficient to transform the premise wffs into the conclusion wff.

8'. Feedback loop: In cryptarithmetic there is genuine feedback after every operation (i.e., substitution and summation). It is, however, local feedback, and decisions regarding movement in the problem space need to satisfy global constraints. In the Moore-Anderson task there is local feedback after every operator application, but it is of limited value. More useful feedback comes after sequences of operator applications.

9'. Costs of errors: In both cases the cost of error is negligible in the sense that a wrong answer may cause the subject some embarrassment, but it will not have social or economic consequences or endanger the lives of other people.

10'. Independent functioning of artifact: Not applicable.

11'. Distinction between specification and delivery: Not applicable.

12'. Temporal separation of specification and delivery: Not applicable.

These nondesign task environments clearly differ from the design task environment in all twelve respects. Incidentally, they also differ from each other with respect to features (1') and (6'), but the consequences of this latter difference are not relevant for our purposes. The psychological consequences of the differences between design task environments and nondesign task environments are summarized in section 4.4 and will be considered in some detail in chapter 5.

I do not mean to suggest that all nondesign task environments will be so radically different. Examples of intermediate cases are the task environments of some of the mathematical problem situations in Schoenfeld (1985). I have chosen to contrast design cases with radically deviant ones. The sharp contrast provided by extreme cases clarifies issues and is thus the right place to start. If something substantive is uncovered, we can move to subtler comparisons.

4.4　Resulting Structure of Design Problem Spaces

A problem space is a computational modeling space created by the interaction of the information processing system with the task environment (see figure 4.1). Strictly speaking, it is characterized in terms of states, operators, evaluation functions, and search strategies. There are three types of states; a start state, a goal state, and intermediate states. Operators are computable functions that move the system from one state to another. Evaluation functions provide a measure of the "goodness" of the current state with respect to the goal or some subgoal state. Search strategies are characterized by two general types: weak strategies and heuristic strategies. Heuristics are domain-specific knowledge structures that are brought to bear on a problem and guide search. In the absence of such heuristic knowledge, weak, general-purpose strategies, such as means-ends analysis, are employed.

Actually, my characterization of the design problem space will not be in terms of low-level predicates, such as states, operators, and evaluation functions, as is standard in many psychological investigations (Newell and Simon, 1972). Rather the characterization will be in a much higher level vocabulary, in terms of a set of invariant features that are common to all design problem spaces. Each can be explained or justified by appealing to the structure of the design task environment and the information processing system. They are listed below and discussed in subsequent chapters:

1. Personal stopping rules and evaluation functions: Because there are no right or wrong answers and no direct feedback from the world, the evaluation functions and stopping rules the designers use will be derived from personal experience and immersion in the profession.

2. Predominance of memory retrieval and nondemonstrative inference: Since there are few logical constraints on design problems, deductive inference plays only a minimal role in the problem-solving process. Most decisions result from memory retrieval and nondeductive inference.

3. Reversing direction of transformation function: Since the task structure is not well specified in advance and the constraints are nonlogical, the designer can negotiate to enlarge, narrow, or simply change problem parameters.

4. Modularity/decomposability: Given the size and complexity of design problems and the limited capacity of short-term memory, one would expect that the problem would be broken into many modules. However, given that connections between modules are mostly contingent, the designer attends to some connections and ignores others.

5. Incremental development of artifact: Interim design ideas are nurtured and developed incrementally until they are appropriate for the task. They are rarely discarded and replaced with new ideas. The principal reasons for this are the size and complexity of problems, the sequential nature of information processing, and the fact that there are no right or wrong answers.

6. Control strategy: Designers use a limited-commitment-mode control strategy that enables them to generate and evaluate design components in multiple contexts.

7. Making and propagating commitments: Since design plans and specifications must be produced in a finite amount of time and interpreted by third parties, designers must make, record, and propagate commitments.

8. Distinct problem-solving phases: Design problem solving can be further subcategorized into problem-structuring and -solving phases. The lack of information in the three components of the design-problem vector requires extensive problem structuring. Problem solving can be further differentiated into three distinct phases: preliminary design, refinement, and detail design. This is probably due to the size and complexity of design problems and the qualitative shift that must occur between the input and the output information.

9. Abstraction hierarchies: The qualitative difference between the input and output information and the several distinct problem-solving phases results in orthogonal abstraction hierarchies.

10. Constructing and manipulating models: Because design typically occurs in situations where it is not possible or feasible to manipulate the world directly, designers usually manipulate representations of the

world. (We only get one "run" on the world, whereas we can get multiple "runs" on models of the world.)

11. Use of many distinct external symbol systems: Given the size and complexity of problems, the need to construct and manipulate external models, and the need for several abstraction hierarchies, designers make extensive use of many distinct symbol systems.

12. Different symbol systems correlate with different cognitive processes: Different symbol systems used by designers have different properties that facilitate or hinder certain cognitive processes.

Although this is an unusual characterization of a problem space, it is necessary. These invariant features do not exist at the level of states, operators, or evaluation functions. They are higher-level psychological constructs, but no less real for that. If the characterization is confined to the more traditional level, nothing interesting emerges. But once one abstracts away to the higher-level constructs, a rich and interesting story can be told. If there is a specifiable mapping between the computational states and operators and our higher-level constructs, all is well. If there is no such mapping, then much remains unexplained. That it is necessary to use this higher-level vocabulary is telling. It may be a harbinger of the more general conclusion toward which we are headed.

4.5   Conclusion

I have made a logical distinction between design (ill-structured) problems and nondesign (well-structured) problems. Design problems can be identified by a cluster of twelve properties. I have analyzed the task environments of design situations and have shown them to be radically different from that of nondesign situations.

I have also suggested that these logical differences will have psychological consequences at the level of the problem space. The next chapter describes a study in which design problem spaces are compared with nondesign problem spaces and articulates cognitive differences between the two.

5

Cognitive Processes Involved in Design Problem Solving

The already known had once more been confirmed
By psychological experiment.
—Robert Frost

In this chapter we will compare data from design problem solving with data from nondesign (cryptarithmetic and Moore-Anderson task) problem solving. The goal is to identify some of the cognitive processes associated with design problem solving and show that they are indeed different from cognitive processes associated with nondesign problem solving.

The results presented here are based on single-subject protocol studies (Ericsson and Simon, 1984). A total of sixteen protocols, twelve from design situations, and four from puzzle-game situations, were examined and compared. The methods of collecting and analyzing data are summarized below and discussed at greater length in appendix A.

5.1 Experiment Design and Procedure

Design Problems: Subjects, Tasks, and Procedures The design protocols were collected from professional designers from the disciplines of architecture, mechanical engineering, and instructional design. The architectural task was to design a self-help, automated post office for the UC-Berkeley campus. The mechanical engineering task was to design an automated postal teller machine for the above post office. The instructional design task was unrelated. It involved designing a self-contained instructional package to teach laypeople a reasonably complicated computational environment.

Each of these tasks is a complex "real-world" design problem having most of the features specified in chapter 4. They differ, however, in two respects. In the experimental situation there was no substantive penalty for being wrong or proposing an inferior solution, as there would be in the world at large. Also, the tasks were such that they required on the order of days to weeks for complete solution specification. But subjects were asked to restrict their sessions to approximately two hours. As a result, solutions were specified to varying degrees of detail.

The procedures for collecting the protocols were the same in each case. Each subject was given a one-page design brief, and any related documents, and asked to specify a solution to the problem, to the degree of specificity allowed by time and resource constraints. They were allowed to use any external drawing aids/tools they desired. All chose to use paper, pencil, and/or pen.

The experimenter was present to answer any questions relating to the experiment and otherwise assumed the role of the client. Subjects were encouraged to ask for clarification as the need arose. The experimenter answered all questions, but never initiated conversation.

Subjects were asked to "talk aloud" as they solved the problem. They were cautioned against trying to explain what they were doing. Rather, they were asked to vocalize whatever was "passing through their minds" at that time. Most of the subjects did not have much difficulty in doing this. When subjects did lapse into periods of silence, the experimenter prompted them by asking, "What are you thinking now?"

The sessions were videotaped. The tapes, along with the written and drawn material, constituted the data.

Coding Scheme   The protocols were transcribed, cross-referenced with the written material, and coded. The coding involved breaking the protocols into individual statements representing single "thoughts" or ideas. Content cues, syntactic cues, and pauses were used to effect this individuation. This resulted in very fine grained units with a mean duration of eight seconds and a mean length of fifteen words. Each statement was coded for the operator applied (e.g., add, delete, justify), the content to which the operator was applied, the mode of output (verbal or written), and the source of knowledge (design brief, experimenter, self, inference).

These statements were then aggregated into modules and submodules, which are episodes organized around artifact components. For example, for the architect subjects, the modules were components like site, building, and services. The site submodules were components like circulation, landscaping, and site illumination. The building submodules included such things as doors, roof, and mail storage. The modules were then further aggregated into design-phase levels. The design-phase level coded for several things, the most important being design-development phases, such as problem structuring, preliminary design, refinement, and detail design. These categories were further coded for the aspect of design development attended to (people, purposes, behavior, function, and structure). The idea here was that artifacts are designed to perform certain functions that are calculated to support certain behaviors that help in the realization of certain goals held by people.

The method of data collection and the coding scheme are detailed in appendix A. It is probably a good idea for the reader to have at least a quick look at appendix A before continuing.

Although all twelve design protocols were examined and coded, the subsequent discussion is based on three of them—one from each discipline. The three were selected on the basis of the completeness of the artifact specification the individuals produced and the fluency of the subjects' verbalization. Throughout the discussion, the architect is referred to as subject S-A; the mechanical engineer is referred to as subject S-M; and the instructional designer is referred to as subject S-I.

Nondesign Problems: Subjects, Tasks, and Procedures   The nondesign protocols were gathered from published sources (Newell and Simon, 1972, appendixes 6.1, 7.1, 9.2, and 10.1). They are from the domains of cryptarithmetic and the Moore-Anderson task and last from fifteen minutes to forty minutes. Two protocols from each domain were chosen, on the basis of their length. The subjects for these studies were undergraduate students. The procedure for collecting the protocols was similar in relevant aspects to the one described above.

The two cryptarithmetic protocols are from Newell and Simon (1972, appendixes 6.1 and 7.1). These subjects will be referred to as NS6.1 and NS7.1 respectively. Both protocols involved solving the following puzzle problem:

DONALD   D = 5
+ GERALD
ROBERT

where each letter stands for a digit and the digits encoded as 'DONALD' and 'GERALD' add up to the digits encoded as 'ROBERT'. The clue given is that 'D' equals five.

The Moore-Anderson task (as already noted) is a string transformation problem isomorphic to theorem proving in the propositional calculus, although the subjects do not know they are proving theorems. The relevant protocols are from appendixes 9.2 and 10.1. The subjects undertaking the tasks will be referred to as NS9.2 and NS10.1. Subject NS9.2 was given the following problem (Newell and Simon, 1972):

L1. $(R \supset \sim P) \cdot (\sim R \supset Q)$
L0. $\sim (\sim Q \cdot P)$

where L1 is the start state (premise) and L0 is the goal state (conclusion). Subject NS10.1 received the following problem (Newell and Simon, 1972):

L1. $P \cdot (Q \cdot R)$
L2. $\sim (P \supset T) \supset \sim (P \cdot Q)$
L0. $T \cdot T$

where L1 and L2 are the start states and L0 the goal state. The rules of transformation for both tasks are the same as specified in figure 4.2 in chapter 4.

Coding Scheme   The nondesign protocols were recoded with a modified subset of the scheme devised for the design protocols. Three changes were required. First, it was found that whereas one could differentiate between problem structuring and problem solving, it was not possible to further differentiate problem solving into preliminary, refinement, and detail phases. Second, the aspect-of-design development category was not applicable. Third, information about the mode of the subject's output (whether written or spoken) was unavailable.

The majority of the coding for both the design and the nondesign protocol was done by the experimenter. However, approximately 20 percent of the data was recoded by a colleague. There was 83 percent agreement between the experimenter and the independent coder.

5.2 The Nature of the Design Problem Space

In the next nine subsections, I note and discuss nine of the twelve invariants in the design problem space. The other three are discussed in subsequent chapters. In each case I ask the following three questions: (1) What is the phenomenon? (2) Why does it occur? (3) What is the supporting data? I also discuss the occurrence or nonoccurrence of the phenomenon in nondesign problem spaces.

5.2.1 Personalized Stopping Rules and Evaluation Functions

Personal preferences play an important role in design problem solving. If and when a certain design component is deemed complete, and whether it is an acceptable solution to the problem, is determined by the designer as opposed to the logical structure of the problem. The decisions are based on personal preference and experience, professional standards and practice, and client expectations. This is undoubtedly because (i) there is not enough information in the problem statement to make these decisions, (ii) there are no right or wrong terminating states, and (iii) there are few, if any, logical constraints. The decisions must be made by the designer in accordance with community practice and/or in consultation with the client.

The important role of personal preferences can be seen in the following protocol fragment from subject S-A:

S-A: The thought I had before, that I might use the . . . . That I am denying now. I don't think it should be carried out. Because it would signify a major intervention on, on the physical form of the building, and, I don't think that deserves it.

Compare this excerpt to the following one, in which one of the nondesign subjects (NS9.2) is proposing and evaluating the series of transformation rules that can be applied to the expressions (numbers 1 through 6 refer to the transformation rules):

NS9.2:   I am looking through them one at a time to see just in what way they might help rearrange the expression.

Now . . .

1

Would be just the idea of switching the idea around, which actually is no help there.

2

Doesn't apply.

3

Doesn't apply.

4

Would apply,

but I can't see in what direction it would help me.

6

Doesn't apply.

As the rules are proposed, it is clear (from the rules and structure of the problem) whether they apply or not. If they do not apply, they must be rejected. If they do apply, a further inference needs to be made about their consequence. While not all evaluations in the Newell and Simon protocols were like this, many were.

The results are as would be predicted by the respective task environments. In the nondesign cases, the evaluation functions are implicitly and/or explicitly supplied by the structure of the problem (because of the completeness of information in the problem vector and the logical nature of the constraints). The same points can be made about stopping rules. The stopping rule for subject NS9.2 was this:

If current state = $\sim(\sim Q \cdot P)$ then stop

There were no such rules for the design subjects. Their stopping decisions were based on what could reasonably be expected in a two-hour session, how tired they were, how interested and motivated they were, whether the resources needed to continue were available, and other pragmatic factors.

5.2.2   Predominance of Memory Retrieval and Nondemonstrative Inference

Only a very small fraction of statements in the design protocols (1.3 percent) are generated by overt deductive inferences. Most seem to be the result of memory retrieval and modification—or what has come to be known as case-based reasoning (Kolodner, 1993)—and nondemonstrative inference. Although the relationship between these two forms of reasoning is unclear, they both seem to be far removed from strict demonstrative inference. Unlike demonstrative inference, they require large amounts of knowledge and probably engage quite different cognitive mechanisms.

The lack of deductive reasoning should come as no surprise. First, deductive systems require axioms (i.e., logical/constitutive/definitional constraints), but most design constraints are nonconstitutive. Second, design activities invariably, but not exclusively, deal with social facts, and there is no a priori reason why the laws of logic should map onto such facts.

The nondesign problem spaces had a much higher proportion of statements generated by strict inference (41 percent). Again, this is expected, given the logical nature of the constraints and the completeness of information in the problem vectors.

5.2.3   Reversing the Direction of Transformation Function

Designers naturally interpret the problem situation through their personal experiences and biases. In addition to this, designers will occasionally stop and explicitly try to change the problem parameters by manipulating both the problem constraints and the client's expectations. I call this "reversing the direction of the transformation function," because rather than transforming the given problem state to a goal state, the designer is in effect transforming the start state and parameters so that they lead to a different goal state. There are two types of reasons why designers may wish to do this. First, they may have some expert knowledge that allows them to see that the specified goal state, *A,* will not support the behaviors or satisfy the desires that the client thinks it will, and they feel professionally obligated to point this out and suggest an alternative goal state, A', that will maximize the client's satisfaction level. The second type of reason is much more mundane. A designer may, for example, suggest an alternative goal state, A'', because it more closely fits that designer's expertise, knowledge, and experience or because there is a bigger fee associated with it.

The following negotiation sequence provides a nice example of an (unsuccessful) attempt to explicitly change the design-brief parameters. Subject S-A is standing on a ninth-floor balcony and has a birds-eye view of the small triangular site he has been given for the proposed post office. He is not content to just build a post office but wants to redesign the whole area.

S-A: So, given the fact we have that triangle over there as a limit. And I cannot exceed that I suppose?

E: Right, that, that . . .

S-A: I have to take that for granted?

E: I, I would think so.

S-A: That's the boundary of. You do not allow me to, to exceed in, in my area of intervention?

E: No, I think you should restrict it to that.

S-A: So, I am constrained to it and there is no way I can take a more radical attitude. Say, well, look, you are giving me this, but I actually, I, I'd come back to the client and say well look, I really think that you should restructure actually the whole space, in between the building. I'd definitely do that, if that was the case. You come to me as a client, and come to me with a triangle alone, I will give you an answer back proposing the whole space. Because, I, I think the whole space should be constructed. So, that there is an opportunity to finally to plan and that space through those, ah, this building, open up Anthropology and, and plan the three buildings together. So, as to really make ah, this ah, a more communal facility.

This kind of episode occurs because design problems are incompletely specified and design constraints are nonlogical and subject to manipulation and negotiation.

Notice that such a sequence simply could not and does not occur in nondesign problem spaces where the problem constraints completely specify the problem, indeed are constitutive of the problem. If it did occur, if the subject requested a change in the problem parameters, we would simply say that he or she could not do the assigned problem and was changing it to a different problem. But it is perfectly appropriate and often desirable in the case of open-ended design problems.

5.2.4 Solution Decomposition into Leaky Modules
A number of researchers have noted the important role played by decomposition in coping with complexity (Alexander, 1964; Simon, 1962, 1973a, 1977). However, there is considerable disagreement as to the extent and structure of decomposition of design problems. Some researchers, particularly in the artificial intelligence community, assume a strict treelike decomposition (Brown and Chandrasekaran, 1989; Flemming, Coyne, Glavin, and Rychener, 1988; Miller, 1985; Mittal, Dym, and Morjaria, 1986). Others have been more perceptive. Alexander (1965), for example, has argued, "A city is not a tree; it is a semilattice." Simon (1981) has made the same point by noting that design solutions are *nearly* decomposable.

In Goel and Pirolli (1989) it was pointed out that designers decompose design solutions into "leaky modules" (i.e., sparsely connected modules) and have two main strategies for dealing with these interconnections: they either (i) block the leaks by making functional-level assumptions about the interconnected modules; or (ii) put the current module on hold and attend to an interconnected module. It was also stressed that partial interconnectivity (as opposed to total connection or total disconnection) is a genuine phenomenon and must be taken seriously. The phenomenon of decomposability is connected to the size and complexity of design problems, the limited capacity of human information processing systems, and the fact that in the world certain things are related to other things.

In discussing design modules, it is important to distinguish between the actual artifact and the representation of the artifact in the problem space. Modularity at the level of the artifact amounts to physical, spatial, temporal, and/or functional boundaries. Modularity at the level of representation amounts to information encapsulation (Fodor, 1983; Goel and Grafman, 1993). The encapsulation at the representational level need not mirror the boundaries at the artifact level, though presumably the former will be some perceived/computed function of the latter.

Any part of the world can be categorized in any number of ways, and any object can be related to any other in as many ways as one likes. There is no a priori way of identifying cognitively relevant boundaries and connections. However, given a specific protocol and knowledge of the domain, we can recognize modules that were cognitively relevant for that designer, during that session. In S-A's protocol, for example, it was possible to identify four major modules and thirty-four sub-modules (see figure 5.1). Each module was the focus of an episode of activity that contained on the average twelve statements and lasted ninety-six seconds.

In asking about "leaks" or connectivity, it is again important to distinguish between the artifact and the representation. In the artifact, connectivity amounts to physical, spatial, temporal, causal, and/or functional connections between modules. In the representations it

1.0 Site

    1.1 Trees

    1.2 Illumination

    1.3 Seating

    1.4 View

    1.5 Circulation

    1.6 Entry/exit

    1.7 Dimensions

    1.8 Building location and orientation

    1.9 Shape and orientation

2.0 Building

    2.1 Open/closed structure

    2.2 Mail storage

    2.3 Services (maintenance, security)

    2.4 Landscape/seating element

    2.5 Number of lines and booths

    2.6 Doors

    2.7 Mail pickup and maintenance

    2.8 Mail storage and transport

    2.9 Independent machines

    2.10 Configuration of booths (plan)

    2.11 Roof

    2.12 Locate equipment

    2.13 Dimension building

    2.14 Dimension equipment

    2.15 Dimension storage

    2.16 Material selection

    2.17 Accessories

    2.18 Wheelchair access

3.0 Services

    3.1 Number of people and service time

    3.2 Number of machines

    3.3 Type and length of lines

    3.4 Mail pickup

4.0 Automated postal teller machine

    4.1 Components

    4.2 Interface

    4.3 Stamping procedure

Figure 5.1
Modules and submodules in subject S-A's protocol

amounts to procedure calls or computational pointers that allow control or data to pass from one module to another. Again, this need not mirror the connectivity at the level of the artifact, but presumably it will be some perceived/computed function of the connections at the artifact level.

What interconnections do our data suggest? It is actually easier to answer the inverse question: What evidence is their in the data for the *lack* of connectivity among modules? There are a number of behavioral indicators of the absence of interconnections between modules in our protocols. Three interesting ones are the following:

1. The designer attends to each module only once.
2. The designer does not refer to any other module within a given module.
3. The designer is able to attend to the modules in an arbitrary order.

Each or any combination of these indicators is reasonable grounds for inferring a certain degree of modularity. The absence of any combination of these behavioral indicators is perhaps reasonable grounds for inferring interconnection among the modules.

One finds evidence for the violation of these indicators in the protocols. In the case of S-A, (a) approximately 50 percent of the modules were attended to more than once, (b) in 88 percent of modules, other modules were referred to, and (c) there was a definite ordering of modules at the macro level. It is implausible that the designer could have attended to them in any arbitrary manner.

This suggests some degree of interconnection among the modules. To investigate the density and distribution of these interconnections, we relied solely on the mentioning of other modules within a module (2). The results are interesting. Subject S-A decomposed his design solution into thirty-four modules clustered in four larger groups. Given these thirty-four modules, there are 1,122 logically possible interconnections that can be made. On average, 7.4 percent of these connections were actually made. Furthermore, there is, as might be expected, a difference between the density of connections internal to major modules (i.e., between submodules within a module) and that of connections between submodules within one module and submodules from another module.

The former connections are considerably denser than the latter (13.4 percent vs. 4.5 percent). These results support observations about the near decomposability of design solutions (Alexander, 1965; Goel and Pirolli, 1989; Simon, 1981).

The same analysis was done on several nondesign protocols. In the case of cryptarithmetic, subjects decomposed the task into modules corresponding to columns of letters. Since the problems only had six columns, there were only six modules (as compared to over thirty for each of the design tasks). But although the number of modules were substantially fewer, the density of interconnections between modules was considerably greater. The procedure above yields the following results for subject NS6.1:

1. Eighty-five percent of the modules are attended to more than once.
2. In 67 percent of the modules, other modules are referred to.
3. The sequence in which the modules are attended to does not seem overly important.

Two out of these three indicators suggest interconnection between modules.

The density of interconnections for subject NS6.1 is greater than that of the design problem space. Twenty percent of the possible connections were made in the former case, as opposed to an average of 7.4 percent in the latter case (subject S-A). The denser interconnectivity of the cryptarithmetic modules is exactly what one would expect given that it is designed as a multiple-constraint satisfaction problem and all the constraints are logical and must be attended to. Perhaps this is why such problems can have relatively few modules and still be very challenging. The reason design problems can have many modules and still be tractable is that the interconnections are contingent rather than logical. The designer has more flexibility in determining which ones to attend to and which ones to ignore.

5.2.5 Incremental Development of Artifact

As partial, interim design ideas and solutions are generated, they are retained, massaged, and incrementally developed until they reach their final form. Very rarely are ideas or solutions forgotten or discarded. This is one of the most robust findings in the literature (Kant and Newell, 1984; Ullman, Dietterich, and Stauffer, 1988). The duration of the incremental development process is to a great extent a function of the resources available.

A number of factors in the design task environment would seem to favor a strategy of incremental development. First, the problems are large and, given the sequential nature of information processing that we assumed earlier, cannot be completed in a single cycle. Second, since there are few logical constraints on design problems and no wrong or right answers, there is little basis for giving up partial solutions and starting from scratch. It makes more sense to continue to develop what already exists. Third, incremental development is compatible with the generation and evaluation of design components in multiple contexts (see subsection 5.2.6).

Incremental development does not occur in the nondesign protocols. While it is true that the nondesign problems were also too large to be completed in a single cognitive step, they nonetheless have an all-or-nothing character. The primary reason for this is that most of the paths searched are wrong. Not only do they not lead to the goal state, they are independent of it. There is no sense in which one builds up to a solution. Once the designer has searched a path and it turns out not to be the solution path, he or she is no better off than before.

The best way to understand what is meant by incremental development is to follow through an example and compare it with an example from the nondesign protocols in which incremental development does not occur. Such examples are offered in the next subsection.

5.2.6 Control Structure

A control strategy for traversing design problem spaces must address a number of issues, including the following:

1. Are the solution modules to be developed in isolation from each other, or is there to be interconnection between the solutions?
2. Is the information to be processed sequentially or in parallel?
3. Are the solutions to be developed incrementally or appear completely formed?

We have already seen how each is to be answered: the solution modules are interconnected to some degree (subsection 5.2.4); the cognitive process is assumed to be sequential (chapter 4); and the solutions are developed incrementally (subsection 5.2.5). A control strategy that accommodates and supports each of these facts is required.

Our data indicate that designers use a limited-commitment-mode (LCM) control strategy, similar to Stefik's (1981) "least-commitment" control strategy. The basic feature of this strategy is that, when working on a particular module, it does not require the designer to complete that module before beginning another. Instead, one has the option of putting any module on "hold" to attend to other related (or even unrelated) modules and returning to the first later. This embedding can go several levels deep. Nor does one commit irrevocably to interim solutions. One can always modify them later (modify not only the particular module being attended to, but any component of the design-so-far: i.e., the surrounding context). This lets the designer take advantage of multiple contexts while generating and evaluating design elements. To specify this more precisely, one needs to show that design elements are indeed considered in different contexts, and trace out the actual control structure showing the LCM control strategy. But first we need a way to individuate elements and contexts.

Individuating Design Elements and Contexts   There is a straightforward mapping between "design elements" and the modules and submodules described earlier. Contexts are not as easy to individuate. They were identified using the following method: The protocol was divided into modules and submodules, and a unique number was assigned to each token occurrence of modules and submodules. Each numbered segment at the level of module or submodule constituted a different context. Whenever module or submodule types were instantiated, it was in a different context.

This notion of context seems to combine both temporal and content components, because whenever a uniquely numbered module or submodule was considered, it was at a unique time t and it was proceeded and followed by a uniquely numbered sequence of modules or submodules (which means there was different information in the problem space). A tracing of modules and submodules and the contexts in which they were considered was developed for each subject. These tracings are best presented in conjunction with control strategies.

Control Strategies   Control strategies can be enumerated at different levels. We used a three-level hierarchical analyses that accounts for the protocols at the level of module, submodule, and individual statement types. As the module and submodule categories are task- and subject-specific, the control structure at these levels will also be task- and subject-specific. Since the categories at the level of individual statements are general across all the tasks and subjects, the control structure at this level will also generalize across tasks and subjects.

We used a recursive transition network (Winograd, 1983) to capture and display the control structure of our subjects. These networks have been widely used in computational linguistics to recognize, parse, and generate natural-language strings. We used them to (manually) recognize the coded protocols.[1]

Some samples of control structure from subject S-A's protocol (one from each level) are presented in networks 1, 2, and 3 (figure 5.2). The salient features of the networks are summarized below, and the reader is invited to examine figure 5.1 for details:

• The control structure naturally decomposes into the three hierarchical levels shown in figure 5.3.

• The first two levels are task-specific; the third is general across all three tasks.

• Within each of the levels, one does not observe a consistent, steady, linear movement through the problem. Rather one sees repetitive, cyclical, flexible control structure at all three levels.

• The effect of this repetition and reiteration is that most modules and submodules are considered several times in several different contexts. For example, in network 1, the site module is considered five times, the building module seven times, the services module four times, and the APTM module four times. Table 5.1 summarizes the multiple occurrences of submodules.

• The single local control structure (LCS) network can recognize all the modules in all the protocols. That is, it can do a flat or local statement-by-statement recognition of all the protocols.

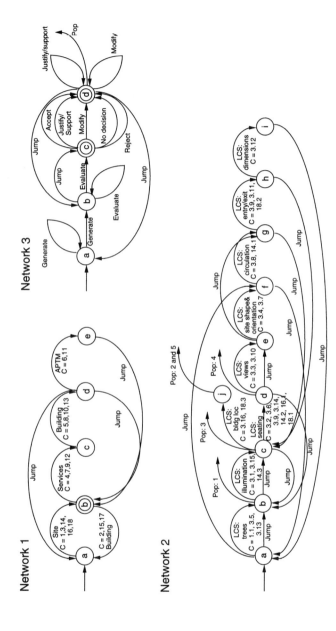

Figure 5.2
Sample of recursive transition networks that recognize subject S-A's protocol. The "C" numbers specify the sequence (and context) in which the arcs are traversed. Network 1 recognizes the complete protocol at the level of the four modules. Network 2 recognizes the "site" submodule. Network 3 recognizes the local control structure of all the submodules.

• Most of the action in the protocols seems to be internal to major modules, at the level of submodules (network 2). The top- and bottom-level networks (networks 1, 3) are rather sparse and simple.

The control strategy for the nondesign problem space also involves cyclical, repetitive, revisitation of modules. However, much of the similarity between it and the LCM control strategy of the design problem space is superficial. One crucial difference is that in the nondesign problem space most of the problem solving occurs internal to modules/episodes. There is little carryover from previous visits to a module or episode. Newell and Simon (1972), in their original analysis of these protocols, claim that in returning to a former state the subject is returning to the previous knowledge state with respect to the problem. If he goes down the wrong path and returns to the previous state, all he knows is that the path just explored does not lead

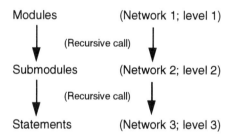

Figure 5.3
Hierarchical organization of control structure

Table 5.1
Occurrences of submodules in multiple contexts for subject S-A

Modules	Number of submodules considered	Percentage of submodules considered more than once	Range	
			High	Low
Site	9	89	7	1
Building	18	28	5	1
Services	4	25	3	1
APTM	3	33	2	1
Total	33	44		

Table 5.2
Trace of the development of knowledge in subject NS6.1's repeated visits to module 6

Visit no.	Concluding knowledge state	Development of knowledge
1	G has to be an even number	Initial proposal
2	No letter in front of R	Connection with first visit unclear
3	G has to be either 1 or 2	Ignore/reverse previous conclusion
4	R has to be greater than 5	Connection to previous visits unclear
5	G is going to be 1	May be connected to visit 3
6	R = 9	May be connected to visit 4
	G = 3	Unconnected to any previous state

Table 5.3
Trace of the development of knowledge in subject S-A's repeated visits to the "seating module"

Visit no.	Concluding knowledge state	Development of knowledge
1	Keep seating below evergreens; do not disturb overall scheme	Initial proposal
2	Keep existing seating	Reaffirm original proposal
3	Incorporate seating elements as part of building structure; relaxation and view of playing field important	Build on first two visits
4	As per third visit but uncouple seating from building structure	Modify third visit
5	Locate seating along borders	Build on fourth visit
6	Counter position seats so as to break up symmetry and not affect circulation	Build on fifth visit

to the goal state. He does not have an enriched understanding of the state he is returning to.

This can be demonstrated by tracing through the repeat visits to a module or an episode and examining the state of knowledge at the end of each visit. Table 5.2 provides such a trace of subject NS6.1's visits to the module column 6. Note the third, "development of knowledge," column. It indicates that there is not a close connection between the current visit to a module or an episode and previous such visits.

In the design case, while problem solving does occur internal to modules, there is also considerable carryover and development of the module from visit to visit, as evidenced by the incremental-development phenomenon and further substantiated by the trace of subject S-A's repeated visits to the submodule "seating" in table 5.3. When the designer cycles back, it is not to a previous knowledge state, but rather to a previous topic or subgoal instantiated in the current context.[2] This suggests some higher-level control structure we have not yet uncovered.

5.2.7 Making and Propagating Commitments

On the one hand, designers need to keep their options open as the design emerges so as not to crystallize too soon (see the discussion of the LCM control strategy above). On the other hand, they also need to make, record, and propagate commitments so as to bring the design to closure. Again, this is dictated by the design task environment. The design plans and specifications have to be in a form that can be interpreted and executed by an independent agent with minimal participation of the designer.

Two possible indicators of commitment are (a) the mode of delivery of the thought or idea, and (b) the "nature" of the written/drawn material. The first seems quite straightforward. Ideas are delivered either verbally or in some combination with marks on paper. The marks on paper are a sign of increased commitment. As will be noted shortly, there is an increase in the number of marks made on paper as the design progresses. The second indicator, the "nature" of the written/drawn material, is actually much more interesting. We will discuss it initially in subsection 5.2.8 in terms of "explicitness and completeness" of the output. A more sophisticated discussion will follow in chapters 6 through 9.

Although commitments are certainly made in the nondesign case, they are only propagated until an evaluation function accepts or rejects them. If they are rejected, there is little that can happen in the way of modification. Because of the localized (episode-internal) nature of nondesign development discussed above, they must be abandoned, and the subject must start fresh.

As an aside, if a designer fails to make and propagate commitments, it becomes painfully obvious. One of the instructional design subjects fell into this category. He did a great deal of talking and hand waving, considering every contingency, every possibility, but was unable to commit himself and use the enormous amount of information he had solicited and generated. As a result, he did not produce much in the way of a lesson specification.

5.2.8   Design Development Occurs in Distinct Phases
The development of a design solution has several distinct phases. First there is a distinction between problem structuring and problem solving. Thereafter, problem solving is further differentiated into preliminary design, refinement, and detailing. This results in four distinct phases. Each is discussed below in turn.

Problem Structuring   Problem structuring is the process of drawing on knowledge from various sources to compensate for missing information in the problem statement and using this knowledge to construct the problem space (Simon, 1973b). It occurs for the obvious reason that design problems are incompletely specified, but the specification of a problem space requires complete information about start states, goal states, operators, and evaluation functions. In Goel and Pirolli (1989), the form and organization of some of this knowledge was examined. Here I want to discuss the extent and location of problem-structuring phases and how these phases differ from problem solving.

The first thing to note is that problem structuring takes up approximately one-quarter of the statements devoted to design development. In the three design protocols, it ranged from 18 percent to 30 percent. In sharp contrast to the design problem space, hardly any problem structuring was evident in the nondesign problem spaces. Only an average of 0.3 percent of the nondesign protocols were devoted to problem structuring.

The second point is that problem structuring occurs at the beginning of the task, where one would expect it, but may also recur periodically as needed. Figure 5.4 shows the temporal distribution, aggregated over five-minute intervals, for the problem-structuring and problem-solving

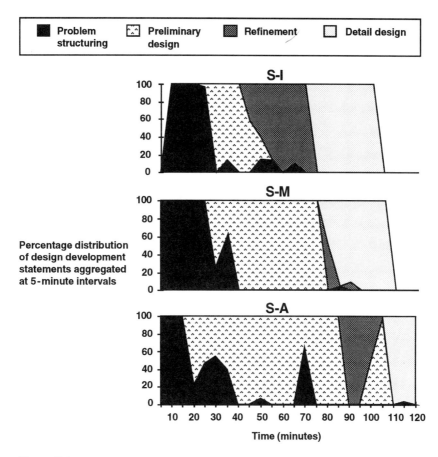

Figure 5.4
Distribution and extent of problem structuring and problem solving for subjects S-A, S-M, and S-I (aggregated over five-minute intervals)

phases for subjects S-A, S-M, and S-I. Figure 5.5 shows the variability in the amount of time devoted to problem structuring versus problem solving across the three subjects.

Although problem structuring is a widely recognized concept, it is often unclear how it differs from problem solving. I offer the following observations based on the data:

1. Aspects of design considered: Table 5.4 presents a breakdown of the aspects of design attended to by noted subjects across the design-

development phases. In general, subjects produced proportionately more statements about people, the purposes of the artifact, and resources during the problem-structuring phases than in problem-solving phases (preliminary design, refinement, and detail design). In contrast, statements about the structure or function of the artifact were more prominent in the problem-solving phases than in the problem-structuring phases. These results suggest that problem structuring in design is associated with attention to how the artifact may be used and what re-

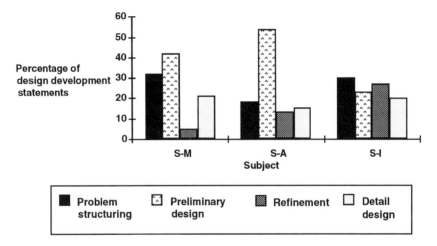

Figure 5.5
Comparative distribution of statements, by design phases

Table 5.4
Percentage of statements made in each design-development phase about various aspects of a design

		Problem solving		
Combined subjects	Problem structuring	Preliminary design	Refinement	Detail design
People	22	11	04	02
Purpose	10	02	00	00
Resource	14	02	00	01
Behavior	08	09	01	03
Function	14	23	32	19
Structure	32	53	63	75

sources are available to form it, whereas problem solving is associated with attention to specification of the function and form of the artifact.

2. Sources of knowledge: The client and design brief are important sources of knowledge during problem structuring but not during problem solving (table 5.5). This is consistent with the claim that problem structuring is substantially a process of bringing new information into the problem space.

3. Commitment to output: A higher percentage of verbal-only statements were generated during problem structuring than problem solving (table 5.6). If the verbal/written distinction is taken as a measure of relative degree of commitment to design decisions, these results indicate a lesser commitment to decisions made during the early problem-structuring phase as compared to those made later during problem solving.

4. Distribution of operators: There is a higher percentage of add and propose operators during problem structuring than during problem solving (figure 5.6). This is also consistent with the claim that problem

Table 5.5
Breakdown of knowledge sources for percentages of statements made in each design-development phase

Combined subjects	Problem structuring	Problem solving		
		Preliminary design	Refinement	Detail design
Design brief	21	00	01	00
Experimenter	25	03	00	00
Self	53	95	96	98
Inferred	01	02	03	02

Table 5.6
Output mode associated with percentages of statements in each design-development phase

Combined subjects	Problem structuring	Problem solving		
		Preliminary design	Refinement	Detail design
Verbal	88	77	61	71
Written	12	23	39	29

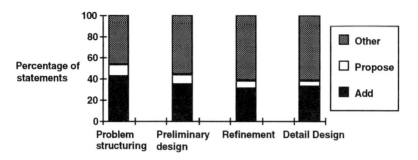

Figure 5.6
Distribution of add and propose operators across design phases

structuring is substantially a process of bringing new information into the problem space.

Problem Solving In addition to the distinction between problem structuring and problem solving, there is a further differentiation of problem solving into preliminary design, refinement, and detail design. Preliminary design statements result in the initial generation and exploration of ideas. Refinement statements serve to elaborate and further an idea, while detailing statements specify the final form of the idea. These categories are standard among designers and are discussed in appendix A.

As might be expected, these phases are generally engaged in sequentially, starting from preliminary design, passing through refinement, and ending with detail design, although it is not unusual for a subject to return to an earlier phase as previously unnoticed aspects emerge (figure 5.4). However, the time subjects devote to each phase varies considerably (figure 5.5). This may account for some of the individual differences in performance.

Generally, the three problem-solving phases differ in at least five ways:

1. The aspects of the problem considered: There is a steady decrease in the consideration of people, purpose, and resource aspects of design development preliminary to detail design and a corresponding increase in the structural aspect (see table 5.4). The behavior and function aspects on average seem to stay relatively constant across the three phases.

2. The primary source of knowledge: There is still some input from the client and/or design brief at the preliminary design stage, but it disappears by the detailing stage (see table 5.5).

3. The degree of commitment made to output statements (as evidenced by the quantity and character of written output): There is a steady increase in the number of verbalizations that are committed to paper as the subject progresses from preliminary design, through refinement, to detail design (see table 5.6). This shows increasing commitment to the emerging design.

4. Level of detail: There is an increase in the degree of explicitness and detailing in the written/drawn material, as demonstrated in subject S-A's development of the floor plan for the post office. Notice the increase in the explicitness of the lines and detailing and dimensioning from figure 5.7 through figure 5.11. In subsequent chapters, we will undertake a much more sophisticated examination of differences in designers' drawings.

5. Transformations: Two types of transformations can be identified in the problem-solving phases, *lateral* transformations and *vertical* transformations. In a lateral transformation, movement is from one idea to a slightly different idea. In a vertical transformation, movement is from one idea to a more detailed version of the same idea. Examples of both are provided in the transformation of figure 5.7 into its final form in figure 5.11.

Figures 5.7 through 5.11 differ not only in their level of detail but also in their relationship to previous diagrams. Figure 5.7 is the first proposed floor plan for the post office. It calls for three separate booths under one roof. Figure 5.8 is a lateral transformation and reorganization of the initial idea in figure 5.7. The three booths are still under one

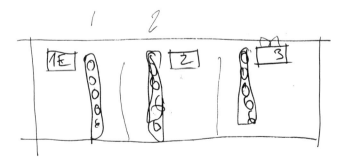

Figure 5.7
Subject S-A, floor plan 1

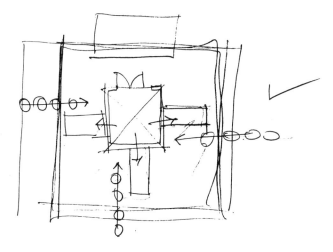

Figure 5.8
Subject S-A, floor plan 2

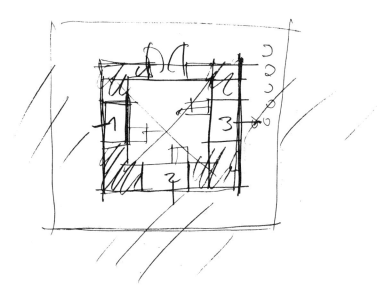

Figure 5.9
Subject S-A, floor plan 3

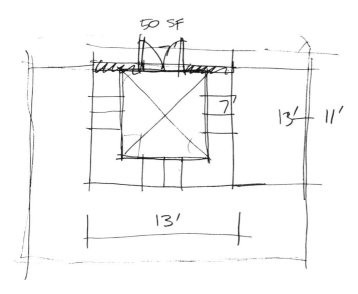

Figure 5.10
Subject S-A, floor plan 4

roof, but now they protrude from a common core. Figure 5.9 is a lateral transformation of figure 5.8. The three booths retain their location but have been internalized into the walls of the main core.

Figure 5.10 on the other hand is a vertical transformation of figure 5.9. There is no modification of the previous idea, only a clarification of lines and an addition of detail (i.e., some dimensions). Similarly, figure 5.11 is a result of a vertical transformation of figure 5.10. Lines and dimensions have been further articulated and some landscaping elements added.

The data indicate that lateral transformations are generally confined to preliminary design phases whereas vertical transformations generally occur in the refinement and detailing phases. For subject S-A, the lateral transformations between figures 5.7, 5.8, and 5.9 occur during preliminary design, whereas the vertical transformation between figures 5.9 and 5.10 occur in the refinement phase, and the vertical transformation between figures 5.10 and 5.11 occurs during the detailing phase.

It seems that these multiple problem-solving phases are required not only because of the size and complexity of design problems but, perhaps more importantly, because of the qualitative shift in the nature of

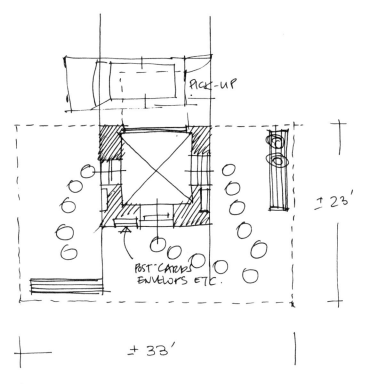

Figure 5.11
Subject S-A, floor plan 5

the information necessary to transform the input to the output. (See abstraction hierarchies below.)

Again, the situation is different for the nondesign problem spaces. Instead of problem solving's comprising distinct phases of different activities, it includes cycles of the same basic activity. The subject is searching for a solution. If the solution is not on the path being searched, the subject must back up and start down another path. The activity as one goes down each path is basically the same.

5.2.9   Abstraction Hierarchies

Finally, there are at least two orthogonal notions of abstraction hierarchies in the design problem space. One deals with the type of information being considered and the other with the level of generality or detail with which it is covered. The latter was captured in the design-development categories (problem structuring, preliminary design, refinement, and detail design) and the former in the aspects of design development categories (people, purposes, behavior, function, and structure). These categories were implicated in 75 percent of the protocol statements.

The two abstraction hierarchies can be viewed as forming the design space in the graph in figure 5.12. Designers differ substantially in the path they take through this space and how quickly or slowly they traverse its various phases. These differences are a function of training, personal preferences and style, familiarity with the task, and other such factors, and account for many of the individual differences between designers. This analysis does not apply to our two examples of nondesign problem spaces.

5.3   Discussion and Summary of the Design Problem Space

In chapter 4 I demonstrated that there are important differences between design and nondesign task environments. In this chapter we have seen that these task environment differences result in substantive cognitive differences at the level of design and nondesign problem spaces. The major features of the two problem spaces are summarized in table 5.7.

In addition to the distinction between design and nondesign problem spaces, a number of observations were also made about the different characters of the design development phases of problem structuring,

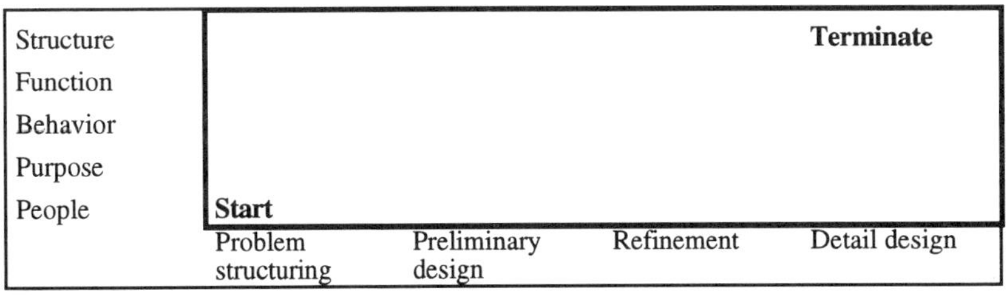

Structure				**Terminate**
Function				
Behavior				
Purpose				
People	**Start**			
	Problem structuring	Preliminary design	Refinement	Detail design

Figure 5.12
Abstraction hierarchies in the design problem space

Table 5.7
Summary of design and nondesign problem spaces

Design problem space	Nondesign problem space
• predominance of personalized stopping rules and evaluation functions	• stopping rules given in problem statement; evaluation functions often (but not always) objective
• few state transformations generated by deductive inference (order of 1%); most result from memory retrieval and nondemonstrative inference	• many state transformations are through demonstrative inference (order of 40%)
• reversal of direction of transformation function as a way of problem structuring	• reversal of transformation function does not occur
• near decomposability of modules: many modules (order of 30); few interconnections (order of 7%); hierarchical clustering of interconnections; subject has flexibility in determining decomposition and interconnections	• near decomposability of modules: fewer modules (order of 6); higher density of interconnections (order of 20%); no hierarchical clustering of interconnections; subject does not have flexibility in determining decomposition and interconnections
• incremental development of artifact	• does not occur
• limited-commitment-mode control strategy	• LCM control strategy not used; much more localized strategy used
• making and propagating of commitments	• commitments made, but propagated only until localized evaluation function accepts or rejects them
• distinction between problem structuring and problem solving with relatively large percentage of time devoted to problem structuring (order of 25%)	• little time devoted to problem structuring (order of 0.3%)
• several distinct problem-solving phases: preliminary design, refinement, detail design	• no distinct problem-solving phases
• manipulation of several abstraction hierarchies	• does not apply

preliminary design, refinement, and detail design. These are summarized in figure 5.13.

Problem structuring is the process of retrieving information from
long-term memory and external memory and using it to construct the
problem space; that is, to specify start states, goal states, operators, and
evaluation functions. Problem structuring, as compared to problem
solving, relies heavily on the client and design brief as sources of information, considers information at a higher level of abstraction, makes
fewer commitments to decisions, and involves a higher percentage of
add and propose operators. One particularly interesting strategy for
problem structuring is reversing the direction of the transformation
function.

In the *preliminary design phase,* alternative solutions are generated
and explored. Alternative solutions are neither numerous nor fully developed when generated. They emerge through the incremental transformations of a few kernel ideas (see subsection 5.2.5). These kernel
ideas are solutions to *other* problems the designer has encountered, or
more generally, ideas and images from the subject's life experience.
When these "solutions" are brought into the problem space, they are,
not surprisingly, out of context or in some way inappropriate and need
to be modified to constitute solutions to the present problem.

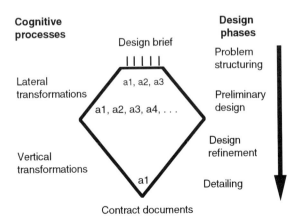

Figure 5.13
The design problem space

This transformation and exploration of alternative solutions is facilitated by the abstract nature of information being considered (a large percentage still concerned with people and behavior), a relatively low commitment to the generated ideas, the coarseness of detail, and a large number of lateral transformations. Lateral transformations are necessary for widening the problem space and exploring and developing kernel ideas.

The *refinement* and *detailing phases* are more constrained and structured. In these phases commitments are made to a particular solution and propagated through the problem space. They are characterized by the concrete nature of information being considered (mostly having to do with the function and structure of the artifact), a higher degree of commitment to generated ideas, attention to detail, and a large number of vertical transformations. Vertical transformations deepen the problem space.

The following aspects of the design problem space do not seem to vary across the design phases, at least at the level of my analysis: the near decomposability of the solution, the limited-commitment-7 mode control strategy, the personalized stopping rules and evaluation functions, and the predominance of memory retrieval and inductive reasoning.

These empirical results about the design problem space constitute the third substantive claim of the monograph and play an important role in the overall argument.

6

A Cognitive Science Analysis of Designers' Representations

No longer in a merely physical universe, man lives in a symbolic universe. Language, myth, art, and religion are parts of this universe. They are the varied threads which weave the symbolic net, the tangled web of human experience.
—Ernst Cassirer

During the course of the first study, several observations were also made about designers' use of external symbol systems. They include the facts that (i) designers manipulate representations of the world rather than the world itself, (ii) designers use many different symbol systems, and (iii) different symbol systems are correlated with different problem-solving phases and cognitive processes. Each of these observations is common knowledge among designers (Albarn and Smith, 1977; Crowe and Laseau, 1984; Goldschmidt, 1991, in press; Laseau, 1989). Unfortunately, most members of the cognitive science community have been raised in a primarily linguistic tradition and find such ideas foreign.

6.1 Designers Manipulate Representations of the World

The input to the design process is a design brief. It is a written or verbal "document" that generally describes the client's current states of affairs, the reason these states are unsatisfactory, and what is required to make them satisfactory. The output of the design process is generally a set of contract documents, consisting of specifications and blueprints. Thus both the input and the output of the design process are representations that describe and/or depict an artifact or process. There are, however, a number of interesting differences between the two descriptions and depictions.

Two differences are of particular importance for our purposes: First, the content of the design brief deals primarily with the people who will use the artifact, the goals they wish to satisfy, and the behavior that will result in goal satisfaction. The contract documents, on the other hand, provide a structural specification of the artifact and information on how it is to be constructed. Second, the design brief is consistent with a number of alternative solutions or artifacts, whereas the contract documents are consistent with at most one of these alternatives.

Design, at some very abstract level, is the process of transforming one set of representations (the design brief) into another set of representations (the contract documents). However, not only are the inputs and outputs of the design process representations, all the intervening transformations are also typically done on representations. This is not an accident. It is dictated by certain features of the design task environment noted in chapter 4. Recall that design typically occurs in situations where it is not possible or desirable to tamper with the world until the full extent and ramifications of the intervention are known in advance. After all, we only get one "run" on the world. Every action is irrevocable and may have substantive costs associated with it. Thus it is not surprising to find that designers produce and manipulate representations of the artifact rather than the artifact itself. All the reasoning and decision making (including performance prediction) is done through the construction and manipulation of models of various sorts, including drawings, mock-ups, mathematical modeling, computer simulations, and so on.[1]

6.2   Multiplicity of Symbol Systems

Designers make extensive use of representations; moreover, these representations encompass many different symbol systems. Examples of systems of representations in the repertoire of architectural designers are illustrated in figures 6.1 through 6.13.

Figure 6.1 is a fragment from a design brief, a document specifying the purpose of the artifact and the various behavioral and functional goals it needs to satisfy. Figure 6.2 is a "bubble diagram" derived from an architectural design brief. It highlights functions and the relationships

I would like two recreational areas in the house. One for the children and one for the adults. The children's room should be well removed from the living areas.

Figure 6.1
Fragment from a design brief

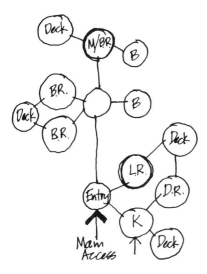

Figure 6.2
"Bubble diagram" (reproduced with permission of Van Nostrand Reinhold from Laseau, 1989, p. 72, 5-6a)

between them. Figure 6.3 is a "layout diagram." It specifies the positions and orientations of the various functional elements. Figure 6.4 is a preliminary attempt to give size and shape to the functional elements. Figure 6.5 is a plan schematic. Figure 6.6 is a conceptual sketch, something the designer might do in the very early stages of a new problem. It is not clear what, if anything, is being depicted. Figure 6.7 is a quick, freehand perspective of a college dormitory. Figure 6.8 is a labeled, freehand sketch of a doorway. Figure 6.9 is a freehand section of a projection table. Figure 6.10 is a window detail. Figure 6.11 is a painting (in perspective) of the Houses of Parliament on the Thames by Monet. Architects are also known to do such quality paintings for various purposes. Figure 6.12 is a wall-section detail executed with drafting instruments. Figure 6.13 is a blueprint of a plan view of the mechanical system of a building.

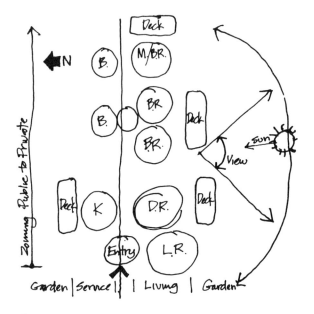

Figure 6.3
"Layout diagram" (reproduced with permission of Van Nostrand Reinhold from Laseau, 1989, p. 72, 5-6b)

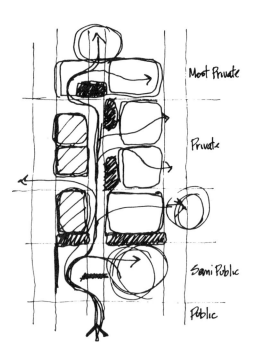

Figure 6.4
First sketch of floor plan (reproduced with permission of Van Nostrand Reinhold from Laseau, 1989, p. 73, 5-6c)

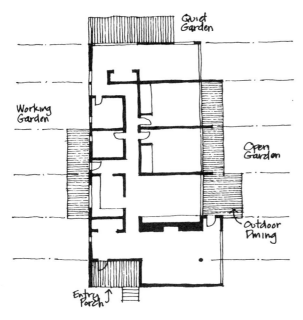

Figure 6.5
Schematic of floor plan (reproduced with permission of Van Nostrand Reinhold from Laseau, 1989, p. 73, 5-6d)

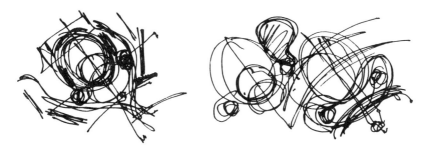

Figure 6.6
Conceptual sketch (reproduced with permission of Van Nostrand Reinhold from Laseau, 1989, p. 8, 1-18)

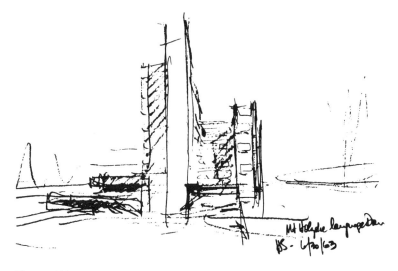

Figure 6.7
Quick, freehand perspective (reproduced with permission of Van Nostrand Reinhold from Laseau, 1989, p. 139,7-17): "By Hugh Stubbins, Mount Holyoke College Dormitories"

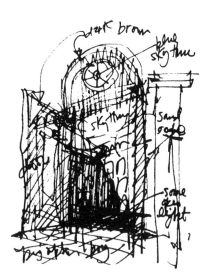

Figure 6.8
Labeled sketch of doorway (reproduced with permission of Van Nostrand Reinhold from Laseau, 1989, p. 3, 1-6): "By Norman Jaffee"

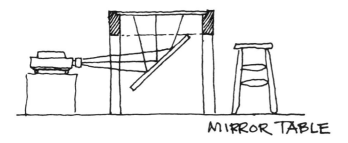

Figure 6.9
Quick, freehand section of projection table (reproduced with permission of Van Nostrand Reinhold from Laseau, 1989, p. 29, 2-30)

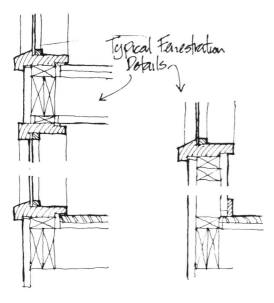

Figure 6.10
Freehand window detail (reproduced with permission of Van Nostrand Reinhold from Laseau, 1989, p. 183, part of 9-15)

Figure 6.11
The Houses of Parliament, by Claude Monet, National Gallery of Art, Washington, D.C.

Designers are certain that there are important differences in their various systems of representation and that these differences affect their thought processes. However, classifying the various representations into types is a nontrivial task. It would be wrong to say that the representations in figures 6.1 through 6.13 are all of the same type and equally wrong to say they are all of different types. We might start out by saying that 6.1 is a fragment of natural-language text and 6.2 through 6.13 are diagrams of various sorts. But this only raises the questions (i) what is the difference between 6.1 and 6.2 through 6.13 that accounts for partitioning them this way, and (ii)

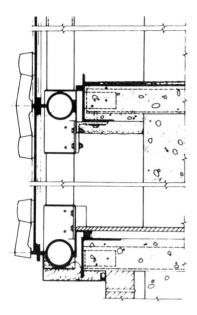

Figure 6.12
Wall section detail (reproduced with permission of Van Nostrand Reinhold from Laseau, 1989, p. 14, 1-26): "Wall Section, Headquarters Building, Smith, Hinchman & Grylls Associates, Inc."

are there no crucial differences between 6.2 through 6.13 that need to be accounted for? For example, does the fact that 6.5 is a freehand perspective and 6.11 is a more "polished" perspective make them members of different symbol systems? What about the fact that 6.5 is a plan, 6.9 is a section, and 6.7 is a perspective? Is this a difference of type? Figure 6.10 is a freehand detail, whereas 6.12 is drafted. Does this constitute a difference of type? Figures 6.2, 6.3, 6.8, and 6.13 are all labeled. Does this put them in the same category? Is figure 6.2 more similar to 6.1 or to 6.5? The questions and possible combinations are many.

Although we can agree that there is considerable richness and variety in the representations in figures 6.1 through 6.13, our intuitions are not secure enough to attempt a classification. We need an explicit classification scheme.

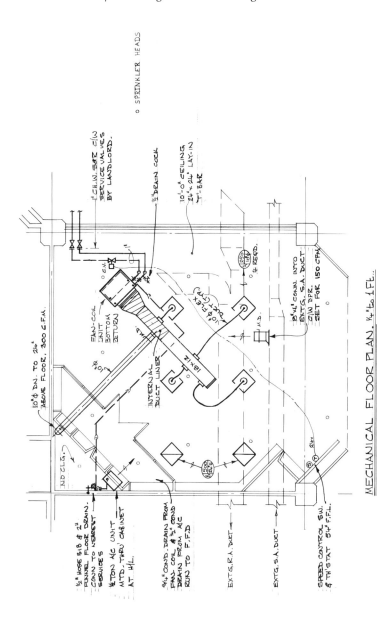

Figure 6.13
Mechanical floor plan blueprint

6.3   Constraints on Classification Schemes

As it turns out, classification schemes are easy to come by. Here is one: All utterances tokened on the surface of the moon belong to symbol system *A;* all those tokened near the surface of the earth belong to symbol system *B;* all inscription tokens that are green and weigh more than five pounds belong to symbol system *C.* But we quickly recognize this as nonsensical and missing the point, suggesting that not just any arbitrary classification scheme will do.

So we see that our intuitions do not go far enough and arbitrary accounts will not do. What is needed is either a theory that begins with our intuitions and extends, develops, and explains them or a theory that offers a nonintuitive categorization motivated and grounded by the theoretical framework of our discipline. This latter theory generally must offer us substantial insights for denying the obvious. The ideal state of affairs would be to have a theory that does justice to both our intuitions and our theoretical framework. Thus a first constraint on a classification scheme must be that it meet one of these criteria.

Another constraint is that the classification scheme not beg the crucial questions. For example, suppose we decide that the distinction between pictorial and linguistic symbol systems is an important one to make. In such a case, it will not do to say that the elements in symbol system *A* have "pictorial properties" and the elements in symbol system *B* have "linguistic properties" and, therefore, *A* is a "pictorial" symbol system and *B* is a "linguistic" symbol system. One can not go in with the notion of linguistic, pictorial, musical, and the like, structures; these (or their theoretical counterparts) must emerge as constructed concepts.

Another issue in the development of a taxonomy is the granularity of individuation. It should not turn out that every representation is of a unique type (i.e., all classes are unit classes) or that all representations are really of the same type. Such results would be just as crazy/arbitrary as the above example. This restriction is required because scientific generalizations predicated over unit classes are not very interesting and we agree that there are differences of type between representational systems. Thus a third constraint is that it provide a reasonable and interesting number of categories (i.e., something other than one or an infinite number).

One method of classifying symbol systems that many cognitive scientists find attractive is on the basis of functionality, that is, on the basis of the cognitive functions that representations serve. Although this method is superficially attractive, it does harbor a serious limitation. It will not allow us to say *why* a particular symbol system serves such and such a cognitive function. That is, suppose we discover that the symbol system of sketching is used in the early, generative phases of design problem solving. What follows? What *should* follow is an account of some of the essential properties of sketching and how they interact with the cognitive system to produce the observed behavior. A functional analysis is not sufficient to allow us to take this step, because it individuates on the basis of observed behavior, not on the basis of important properties of symbol systems. This suggests a fourth constraint: that the scheme individuate on the basis of important, preferably constitutive, properties of symbol systems.

A fifth constraint on a classification scheme is that it be readily applicable. By "readily applicable" I mean we should be able to apply it with a modest (i.e., something less than complete) knowledge of the world. If complete knowledge of the world is a prerequisite for applying the scheme, it will be of little value.

A sixth constraint is that it be widely applicable. By "widely applicable" I mean it needs to be such that it can be applied to all symbol systems. If it is not widely applicable in this sense, it will not result in a general typology of symbol systems.

One might consider these six constraints—(i) grounding of the categories, (ii) not question begging, (iii) plural but finite number of categories, (iv) individuating on the basis of important properties of symbol systems, (v) applicability in the face of limited knowledge, and (vi) wide-ranging applicability—as minimal, general constraints on any satisfactory classification scheme.

For the purposes of cognitive science, we need to introduce two additional constraints. Our seventh constraint is that the distinctions made by the classification scheme be (potentially) detectable by our behavioral data and methodology. The eighth constraint is that the distinctions the classification scheme makes be compatible with our explanatory appeal to computation. Thus we have a total of eight constraints that any classification scheme adequate for the purposes of cognitive science must satisfy.

Notice the difference in the status of the first six general constraints and the two specific ones. The first six seem to carry more weight, because they are motivated by our intuitions and general assumptions about the nature of the world and scientific explanations. It would require a great deal to overthrow these assumptions. We expect no contradictions in satisfying all six simultaneously. The last two constraints are motivated by discipline-specific theoretical assumptions, the status of which (in this case) is much less secure. Since they have a common motivation, it is reasonable to expect that they, too, may be satisfied simultaneously. But given the different motivations of the first six and last two constraints, there is no a priori reason to believe that both sets *can* be satisfied simultaneously. Furthermore, in the case of a conflict, and in the absence of compelling reasons to the contrary, one would have to favor the first six constraints and be prepared to modify the discipline-specific theoretical assumptions.

We now examine the major approach used by cognitive scientists to classify symbol systems—that of informational and computational equivalence—and evaluate it with respect to each of these constraints.

6.4 Informational and Computational Equivalence

6.4.1 Summary of Approach

Simon's (1978) approach to defining and classifying symbol systems is reflective of much of the cognitive science community. On this account, the closest thing we get to a definition of symbol systems is the following: "Defining a representation means (1) specifying one or more data types, and (2) specifying the primitive (i.e., "fast") operations that can be performed on information in those data types. . . . [T]he declaration of a data type means that certain primitive operations are available for accessing, storing, and modifying data" (Simon, 1978, pp. 7–8). For example, *car* (return the first element in the list) and *cdr* (return the list minus the first element) are primitive operations in the list-type data structures found in the computer language, LISP. Finding an arbitrary element in a list data structure is not a primitive operation, but finding an arbitrary element in an array data structure is.

The classification of symbol systems begins with a distinction between informational equivalence and computational equivalence. Simon defines them as follows:

Informational Equivalence. Two representations are informationally equivalent if the transformation from one to the other entails no loss of information, i.e., if each can be constructed from the other. (1978, p. 4)

Computational Equivalence. Two representations are computationally equivalent if the same information can be extracted from each (the same inferences drawn) with about the same amount of computation. (1978, p. 5)

The idea is that two representations that are informationally equivalent may be computationally differentiable. Furthermore, the claim is that cognitive science should differentiate representations at the computational level, in terms of the processes defined over them. More generally, the differences picked out by this classification scheme amount to computational considerations, such as resource allocations, primitive operations, and control mechanisms. This results in the typology in figure 6.14.

Anderson (1983) is also convinced that the appropriate way to differentiate representational systems is by the *processes* defined over them. He writes,

The central issue is the distinction between representations from the point of view of the process defined on them and representations from the point of view of the notations used to express them. . . . It is impossible to identify whether a

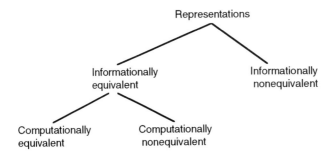

Figure 6.14
Informational- and computational-equivalence classification scheme

particular notation correctly expresses the structure of a representation or whether different knowledge structures are encoded according to different notations. . . . It is possible to decide that different knowledge structures have different processes defined upon them. . . . [R]epresentations can be defined in terms of the processes that operate on them. (1983, p. 46)

Anderson goes on to specify five theoretically relevant processes (within the ACT* theory) that interact with representational structures in working memory: (i) encoding process ("deposits" representations of the environment into working memory); (ii) storage process ("deposits" records from working memory into declarative memory); (iii) retrieval process (returns records from long-term memory into working memory); (iv) match process (determines which productions will apply to the contents of working memory); (v) execution (creates new working-memory structures through the firing of productions). Insofar as representational structures are treated differently by one or more of these computational processes, they constitute different representation types for Anderson. To the extent they are treated identically, they are the same type.

Lindsay (1988) is also impressed with processing. His suggestion, specific to imagery and propositional representations, is that the latter will support deductive inference procedures, whereas the former requires nondemonstrative inference procedures. Again, the way to differentiate between representational systems is by the procedures defined over the data structures.

6.4.2   Applying the Apparatus: Larkin and Simon (1987)

Larkin and Simon (1987) use the informational- and computational-equivalence apparatus to try to discern the differences in the respective cognitive roles played by "diagrammatic" and "sentential" representations, which they define as follows:

1. In a *sentential* representation, the expressions form a sequence corresponding, on a one-to-one basis, to the sentences in a natural-language description of the problem. Each expression is a direct translation into a simple formal language of the corresponding natural-language sentence.

2. In a *diagrammatic* representation, the expressions correspond, on a one-to-one basis, to the components of a diagram describing the problem. Each expression contains the information that is stored at one particular locus in the diagram, including information about relations with the adjacent loci. (Larkin and Simon, 1987, p. 66)

Figure 6.15a offers an example of a diagrammatic representation of a pulley system; figure 6.15b is an sentential representation of the same system. The difference between the two is this:

[T]he diagrammatic representation preserves explicitly the information about the topological and geometric relations among the components of the problem, while the sentential representation does not. A sentential representation may, of course, preserve other kinds of relations, for example, temporal or logical sequence. An outline may reflect hierarchical relations. (p. 66)

The idea is that, given two such representations that are informationally equivalent, they can be mapped onto, or translated into, two data structures *DS* and *DS'*. In the data structure for the sentential representation, the "elements appear in a single sequence," and in the data structure for the diagrammatic representation, the "information is indexed by two-dimensional locations" (p. 68). One can then observe the interaction of these data structures with some procedure and make observations about relative computational efficiency (see figure 6.16). This is illustrated more concretely in figure 6.15 with the "pulley example" taken from Larkin and Simon (1987). The representation in 6.15a is translated into the data structure in 6.15c (though the lettering schemes in 16.5a and 16.5c do not correspond, see figure 2 in Larkin and Simon [1987, p. 79]), and the representation in 6.15b is translated into the data structure in 6.15d. The data structures in 6.15c and 6.15d are then compared with respect to computational equivalence. More precisely, the productions in 6.15e are used to search each of the data structures, and, because of different indexing in the two cases, search and solution times are found to vary considerably.

All in all, this is not a very satisfying account. One is left with the feeling that something important has been missed. In the balance of this chapter, I evaluate the approach and identify some of the sources of dissatisfaction.

Figure 6.15 (opposite page)
(*a*) Diagrammatic representation of a pulley system (*b*) Sentential representation of a pulley system (*c*) Data structure for diagrammatic representation (*d*) Data structure for sentential representation (*e*) Procedure defined over diagrammatic and sentential data structures (Reproduced from Larkin and Simon [1987] with permission of Ablex Publishing)

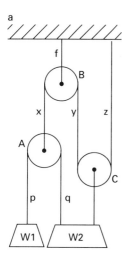

b

Consider a problem given in the following natural-language statements. We have three pulleys, two weights, and some ropes, arranged as follows:

1. The first weight is suspended from the left end of a rope over pulley A. The right end of this rope is attached to, and partially supports, the second weight.

2. Pulley A is suspended from the left end of the rope that runs over pulley B and under pulley C. Pulley B is suspended from the ceiling. The right end of the rope that runs under pulley C is attached to the ceiling.

3. Pulley C is attached to the second weight, supporting it jointly with the right end of the first rope.

The pulleys and ropes are weightless; the pulleys are frictionless; and the rope segments are all vertical, except where they run over or under the pulley wheels. Find the ratio of the second to the first weight, if the system is in equilibrium.

c

	(weight a) (rope b) (rope c) (pulley d)
(1a.1)	(hangs a from b)
(1a.2)	(pulley-system b, d, c)

	(weight e)
(1b.1)	(hangs e from c)

	(rope f) (pulley g) (rope h) (pulley i) (rope j) (rope k) (rope l) (ceiling m)
(2a.1)	(hangs d from f)
(2a.2)	(pulley-system f, g, h)
(2a.3)	(pulley-system h, i, j)
(2b.1)	(hangs g from k)
(2b.2)	(hangs k from m)
(3a.1)	(hangs j from m)
(3a.2)	(hangs l from i)
(3b)	(hangs e from l)
(4.1)	(value a 1)

d

	(weight W1) (rope Rp) (rope Rq) (pulley Pa)
(1a.1)	(hangs W1 from Rp)
(1a.2)	(pulley-system Rp, Pa, Rq)

	(weight W2)
(1b.1)	(hangs W2 from Rq)

	(rope Rx) (pulley Pb) (rope Ry) (pulley Pc) (rope Rz) (rope Rt) (rope Rs) (ceiling c)
(2a.1)	(hangs Pa from Rx)
(2a.2)	(pulley-system Rx, Pb, Ry)
(2a.3)	(pulley-system Ry, Pc, Rz)
(2b.1)	(hangs Pb from Rt)
(2b.2)	(hangs Rt from c)
(3a.1)	(hangs Rx from c)
(3a.2)	(hangs Rs from Pc)
(3b.3)	(hangs W2 from Rs)
(4.1)	(value W1 1)

e

P1. **Single-string support.** (weight <Wx>) (rope <Ry>)
(value <Wx> <n>) (hangs <Wx> <Ry>)
~(hangs <Wx> <Rx>)
→ (value <Ry> <W-number>)

P2. **Ropes over pulley.** (pulley <P>) (rope <R1>) (rope <R2>)
(pulley-system <R1> <P> <R2>) (value <R1> <n1>)
→ (value <R2> <n1>)

P3. **Rope hangs from or supports pulley.** (pulley <R1>) (rope <R1>) (rope <R2>)
(pulley-system <R1> <P> <R2>) { (hangs <R3> from <P>) or (hangs <P>
from <R3>) } (value <R1> <n1>) (value <R2> <n2>)
→ (value <R3> <n1 + <n2>)

P4. **Weight and multiple supporting ropes.** (weight <W1>) (rope <R1>) (rope <R2>) (hangs
<W1> <R1>) (hangs <W1> <R2>) ~(hangs <W1> <R3>)
(value <R1> <n1>) (value <R2> <n2>)

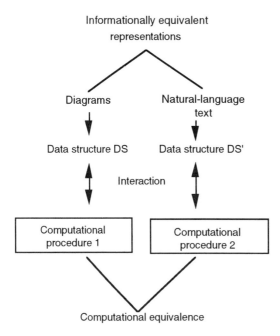

Figure 6.16
Larkin and Simon's analysis of diagrams and sentential representations

6.4.3   Critique of the Informational- and Computational-Equivalence Approach

Although differentiating symbol systems on the basis of informational and computational equivalence is a standard and deeply entrenched approach in the cognitive science literature, it leaves much to be desired. It is here evaluated with respect to the eight constraints on classification schemes proposed in section 6.3. It fails on most counts.

Grounding/Justifying the Categories   The first constraint on classification schemes required that the resulting categories be grounded in a set of intuitions or be motivated by the theoretical framework of the discipline. The categories resulting from individuation on the basis of informational and computational equivalence are certainly not grounded in intuitions. For example, if I have two books that are identical except that one has a standard alphabetical index whereas the other index is ordered by the page numbers on which the items appear, then I have two different *types* of representational systems by the computational criterion. This strikes me as odd, because when we individuate symbol systems intuitively, we list categories like painting, music, algebra, and natural language. Both books, on any intuitive classification, would fall into the same category.

These results seem to be arbitrary, but in context they are not. We have a theory of cognitive processes that characterizes them as computational processes and justifies categorization based on information processing resources and effort. This might well lead one to believe that our cognitive theory alleviates the need to account for our intuitive categories.

As it turns out, it does not. Most cognitive scientists continue to believe that intuitive categories like "linguistic" and "pictorial" are relevant and important to cognitive science, that there will be important cognitive differences along these dimensions. Even Larkin and Simon are, after all, making claims about *sentential/linguistic* and *diagrammatic* representations. As long as we continue to use the intuitive categories in our professional discourse, we will be obligated to develop a classification scheme that captures, systematizes, and extends them.

Begging the Questions   The second constraint required that we not beg the question as to why a certain representation belongs to a certain category. The informational- and computational-equivalence approach is in danger of doing so on several counts.

First, Larkin and Simon (1987) define "sentential representation" in terms of "sentences in a natural language" and "diagrammatic representation" in terms of "diagrams." This is not helpful and begs the question in the most obvious way. I take it that the assumption is that it is painfully obvious what is and is not a sentence or diagram. But as noted above, this is clearly not the case. (Which of the representations in figures 6.1 through 6.13 constitute pieces of linguistic description and which constitute diagrams? If the answer is that 6.1 is a piece of natural language and everything else is a diagram, then the questions are why? and are there no differences of kind among figures 6.2 through 6.13?)

If we continue to believe that our intuitive categories like "linguistic" and "pictorial" are relevant and important to cognitive science, we must come up with a classification scheme that accounts for them. We can either have an explicit theory or beg the question.

Second, we now also need to be able to map from the intuitive categories to *equivalent* formal data structures to which the computational equivalence criterion can be applied. In the Larkin and Simon example in figure 6.15, this corresponds to the mapping from 6.15a to 6.15c and from 6.15b to 6.15d. This again requires an additional theory, one that specifies which properties of a computational data structure and procedure make it correspond to an intuitive category like "linguistic" or "pictorial." But, as noted in the introductory chapter, there are no reasons to believe that all external symbol systems can be mapped onto equivalent formal expressions, and many reasons to believe they cannot. Thus there is little reason to believe we will ever have such a theory.

The "theory" that Larkin and Simon (1987) offer for this step is trivial and situation-specific. On their account a "diagrammatic" data structure explicitly encodes information about "topological and geometric relations," whereas a "sentential" data structure encodes information about other relations, such as "temporal or logical sequence." There are two problems with this claim. First, we really do not have a good working account of implicit and explicit encoding of information in computational systems (Kirsh, 1990). Second, the properties of "topological and geometric relations" and "temporal or logical sequence" seem neither necessary nor sufficient to distinguish diagrammatic and sentential structures *generally*. For instance, what "topological and geometric relations" are explicitly encoded in the conceptual diagrams in figure 6.6, and what "temporal or logical sequence" is explicitly encoded in the text in figure 6.1?

One could of course argue that there is no need to talk about the intuitive categories as far as cognitive science is concerned and avoid both these difficulties, but given the extent to which our scientific discourse relies on intuitive categories, this is not a serious option at the moment.

Unit or Arbitrary Categories   The third constraint on a classification scheme required that it result in an interesting number of categories (i.e., not one or an infinite number). Unfortunately, individuating representations on the basis of computational equivalence—without the guidance of intuitive categories and a theory to map the computational-equivalence categories onto the intuitive categories—will leave us with unit classes if we interpret "equivalence" strictly, or it will leave us with arbitrary classes if we interpret "equivalence" loosely.

All procedures computing different functions are informationally nonequivalent and constitute disjoint classes. Within each class of informationally equivalent procedures will be many computationally nonequivalent procedures. But there is no accepted interpretation of computational equivalence. If we take equivalence in the sense of strict identity, then each procedure will constitute a unit class. If two procedures are computationally identical, then they are just different instances/tokens/copies of the same single procedure—like two copies of the Microsoft Word program. If there is the slightest difference between them, such as a change in variable name, or more drastic differences, such as the language they are written in or the algorithm they implement, they will be computationally different procedures, because they will make different demands on machine resources.

We can of course loosen up our notion of sameness, but the problem is, in the absence of the theories mentioned above, where do we stop? On what basis do we say that the difference in memory allocation between two programs that are identical except that one uses different (and longer) variable names is irrelevant, but that memory differences between two word-recognizing programs, one of which stores a list of roots and generates plurals and tenses while the other also stores plurals and tenses, are relevant?

Individuation Based on a Single (Questionable) Property   The fourth constraint required that a classification scheme for symbol systems individuate on the basis of important, preferably constitutive, properties of symbol systems. This requires some understanding of the various components and relations of a symbol system and how they can vary.

The informational- and computational-equivalence criterion is based, unfortunately, on some rather impoverished and mistaken assumptions in this regard.

Simon (1978) defines representations in terms of data structures and procedures. Although both components are necessary for representational systems, they are not sufficient. The referential aspect is all-important and must be incorporated in any analysis. It is the whole purpose of a representation. Without it the concept of a representational system is incoherent.

The referent has simply dropped out of the computational-equivalence analysis. It is this serious omission that leads Anderson to make the erroneous claim that "The central issue is the distinction between representations from the point of view of the process defined on them and representations from the point of view of the notations used to express them" (1983, p. 46). Notation and processing/inferencing are the only issues even considered. It is further conceded that in the case of mental representations, issues of "notation" or syntax are not decidable with our methodology and database. This leaves processing or inferencing as the sole basis of individuation on this account.

In restricting themselves to inferencing/processing issues, these researchers have restricted themselves to one of many representational issues. This is unnecessary and distorts the subject matter. In the next chapter, we will see that it is possible to say something interesting about a number of the components and relations of symbol systems, including the central compliance relation, on the basis of behavioral data.

A further difficulty with this approach is that it is not clear whether processing or computational concerns are bona fide semantical issues. Information equivalence is defined in terms of entailment (Simon, 1978). Entailment, in turn, is concerned with truth: S entails S' if and only if when S is true, S' is also true. As such, both entailment and information equivalence are concerned with truth and are genuine semantical notions. However, it is not clear that the same can be said about computational equivalence. It would surely be perverse to suggest that there is no relationship between computational equivalence and representation, and equally perverse to suggest that the notion of computational equivalence will be the center of a theory of representation. Whatever the relationship between representation and computational equivalence, it is neither trivial nor obvious. Much work needs to be done to explicate and reconstruct this relationship. It seems to me the onus is on the advocates of this classification scheme to try to tell this story.

Applicability of Criteria Requires Complete Knowledge of the World
The fifth constraint on a classification scheme was that it not require complete knowledge of the world for its application. The informational- and computational-equivalence criterion fails this constraint also.

First, as already noted, the classification scheme assumes that all external symbol systems can be translated into *equivalent* expressions in a formal language (i.e., with no loss of cognitive significance). There is absolutely no reason to believe that this is possible and many reasons to vigorously deny it. Try it with a Shakespearean sonnet.

Second, the computational criterion can be applied only to representations that are deemed to be informationally equivalent. But determining information equivalence is not trivial. It requires much more than knowing the symbol system in effect; it requires an explicit theory of the domain of application. In fact, computational equivalence is not a claim about the system of representation at all. It is a claim about the domain. We have such domain theories for subsets of mathematics, logic, and some fragments of science. So we can, as Simon (1978, p. 4) notes, say that "appropriately axiomatized formulations of Euclidean geometry and analytic geometry" are informationally equivalent. It is such an implicit domain theory about physics problems that allows Larkin and Simon to claim informational equivalence of their "sentential" and "diagrammatic" representations in figures 6.15a and 6.15b. But we simply do not have domain theories for most domains and thus cannot even entertain the question of informational equivalence. To have such theories, we would need to know all there is to know about the world.

To see this clearly, consider the all-too-common situation in which we know the symbol systems involved but do not have a theory of the domain. Take two English translations of Goethe's *Faust,* one by

Bayard Taylor and the other by Madison Priest. As native speakers of English, we have considerable knowledge of the language in which they are written. But having no domain theory of literature, we have no idea how to determine informational equivalence. In fact, we cannot even make sense of the question. If we cannot determine informational equivalence of the works, we cannot categorize them.

This is clearly unsatisfactory. The classification of symbol systems should transcend the specifics of what is being said in them. If it does not, we will not get a classification scheme until we complete our science of the world—until we know all there is to know.

Lack of Wide-Ranging Applicability   The sixth constraint on a classification scheme was that it be widely applicable. Once again, the informational- and computational-equivalence approach fails.

As noted above, a domain theory is required to determine informational equivalence. If we can not determine informational equivalence, we can not apply the criterion. Since for most domains we can not determine informational equivalence, we can not use the apparatus.

Worse yet, suppose we did have domain theories for literature and music. Presumably such theories would tell us that Shakespeare's *Hamlet* and *Macbeth*, and Beethoven's Ninth and Fifth Symphonies, are not informationally equivalent. This classification scheme would not even be able to group them into two categories (corresponding to language and music). Or suppose that our domain theory of literature tells us that every literary work in the English language is informationally nonequivalent to every other. What do we do?

More generally, information equivalence is a content notion; it is concerned with what specific information is represented in a specific situation rather than what *types* of information can be represented in systems of various types or *how* the information is represented. Individuation on the basis of specific information content will not result in a general typology of symbol systems.

Accessibility to Behavioral Data   The seventh constraint was that the distinctions made by the classification scheme be detectable on the basis of behavioral data. Because computational differences in processing result in space and time differences, which show up in behavioral data, the differences picked out by the computational-equivalence criterion are to some extent accessible to our methodology and database. Just how transparent computational differences are in behavioral data is, however, disputed among psychologists. See Palmer (1978) for a skeptical view.

The Computational Connection   The eighth constraint was that the distinctions made by the classification scheme map onto computational systems. Differentiation on the basis of computational-resource allocation is tailor-made for satisfying this constraint.

6.5   Summary

Cognitive science proposes a classification scheme grounded in assumptions about the computational nature of cognitive information processing. The resulting categories are very nonintuitive. This in itself need not be a problem. But as it turns out, it is a problem because the informational- and computational-equivalence framework is insufficient to do the job. It requires four additional theories for its application (see figure 6.17): (1) it needs to appeal to a classification scheme that can pick out the intuitive categories; (2) a theory is needed to map our intuitive categories onto the categories individuated by the computational-equivalence criterion; (3) a theory of computational equivalence is necessary; (4) a domain theory of every domain to be examined is needed. Unless we can construct these four theories, we have no basis for using the informational- and computational-equivalence apparatus.

Notice what has happened here. We initially needed a theory of classification to capture and extend our intuitive categories. Instead of seriously pursuing this goal, we opted for a classification scheme motivated by concerns of computational information processing. The result is that we now need four additional theories—including the original one we were looking for. This is not progress.

The reason for the regression seems to be that in originally approaching the problem, we paid more attention to the demands of the computational constraint than to any of the other constraints, or even to the

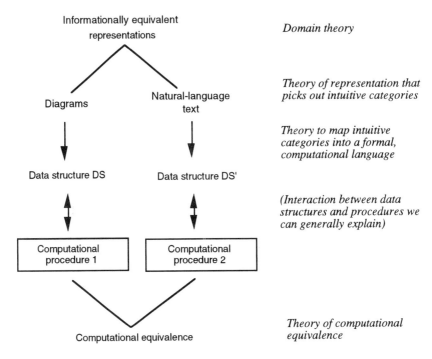

Figure 6.17
Additional theories necessary for applying informational- and computational-equivalence criteria

problem at hand. The result was an inability to satisfy the six general constraints. This is not to suggest that there is necessarily a contradiction in the simultaneous satisfaction of the first six general constraints and the eighth constraint, only that this particular approach will not do the job.

As a final demonstration of the scheme's inadequacy and, perhaps more strongly, its irrelevance, let us try to apply it to the representations in figures 6.1 through 6.13 and see what light is shed. The fact of the matter is that we can not even get started. Notice that this is not simply because the representations are not representations of the same artifact and thus not informationally equivalent. Figures 6.2 through 6.5 are indeed representations of the "same artifact"—they chronicle a series of transformations from a program to a plan schematic—as it is being developed by a single designer, during a single problem-solving session. Even where we have representations from a single subject engaged in a single design session, there may still be no sense in which any two representations are informationally equivalent. Every subsequent drawing is associated with different states in the problem space and as such introduces and highlights new and different information. It simply cannot be informationally equivalent to a previous or a subsequent drawing. If the drawings are not informationally equivalent, the computational criterion cannot be applied.

In the next chapter, I propose and develop an alternative account based on the work of Nelson Goodman. In keeping with earlier remarks, we will develop a scheme that first satisfies the six general constraints and worry about the discipline-specific constraints later. In particular, we will begin by focusing on the major components and relations of symbol systems noted in chapter 1 and then see how they can vary, independent of any computational concerns.

7

Goodman's Analysis of Symbol Systems

For there is an unexplored possibility of genuine semantic beyond the limits of discursive language. . . . We are not talking nonsense when we say that a certain musical progression is significant, or that a given phrase lacks meaning, or a player's rendering fails to convey the import of a passage.
—Susan Langer

Having pointed out a number of shortcomings with the cognitive science practice of classifying symbol systems, it is necessary to suggest an alternative that avoids these difficulties. In this chapter, I want to provide an outline of a better and more complete classification scheme. I will summarize a classification system developed by Nelson Goodman (1976) in his groundbreaking work *Languages of Art: An Approach to a Theory of Symbols,* which is perhaps the deepest, most rigorous analysis of symbol systems to date. My contribution is limited to (i) bringing it to the attention of the cognitive science community, (ii) showing that it does meet each of the six general constraints proposed in chapter 6, (iii) showing the work it can do for cognitive psychology, (iv) showing that the distinctions it makes can be made largely on the basis of behavioral data (the seventh constraint), and (v) connecting the theoretical apparatus to the Computational Theory of Mind. In fact, we have already encountered the connection between Goodman's theoretical apparatus and the Computational Theory of Mind in chapter 3, albeit in a disguised form. I will specify the connection more explicitly at the end of this chapter.

Over the past fifty years, Goodman has developed an impressive apparatus for talking about and classifying symbol systems, which addresses many of the issues/questions to which a theory of representation needs to do justice.[1] The apparatus includes the following:

Theory of notationality
    Syntactic criteria
        Disjointness
        Effective differentiation
    Semantic criteria
        Unambiguity
        Disjointness
        Effective differentiation
Density
    Syntactic
    Semantic
Modes of reference
    Denotation
    Exemplification
    Expression
Repleteness

Goodman's primary concern in *Languages of Art* is the age-old question of what distinguishes description from depiction, linguistic from pictorial symbol systems. It is a question that is not unfamiliar to cognitive scientists. Goodman begins by providing a devastating critique of the standard answer—pictures resemble what they represent, whereas linguistic strings denote by convention—and concludes by proposing an alternative embedded in some nice intuitions about the identity conditions on works of art. However, the primary attraction of the apparatus, for our purposes, lies in its cognitive and computational implications. Little of consequence—for present purposes—hangs on its success in definitively capturing the distinction between description and depiction. I downplay the latter aspect in my presentation of the apparatus.

I begin by introducing the distinction between denotation and exemplification and expression. Thereafter, I introduce the theory of notationality and the notions of density and repleteness. The latter are best understood as a three-tiered classification scheme. At the first level, symbol systems are sorted out by the theory of notationality. At the second level, some categories are further differentiated by the criterion of density. Finally, some of these categories are further differentiated by the criterion of repleteness. This apparatus allows Goodman to engage in a sophisticated discussion about the relationships among such diverse systems as natural language, diagrams, musical scores, paintings, and so on. It strikes me as just the kind of apparatus we could benefit from in cognitive science.

7.1   Modes of Reference

Denotation is the core of representation for Goodman. It is his basic unanalyzed relation of reference. A character x refers to an object y because x denotes y. Denotation serves as the sole notion of reference in most theories. In addition to denotation, Goodman introduces another species of reference called *exemplification,* reference by a symbol to a label that applies to (or denotes) that symbol. The symbol in figure 7.1 instantiates certain labels or possesses certain properties.[2] Among these labels are 'black', 'small', and 'square'. If the symbol belongs to a system in which it is also denoted by the labels, then the symbol is said to exemplify these labels.

Goodman's favorite example is a tailor's swatch. The swatch not only represents certain (but not all) properties of the roll from which it was cut (e.g., color, texture, and weight of the fabric), it actually possesses, hence exemplifies, these properties. But notice that the swatch possesses many other properties—size, date of manufacture, ownership,

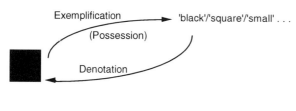

Figure 7.1
Exemplification: reference by a symbol to a label that applies to that symbol

and so on—but within the symbol system that it is used, these properties do not denote the sample, so although these properties are possessed, they are not exemplified. Exemplification is possession plus denotation. Just which of the many properties of a sample are exemplified depends on the symbol system in effect.

Where the instantiation of a label is metaphorical, the symbol/sample is said to *express* the label. Thus expression is metaphorical exemplification. Properties that are metaphorically possessed, while not literally possessed, are transferred onto the symbol system from another realm, and thus are *actually* possessed. They do belong to the symbol. For example, Daniel Maclise's painting *The Origin of the Harp* literally possesses, thus exemplifies, the property of having a dark greenish background with a central, foregrounded figure. But it does not literally possess the properties of quiet solitude and tenderness. Since the labels 'quiet solitude' and 'tenderness' are referred to by the painting and metaphorically denote the painting, the painting is said to express quiet solitude and tenderness.

One of the most enlightening aspects of Goodman's theory of representation is that labels are not restricted to linguistic symbols. They can be drawn from any symbol system. Thus exemplificational and expressive properties of nonlinguistic symbols (and even linguistic symbols) are not subsumed under linguistic descriptions. This is as it should be. There are no reasons to believe that all the properties exemplified or expressed by a pictorial work can be picked out by nonpictorial labels, or that all properties exemplified or expressed by a linguistic work can be picked out by nonlinguistic labels, and so on for other symbol systems.

Since the labels that are instantiated and the samples/symbols in which they are instantiated can be from any symbol system, it follows that exemplification (and expression) can say nothing about the description versus depiction issue. All types of symbol systems can exemplify and express various properties. Some further examples may help. The following sequence of statements from the propositional calculus exemplify implication:

$$p \rightarrow q$$
$$\underline{p}$$
$$q$$

The work *Hamlet* exemplifies, among other labels, 'Shakespeare's greatest work' and 'a study in indecisiveness'. Among the labels it expresses might be 'melancholy'. Beethoven's Ninth Symphony exemplifies such labels as 'melody', 'harmony', and 'glorious'. The fourth movement expresses such labels as 'pomp' and 'passion'. The architectural works of P. L. Nervi exemplify such labels as 'economy', 'elegance', 'structural strength', and 'innovative use of concrete' and express such labels as 'harmony' and 'fluidity'. Tiepolo's painting *Venus and Time* exemplifies the label 'beautiful' and expresses the label 'youth'.

Exemplification is potentially a very important notion for cognitive science. It may be what much of the work on "mental models" (Johnson-Laird, 1983) is trying to get at. (What sense can be made of it with respect to computational systems, however, still needs to be worked out. There is little room for it in the accounts of computation provided by physical symbol systems.) It also seems to underlie many attempts to differentiate between "propositions" and "images." Palmer (1978), for example, advances a distinction based on "intrinsic" and "extrinsic" relations, which may be profitably understood in terms of exemplification.

In intrinsic representations "the representing relation has the same inherent constraints as its represented relation. That is, the logical structure required of the representing relation is intrinsic to the relation itself rather than imposed from outside" (Palmer, 1978, p. 271). So, for example, scheme B in figure 7.2 is an intrinsic representation of realm A, because there is a correspondence between the relative heights of the lines in B and the relative heights of elements in A, and the "longer-than" relation preserves the logical properties (i.e., asymmetry and transitivity) of the "taller-than" relation to which it corresponds. (The example Palmer gives is only of logical properties. It is not clear whether nonlogical properties are also included in the "inherent constraints.")

Extrinsic representations are those in which the "inherent structure of a representing relation is totally arbitrary and that of its represented relation is not" (Palmer, 1978, p. 271). An example of this type of representation is scheme G in figure 7.2. Here the "taller-than" relation is modeled by an arrow, but "arrow-connectedness" is neither necessarily

Scheme   **Realm**

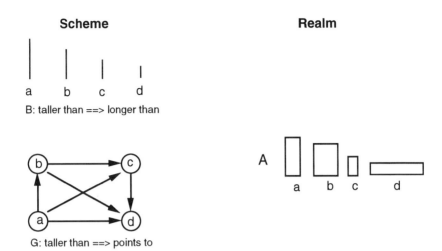

B: taller than ==> longer than

G: taller than ==> points to

Figure 7.2
Subset of figure 9.1 from Palmer (1978, p. 263)

transitive nor asymmetric. The logical structure of "taller-than" is imposed on it from the outside.

The intrinsic/extrinsic distinction is rather interesting. However, there is considerable confusion introduced by the underlying assumption that if the representing world shares some properties with the represented world (either concrete or logical), that is necessary and sufficient to underwrite "pictorial" reference; where such properties are not shared, the reference is extrinsic or "propositional." This is problematic at best. There are actually two readings that need to be considered:

1. *x* represents *y* because *x* resembles or shares properties with *y*
2. *x* represents *y* because I experience *x* as resembling or sharing properties with *y*

On the first reading it is easy to show that any two objects resemble each other in any number of ways (or share as many properties as you like), thus resemblance or sharing of properties can not be the basis of reference. Furthermore, even if you do not accept such arguments, it is still easy to show that resemblance or sharing of properties is neither necessary nor sufficient for reference. For example, The Macintosh personal computer in my office resembles, or shares many properties with, the Mac PC in the next office, but it does not represent the Mac PC next door. Conversely, Willem de Kooning's painting *Woman 1* does not resemble, or share many properties with, a woman, but it does represent a woman. The reader is referred to Goodman (1976) for a complete critique.

The second reading is of course immune from these criticisms, for the claim here is not about the world but about our representation/perception of the world. Here, there is no denying the *experience* of resemblance, but the experience can not be used as an explanatory notion. Surely it is what needs to be explained.

Despite these difficulties, there is something right about the intrinsic/extrinsic distinction. One way to understand Palmer is that extrinsic representations are those that merely denote, whereas intrinsic representations actually exemplify. Interpreted as such, it becomes a clear and important distinction for any theory of representation to make.

Unfortunately, Palmer cannot accept this reformulation. For one thing, exemplification requires (or subsumes) denotation, which means that intrinsic representation would require extrinsic representation. But Palmer puts intrinsic and extrinsic forward as conflicting requirements, because he thinks that (in the case of intrinsic symbol systems) possessing a property is a necessary and sufficient condition for representing that property. Apart from being false, this unnecessarily conflates issues of "roots of reference" with issues of "structure of reference." The two are logically independent. Finally, even if Palmer is prepared to accept this reformulation, the denotation/exemplification distinction can not, as should be clear from the above examples, do the work of differentiating between description and depiction, which is the work Palmer wants the intrinsic/extrinsic distinction to do.

7.2   Theory of Notationality

The theory of notationality encompasses the major components and relation of a symbol system: scheme, realm, and reference link. It classifies symbol systems according to whether they meet or fail some combination of five logically independent criteria.

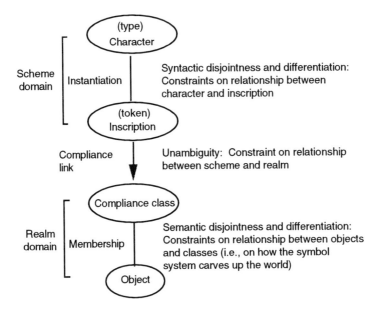

Figure 7.3
Components and relations of symbol systems considered by the theory of notationality

   Two of the criteria are syntactic and three are semantic: (i) syntactic disjointness, (ii) syntactic finite differentiation, (iii) semantic unambiguity, (iv) semantic disjointness, and (v) semantic finite differentiation. A notational scheme (also called a discursive language) must meet the first two. A notational system must meet all five. As noted in figure 7.3, criteria (i) and (ii) are constraints on the structure of the scheme elements, criteria (iv) and (v) are constraints on the structure of the realm, and criterion (iii) is a constraint on the structure of the reference link. The reader will note the overlap between these five properties and the CTM-properties.

7.2.1   Syntactic Criteria

The first requirement of notationality is *syntactic disjointness*, where disjointness is a relationship between classes of character-indifferent or syntactically equivalent inscriptions. Two inscriptions are said to be character-indifferent if "neither one belongs to any character the other does not" (Goodman, 1976, p. 132). This means that all marks that belong to the same character constitute an equivalence class (i.e., they satisfy the requirements of reflexivity, symmetry, and transitivity). Thus character-indifference insures that all inscriptions of a character are "true copies" of each other, that any inscription of a character is as valid as any other inscription of that character. How it is achieved is a separate matter, although Goodman points out that it need not be by virtue of any "simple function of shape, size, etc." (Goodman, 1976, p. 138).

Given two sets of character-indifferent marks, such sets must be disjoint; no mark outside of a set will be character-indifferent with members of it. Or as Goodman puts it, a "character in a notation is a most-comprehensive class of character-indifferent inscriptions" (Goodman, 1976, p. 132). Disjointness ensures that no mark genuinely belongs to more than one character.

The second criterion for notationality is *syntactic finite differentiation*. Goodman states it as follows: "For every two characters k and k' and every mark m that does not actually belong to both, determination either that m does not belong to k or that m does not belong to k' is theoretically possible" (1976, pp. 135–36; italics omitted). The phrase "theoretically possible" is rather interesting and should immediately be qualified. According to Goodman, "theoretically possible" may be interpreted in "any reasonable way." As he goes on to note, whatever the interpretation, "all logically and mathematically grounded impossibility . . . will of course be excluded" (1976, p. 136).

Finite differentiation does not imply finite number of characters. Schemes of an infinite number of characters can be finitely differentiated (e.g., Arabic fractional notation). There can also be schemes of two characters that are not finitely differentiated (e.g., a scheme whereby all marks not longer than one inch belong to one character and all marks longer than one inch belong to the other character).

Disjointness and finite differentiation are independent requirements. The former is ontic, the latter epistemic. A scheme of straight marks in which every difference in length—no matter how small—counts as a difference of character is disjoint but not finitely differentiated. (It is disjoint because by definition we know that no two characters have an inscription in common. It is not finitely differentiated because it is theoretically impossible to do a mapping from the marks to the characters.) A scheme in which all the marks are perceptually different but two characters have at least one inscription in common is finitely differentiated but not disjoint. (It is not that the differentiation can not be made, it is simply that the inscription genuinely belongs to more than one character.) In the case of disjointness, the issue is one of having equivalence classes of inscriptions that do not satisfy the requirements of intersection or inclusion. In the case of finite differentiation, the issue is one of being able to specify theoretically the correspondence from inscriptions to characters.

Thus far we have been talking about atomic characters. Most symbol schemes have rules of composition that allow for the combination of atomic characters into compound characters. The above criteria of notationality work exactly the same for compound characters.

Jointly, the two requirements are quite strong. They ensure a one-to-one mapping between inscriptions and characters and thus enable *the collapse of the distinction between inscription and character*. In a notational scheme, manipulating the inscription is identical to manipulating the character.[3]

7.2.2   Semantic Criteria

The first semantic criterion of notationality is *unambiguity*. It applies to the reference/content or, more generally, the compliance link. It states that every inscription must have the same, single compliance class in each instance, irrespective of context. Thus "a mark that is unequivocally an inscription of a single character is nevertheless *ambiguous* if it has different compliants at different times or in different contexts, whether its several ranges result from different literal or from literal and metaphorical uses" (Goodman, 1976, p. 147).[4]

A character is unambiguous if all its inscriptions are unambiguous and if they all have the same compliance class. The common compliance class of the inscriptions is the compliance class of the character. This means that *if a system is unambiguous, syntactic equivalence will ensure semantic equivalence*. Since the inscriptions of an unambiguous character are syntactically and semantically equivalent, one can "speak of the character and its compliance-class without bothering to distinguish among its several instances" (Goodman, 1976, pp. 147–48).

The second semantic criterion of notationality is the *disjointness* or nonintersection of every two compliance classes in the system. It stipulates that "no two characters have any compliant in common" (Goodman, 1976, p. 151, italics omitted). This is a rather severe restriction. It enforces a semantic segregation of characters in the system by disallowing such semantically intersecting terms as 'doctor' and 'man' (i.e., some doctors are men, and some men are doctors). But it does not imply discreteness of compliants. It is permissible for compliants of one character to be parts of compliants of another character. Thus it is acceptable to have the characters 'man' and 'leg' in the system, because no man is a leg and no leg is a man.

The final requirement for a notational system is *semantic finite differentiation*. It is stated as follows: "for every two characters K and K' such that their compliance-classes are disjoint, and every object h that does not comply with both, determination either that h does not comply with K or that h does not comply with K' is theoretically possible" (Goodman, 1976, p. 152, italics omitted). The interpretation of "theoretically possible" is as above.

An example Goodman offers is that of fully reduced Arabic fractional numerals correlated with objects, based on their weights in fractions of an ounce (Goodman, 1976, p. 153). In this system, since there is no preset limit as to what constitutes a significant difference in weight, for many characters it will not be possible to determine that the object does not comply with them all (i.e., it will not be possible to assign a given object to a single class). Such a system meets the criteria of syntactic disjointness and finite differentiation as well as the semantic requirements of unambiguity and disjointness but fails the requirement of semantic finite differentiation. Even a system containing two characters a and b, where a is correlated with all objects weighing a pound or less and b is correlated with all objects weighing more than a pound, fails semantic finite differentiation.

It should be kept firmly in mind that *these five constraints are constraints on schemes and systems, not on the internal structure of individual symbols.*[5] It does not make sense to ask whether a given symbol or character x is syntactically disjoint and finitely differentiated; unambiguous; and semantically disjoint and finitely differentiated. There is no basis for understanding, much less answering, such a question. Rather, the questions that need to be asked are about the *systems* to which the symbols belong (see chapter 1).

Goodman's theory of notationality arranges and orders symbol systems in a matrix of thirty-two cells, on the basis of which combination of the five criteria they meet or fail to meet. But most of the cells are occupied by relatively uninteresting symbol systems generated solely for illustration purposes.[6] However, three of the categories are of special interest: notational systems, discursive languages, and non-notational systems (see figure 7.4).

Notational systems meet all five criteria. The characters/inscriptions and compliance classes are disjoint and finitely differentiable, and the correlation between inscriptions and compliance classes is unambiguous. Some of our artificial languages—ZIP Codes, telephone numbers, musical scores—fall into this category. Discursive languages meet the two syntactic criteria but fail the three semantic criteria. Examples of such systems are natural languages—English, French, German, and so on—and some artificial languages like the predicate calculus. Subsets of

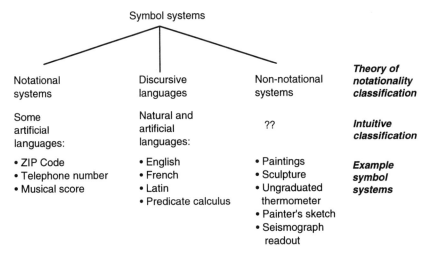

Figure 7.4
Three interesting categories resulting from the theory of notationality

discursive languages, chosen for unambiguity, semantic differentiation, and disjointness, can of course be notational systems. Notational systems and discursive languages can be further differentiated on the basis of their syntactic and semantic rules. Finally, the non-notational systems fail all five criteria. They include a wide assortment of symbol systems, including paintings, sculpture, ungraduated thermometers, sketches, seismograph readouts, and much more. This motley collection does not seem to correspond to any intuitive category as do the above two. However, it is possible to sort out this category by applying additional criteria, such as density.

7.3   Density

A scheme or system can fail the finite-differentiability criterion in a number of ways. One such way is through density. A scheme is considered *dense* if it "provides for infinitely many characters so ordered that between each two there is a third" (Goodman, 1976, p. 136). A field of reference is dense if between any two referents there is a third.[7] Density is sufficient but not necessary to destroy finite differentiation.

If differentiation is destroyed through density, the result is a category whose members we would intuitively classify (very roughly) as pictorial symbol systems. The category would include paintings, sculpture, ungraduated thermometers, and seismograph readouts. It is not clear that we have a intuitive label for the nondense class. It would include symbol systems such as the following: a scheme of two characters in which all marks less than or equal to one inch belong to one and all marks greater than one inch belong to the other. If these characters are correlated with weights such that everything less than or equal to one pound correlates with one and everything heavier than one pound with the other, then the system would be nondense and non–finitely differentiable.

7.4   Repleteness

The final criterion Goodman offers us is *repleteness*. It is a syntactic criterion having to do with which features of a character are constitutive of that character in the particular scheme and which can be dismissed as contingent. Unlike the notationality and density criteria, repleteness is a matter of degree. A scheme in which little can be ruled out as contingent is called replete. A scheme in which much can be ruled out is considered *attenuated*.

For example, if we compare a seismograph readout with a pencil outline of a cityscape by Frank Lloyd Wright, all that matters in the former are the coordinates of the points that the center of the line passes through. The color of the ink, the weight of the paper, the size of the graph, and so on, do not matter. However, in the latter system, little can be dismissed as irrelevant.

This gives us our final criterion and allows us to differentiate paintings, sculpture, sketches, and the like, from seismograph readouts and ungraduated thermometers (see figure 7.5).

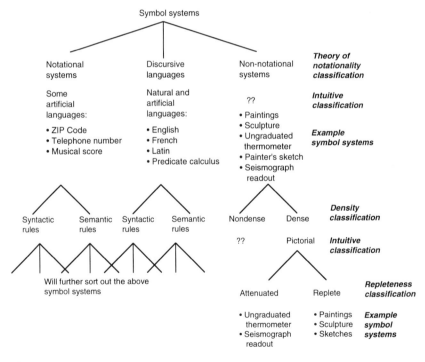

Figure 7.5
Classification of symbol systems using Goodman's apparatus

7.5   Evaluating the Goodman Apparatus

Having outlined much of Goodman's apparatus, I will now evaluate it against the six general and two discipline-specific constraints proposed above. It fares well on all accounts.

7.5.1   Grounding the Scheme in Intuitive Categories

The Goodman apparatus results in categories that both do justice to and extend our pretheoretical intuitions. It gathers together artificial symbol systems, such as postal ZIP Codes, telephone numbers, and musical notation into one category; the various natural languages and some artificial languages, like the predicate calculus, into another category; and paintings, sculpture, and sketches into a third category.

7.5.2   Not Begging the Questions

The classification scheme does not presuppose the resulting categories. The assignment of symbol systems to categories is not based on an appeal to unspecified/unexplained properties of the intuitive categories (such as "linguistic" properties and "pictorial" properties). The intuitive categories are reconstructed on the basis of whether the symbol system in question meets a number of well-specified syntactic and semantic criteria, which are themselves defined independently of the intuitive categories.

7.5.3   Reasonable Granularity of Individuation

The classification scheme results in an interesting number of categories (greater than one and less than infinity). The theory of notationality on its own results in thirty-two possible categories. Most of these are cognitively irrelevant, but three of them do correspond to intuitive categories. This number is multiplied when issues of exemplification/denotation, density, and repleteness are considered, but it remains very manageable.

7.5.4   Individuating on the Basis of Relevant/Important Properties

The Goodman classification scheme encompasses the whole range of components, relations, and issues we associate with representation—

including the all-important reference link. It individuates symbol systems on the basis of certain variations in (i) the structure of the syntactic elements (in terms of disjointness, finite differentiation, density, and repleteness), (ii) the structure of the semantic realm (in terms of disjointness, finite differentiation, and density), and (iii) the structure of the reference link (in terms of ambiguity and denotation/exemplification/expression). As we will see in the next chapter, these properties have important cognitive and computational consequences.

7.5.5   Limited Knowledge of World Required to Apply the Scheme

To apply the information-equivalence criteria, we need to know the content/referent of the representation so we can make the determination of equivalence. And to actually determine equivalence we need a theory of the domain.

To apply the Goodman apparatus, we need to answer only a limited number of questions. For the theory of notationality, we need to answer the following questions:

1. Syntactic disjointness: Does the character x belong to a symbol system that contains the character x', such that the equivalence classes of marks that belong to x and x' intersect?

2. Syntactic finite differentiation: Does the character x belong to a symbol system that contains the character x', such that for any mark m that does not actually belong to both x and x', it is possible to determine that m does not belong to x or that m does not belong to x'?

3. Unambiguity: Does the character x belong to a symbol system in which it has the same referent in every context in which it appears?

4. Semantic disjointness: Does the character x belong to a symbol system that carves up the world in such a way that no two compliance classes intersect?

5. Semantic finite differentiation: Does the character x belong to a symbol system that carves up the world in such a way that, given the character x' (whose compliance class is disjoint from the compliance class of x) and the object o which does not belong to both compliance classes, it is possible to determine that o does not belong to x or that o does not belong to x'?

For exemplification the question is which of the labels referred to by a symbol/sample denote it? For density the question is does the symbol system have a densely ordered set of characters or compliance classes? For repleteness one needs to know whether, in the symbol system to which the character belongs, relatively many or relatively few of the syntactic features of the character are constitutive of the character.

How we come to know the answers to these questions is an independent issue and is discussed in subsection 7.5.7. What is required is a knowledge of the symbol system in effect, but knowledge in the sense that native speakers of English know how to use English, not in the sense of having a theory of its use. If we can agree on the symbol system that is in use, we can agree on the answers to the above questions, and hence agree on which category the symbol system falls into.

In the cases of some artificial symbol systems (e.g., postal ZIP Codes, telephone numbers, the predicate calculus), the answers to these questions are given to us in the definitions of these systems. In the case of more complex symbol systems (e.g., the drawing and drafting systems of architecture, natural language, painting), the ability to answer these questions can require considerable immersion in the culture and practices of the community in which the system is being used. Since we do not have to determine information equivalence in either case, we do not need a theory of the domain.

7.5.6 Wide Applicability of Scheme

The Goodman scheme has wide-ranging applicability and results in a general typology of symbol systems. See figure 7.5 and the preceding discussion. See also chapter 8.

7.5.7 Accessibility of Criteria to Empirical Methodology and Database

The first discipline-specific constraint on a classification scheme was that the distinctions made by the scheme be accessible to our behavioral data and methodology. That is, given a symbol system in use, we should be able to classify it on the basis of the data available to us. There are three different cases that need to be dealt with: (i) external symbol systems where we know the system in effect, (ii) external symbol systems where we do not know the system in effect, and (iii) the internal symbol systems postulated by cognitive science.

In the case of external symbol systems where we know the system in effect to the extent that we can answer the questions in subsection 7.5.5, we can unproblematically classify the system independently of any behavioral data. For example, those of us who know the American Social Security numbering system can agree that it is a fully notational system that lacks density and repleteness and exemplifies or expresses few properties. Similarly we can agree that the system of western painting is a completely non-notational symbol system with much density and repleteness, and is capable of exemplifying and expressing many properties.

In the case of external symbol systems where we do not know the system in effect, because it is either a totally foreign system or some specialized subset of a known system, we must discover it before we can classify it. How is this to be done? First of all, it is clear that it can be done. We do it all the time. We routinely learn new, unknown symbol systems—everything from foreign natural languages to the specialized systems of drawings used by architects. The easiest way to do so is through immersion and interaction in the community in which the systems are used.

But such learning can also be done in more formal "experimental settings" where only unobtrusive behavioral observations, rather than full-fledged interactions, are allowed. Field linguists and anthropologists do this for a living. This is not to suggest that figuring out an unknown symbol system from behavioral data is a trivial task—after all, behavioral data will always underdetermine meaning—but it is a possible task because we also have knowledge of the mental states and concepts of the creators and users of the symbol system. As is generally the case in empirical work, we make the best inference given our knowledge and data and look for additional corroborating and conflicting evidence. Once the system is known, the questions in subsection 7.5.5 can be answered as above.

Although it is important that the criteria can be applied to known and newly discovered external symbol systems, cognitive science is ultimately interested in internal symbol systems. As with external symbol systems, we have to know the symbol system in effect before we can apply the scheme. The only way we have of knowing the internal symbol system is on the basis of behavioral data. We infer the structure of internal systems that underlie some specific behavior on the basis of the subject's utterances, symbolic marks, and gestures, and a host of contextual cues. Thus, getting to know an internal symbol system is, in many ways, very much like getting to know an unfamiliar external symbol system.

One important difference between the internal and the unfamiliar external symbol systems is that, in the internal case, the behavioral data will allow us to determine only the semantic properties. It is not sufficient to allow us to determine syntactic disjointness and density and relative repleteness of mental tokens, although such issues may be accessible to some combination of neurophysiology and behavioral data at some future date. Once we have inferred the semantics of an internal symbol system, we can actually go back and sometimes infer its syntactic structure by arguing that there are good reasons to suppose a match between the syntactic and the semantic notational properties.

For example, suppose we discover a symbol system that satisfies the semantic constraints on notational systems (i.e., unambiguity, semantic disjointness, and semantic differentiation). What can we say about its syntactic properties? The syntactic and semantic properties are logically quite independent (in fact, as already noted, each of the five notational criteria is logically independent of the others). But in practical terms, it does not make sense to develop a symbol system that is semantically notational but syntactically non-notational. If the set of characters is dense, the full distinguishability of objects in the reference domain will not guarantee semantic differentiation. A dense ordering of characters means a dense ordering of compliance classes, which means that for any object that genuinely does not belong to two compliance classes it will not be possible to say which one it does not belong to.

One can get around this, but at the expense of undermining the force of the non-notational syntax. For example, one could arbitrarily correlate each object with one character. But the result would be inefficiency. Infinitely many characters would be vacant. Alternatively, one could correlate objects with marks that deviate from each other within certain tolerances. But this would result in waste or redundancy. Most of the characters allowed for by the scheme would not be used. Thus on grounds of efficiency and economy it is reasonable to argue that a semantically notational system will also meet the syntactic criteria of notationality.

What about the reverse case, in which we have a system that does not meet the semantic criteria of notational systems? What can we infer about the syntax of such systems? Is it possible to pick out densely ordered objects with a disjoint and finitely differentiated set of characters? On the surface, the answer would again seem to be no. After all, one result would seem to be incompleteness and inaccuracy of coverage. However, this is not the case. Natural languages have actually solved this problem by introducing combinatorial syntax and semantics. Therefore, there is no basis for inferring syntactic structure from non-notational semantic structures.

Furthermore, as we will see in the last chapter, it is possible to draw certain conclusions about the structure of internal symbol systems from the structure of external symbol systems.

7.5.8 The Computational Connection

The second discipline-specific constraint on a classification scheme is that there be a connection between the classification scheme and our notion of computational information processing. This constraint is undoubtedly the most important one for advocates of the informational- and computational-equivalence approach. Given the discussion is part I, it is easy to see why.

As it turns out, there is a straightforward mapping between the five constraints on symbol systems provided by Goodman's theory of notationality and the seven CTM-constraints on computational systems proposed in chapter 3. The CTM-constraints incorporate four of the five constraints on notational systems (syntactic disjointness [CTM2], syntactic differentiation [CTM3], unambiguity [CTM5], and semantic differentiation [CTM6]). Semantic disjointness was not included as one of the CTM-constraints, because the type of interpretation called for by RTM'-constraints on a theory of mind does not require that one be able to go from the referents back to the computational states. In addition, since computational systems are dynamical rather than static systems, it was necessary to add two causal constraints (CTM1 and CTM4) and a constraint that maintains the other six across instantaneous descriptions of the system (CTM7). In the subsequent discussion, when I speak of static symbol systems—such as marks on paper—as having or lacking the CTM-properties, CTM1, CTM4, and CTM7 are not applicable. When I am speaking of dynamical symbol systems, all seven apply.

Our account of CTM-systems did not address the properties of exemplification, expression, and repleteness. However, I do not think there is a substantive role for these properties in current computational notions of semantics. I can imagine how one might begin to develop a story of exemplification in computational systems. For example, a correspondence between numerical value and cardinality of a set of bits and a causal account that quantified over this fact would get us started on the road to exemplification. However, how far such an account can be taken is not at all clear to me.

Expression, which is metaphorical exemplification, is much more difficult to make sense of in computational systems. I think we can no more account for it than for metaphor in general. Repleteness is an equally difficult concept for computational accounts. In a replete system, many properties of the symbol tokens are semantically (and thus causally) relevant in the functioning of the symbol. Few properties can be set aside as irrelevant. This raises a number of problems. First, different properties of tokens may be semantically (and causally) relevant in different symbols, even among those belonging to the same symbol system. Second, there may be no agreement as to which ones are relevant. Third, within symbols there may be inconsistency in the semantic import of different properties of the token. Fourth, it is always possible that new semantically relevant properties will be discovered in existing symbols.

In building a machine whose behavior is sensitive to the physical/syntactic properties of its symbols (i.e., a physical symbol system), we need to specify in advance which properties of the physical states are the relevant or causally efficacious ones (e.g., weight, color, and shape); once this specification has been made, it must be fixed. One needs to know the semantic import of each physical property of the token, and there can be no inconsistency in the semantic import of various properties belonging to individual tokens. Finally, the same set of properties must be semantically and causally relevant for every computational state. That is, it cannot be the case that during the instantaneous description of the system at t_1 the semantically/causally relevant property is the weight of the tokens, while at t_2 it is the height of the tokens, and at t_3 it is the disjunction of color and weight.

To summarize, we see that the Goodman apparatus fares better than the informational- and computational-equivalence approach with respect to each of the constraints on a classification scheme for symbol systems. Whether Goodman has succeeded in capturing the distinction between depiction and description with the theory of notationality is not the crucial issue for our purposes. The connection between the theory of notationality and the CTM-properties is in itself sufficient to justify using these criteria to classify symbol systems. However, it still remains to be seen what work the apparatus can do for us over and above the informational- and computational-equivalence approach and what some of its cognitive implications are. We turn to these questions in the next chapter, in which the apparatus is applied to the representations in figures 6.1 through 6.13.

8

Virtues of Non-Notational Symbol Systems

I am, in fact, strongly inclined to doubt the very intelligibility of the suggestion that there is a stage at which cognitive processes are carried out in a medium which is fundamentally nondiscursive.

—Jerry Fodor

8.1 Sorting Designers' Representations

With the Goodman apparatus in hand, let us return to the variety of representations used by designers and try to sort them out. To start with, we can classify the design brief (i.e., the input) as a document written or verbalized in a discursive natural language. Natural languages, such as English, meet two of the five notationality criteria. They are syntactically disjoint and differentiated but fail the semantic criteria of unambiguity and semantic differentiation. For instance, none of the marks in English belong to more than one symbol. Expressions spelled the same way are interchangeable. It is also theoretically possible to determine which symbol a mark belongs to, although in practice it may be difficult (e.g., because of sloppy handwriting). The important point is that the scheme does allow for such effective differentiation. The ambiguity of natural language is widely recognized and requires little comment (e.g., 'bank' may refer to a financial institution or a riverbank, depending on context). Furthermore, natural languages do allow for semantically intersecting expressions, such as 'man' and 'doctor', where some men are doctors. Finally, natural languages allow for densely ordered semantic fields. One can generate expressions such that between any two referents or contents there is a third. For example, the predicates 'colder than' and 'warmer than' can be used to pick out densely ordered compliance classes of temperatures.

The final output of the design process are the contract documents. They consist of the specifications and blueprints. Both are largely denotative and notational. The specifications are written in a subset of a discursive language that tries to approximate notationality, by avoiding ambiguous, intersecting, and densely ordered expressions. There are conventionalized forms, expressions, and contexts agreed to by the community and the courts that facilitate unambiguous interpretation.

The contract drawings or "blueprints" are a combination of drawings, specialized symbols or icons,[1] numbers, and labels, but they nonetheless approximate a notational system. The linguistic labels used on blueprints are generally an unambiguous, semantically disjoint, and differentiated subset of natural language. The system of drawing itself is not a notational system, but the full system is not in effect in the case of blueprints. Contract drawings indicate only (and very roughly) relative size, shape, and location. Each drawing is clearly marked with the warning "Do not scale." Measurements of lengths, areas, weights, and the like, are indicated in Arabic numerals, which are syntactically disjoint and differentiated and refer unambiguously to disjoint classes of numbers, but have densely ordered semantic fields. However, since accuracy of measurements is limited by convention to discernible limits (e.g., one-sixteenth of an inch) the classes of lengths and weights to which the numbers refer are not densely ordered. The linguistic labels used on blueprints are generally a notational subset of natural language. The specialized symbols or icons (e.g., water closets, electrical outlets, doorways, and heating ducts), although they may look "diagrammatic," on closer inspection have more in common with ZIP Codes and telephone numbers than with sketches and do constitute a notational system. Thus the constitutive properties of the blueprints are specified in a (near) notational system.

What can be said about the intermediate drawings, the sketches that help transform design briefs into artifacts (or processes) specified by the contract drawings? First, exemplificational and expressive properties play a much more important role in designers' sketches—especially the early, explorative ones—than in the contract drawings. Many of the early and intermediate sketches not only denote but also exemplify such labels (properties) as 'shape', 'relative size', 'relative location', 'fluid', 'rigid', 'elegant', and so on. They also express such labels as 'bold', 'uncertain', 'hurried', and the like.

Second, most of the sketches made during the early phase of the design process belong to non-notational symbol systems and fail finite differentiation through density. That is, the marks belong to symbol systems that are syntactically and semantically disjoint, densely ordered, and ambiguous.

The symbol system of sketching fails syntactic disjointness, because each mark (token) may belong to many characters (types) at the same time. That is, in the absence of any agreement as to the constitutive versus contingent properties of these marks, there may be no fact of the matter as to which equivalence class they belong. For example, what equivalence class does mark a in figure 6.6 in chapter 6 belong to? Do marks a and b belong to the same equivalence class? There may be no agreed-on answers to these questions.

Sketching fails syntactic differentiation through density. Because the symbol system allows for a dense ordering of characters or types (i.e., between any two characters there is a third), it is not always possible to tell which equivalence class a mark belongs to. Even if we agree that the mark a in figure 6.6 does in fact belong to only one equivalence class, it may not be perceptually possible to tell which of several classes it does or does not belong to.

Sketching is ambiguous, because characters do not have the same referent or content in every context in which they appear. Does mark a in figure 6.6 represent the beginning of a floor plan or the head of an insect?

Sketching fails semantic disjointness for the same reason as natural language: it allows referred objects to belong to intersecting classes. For example, the structure picked out by figure 6.7 belongs to the class of buildings but also to the class of residential buildings.

The system of sketching allows for a dense ordering of compliance classes and thus fails semantic finite differentiation. When this is the case, it is not possible to tell which class a particular object belongs to. For example, in a perspective drawing of a building, every height mark would correspond to a different class of heights of buildings in the world, and these classes of heights are of course densely ordered. It would not be possible to tell which class a particular building height belongs to.

Finally, some of the designer's marks belong to symbol systems that are more replete than others (e.g., presentation drawings vs. window details), where little can be dismissed as irrelevant. The various symbol systems and the sequence in which they are used is summarized in figure 8.1.

If we now return specifically to figures 6.1 through 6.13 and apply the Goodman apparatus, we get the following results: 6.2, 6.10,

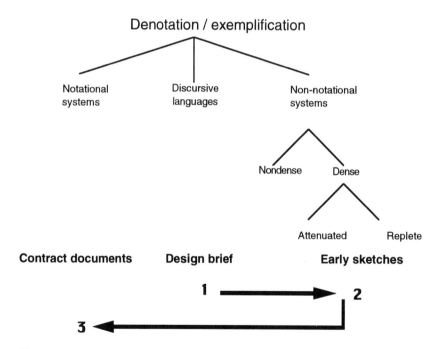

Figure 8.1
Classifying architectural symbol systems and the sequence in which they are used

6.12, and 6.13 belong to notational systems, they lack repleteness and expressiveness, and they exemplify few properties. The figures do differ in the properties that are exemplified. For example, 6.10, 6.12, and 6.13 exemplify relative shapes, sizes, and locations of structural elements, whereas 6.2 does not. Figures 6.1, 6.3, 6.4, and 6.5 belong to discursive languages, though again, they exemplify different properties. For example, the characters in 6.3 exemplify relative position and orientation of rooms, whereas shapes and relative sizes are exemplified in 6.5. From the fragment given, it is not clear what labels the design brief (6.1) might exemplify. Figures 6.6, 6.7, 6.8, 6.9, and 6.11 all belong to non-notational symbol systems, but they differ not only in the labels exemplified but also in the labels expressed and in relative repleteness. For example, 6.7 exemplifies the label 'lucid', and 6.11 expresses the labels 'mysterious' and 'somber', among others. Both are much more replete than 6.9 and 6.11 is much more replete than 6.7.[2]

What emerges from this analysis is an account that, unlike the informational- and computational-equivalence criteria, begins to do justice to the richness and intricacy of human symbolic functioning. It also allows us to see that some of the symbol systems that designers use—such as the subset of natural language used in specifications and the contract drawings—share the properties that the Computational Theory of Mind claims the language of thought possesses, specifically syntactic disjointness, syntactic and semantic differentiation, and unambiguity; other representations (early and intermediate sketches) belong to symbol systems characterized by the lack of these very properties and the possession of additional properties of density, repleteness, and enriched exemplificational and expressive capabilities. The discursive design brief falls somewhere between these two extremes. These results are summarized in table 8.1, in a slightly different format.

Before continuing with the argument, I would like to compare the line of thought I am developing with the vast imagery literature in cognitive science. The comparison will highlight a number of important features of our results.

Table 8.1
Comparing properties of drafting, natural-language, and sketching systems with the properties of CTM-systems

	Symbol systems			
	CTM-systems	Drafting systems	Natural language	Sketching systems
Syntactic properties				
Demarcation of types	Disjoint	Disjoint	Disjoint	Nondisjoint
Ordering of types	Differentiated	Differentiated	Differentiated	Undifferentiated
Semantic properties				
Compliance link	Unambiguous	Unambiguous	Ambiguous	Ambiguous
Demarcation of compliance classes	Disjoint	Disjoint	Nondisjoint	Nondisjoint
Ordering of compliance classes	Differentiated	Differentiated	Undifferentiated	Undifferentiated
Density	No	No	Semantic	Syntactic and semantic
Repleteness	No	No	No	Yes
Mode of reference	Denotation, exemplification?	Denotation and exemplification	Denotation, exemplification, expression	Denotation, exemplification, expression

8.2   Relationship to Imagery Literature

The reader may be a little puzzled by the fact that I have conducted my argument without addressing the large literature on the imagery debate and the related literature on picture/word processing. In fact, I did refer to this literature in chapter 1 but only to defer discussion. We are now in a position to see why it is not particularly germane to my argument.

The modern imagery debate began twenty years ago. Over the years it has covered considerable ground and undergone a number of transformations. Diverse studies have been brought to bear on the issues: sophisticated philosophical arguments (Block, 1981; Dennett, 1981; Rollins, 1989; Tye, 1984), elegant psychological data (Finke and Pinker, 1982; Finke, Pinker, and Farah, 1989; Kosslyn, 1980, 1981, 1983; Kosslyn et al., 1981; Kosslyn and Pomerantz, 1981; Metzler and Shepard, 1974; Paivio, 1977; Shepard, 1982; Shepard and Cooper, 1982; Shepard and Metzler, 1971), neuropsychological data (Farah, 1984, 1989; Kosslyn, Alpert, Thompson, Maljkovic, Weise, Chabris et al., 1993), and impressive computational models (Funt, 1983; Glasgow and Papadias, 1992; Shwartz and Kosslyn, 1982). I will not even pretend to survey, summarize, or critique this literature. I will, however, identify the critical issues and relate them to my argument.

Three crucial claims are associated with the literature; one addresses cognitive architecture, one addresses the "format" of the representations, and one addresses the relationship between the representation and the represented object. They have spawned several subfields of research.

The architectural issue has two components. One raises the question whether there exist cognitive structures and processes dedicated to processing visual information or if such processing is handled by general-purpose structures and procedures. This question seems to be the primary focus of the picture/word processing literature (Kroll and Potter, 1984; Paivio, 1977; Potter, So, Eckardt, and Feldman, 1984; Snodgrass, 1984; Snodgrass and Vanderwart, 1980; Vanderwart, 1984). I think there are some conceptual problems with this literature and refer the reader to Kolers and Brown (1984) for an interesting critique.

The second component addresses the claim that imagery utilizes the same cognitive structures and processes, possibly even the same neural pathways, as the visual-perception system (Finke and Shepard, 1986; Kosslyn et al., 1993).

The "format" of images has been most extensively investigated by Shepard (Shepard, 1982; Shepard and Cooper, 1982; Shepard and Metzler, 1971) and Kosslyn (1980). The issue seems to be whether the processing of images involves (1) computations defined over geometric data structures specified in terms of points, vectors, surfaces, or volumes, which can support geometric operations, such as rotation, translation, zooming, perspective transformations, and the like, or (2) relational structural descriptions of some kind (e.g., under [ball, table]), which support logical inferences. Presumably, relational structures are specified in geometric terms at *some* point, and geometrical structures have labels at some point (see figure 8.2). So the issue has to be at what point in this hierarchy the relevant cognitive/computational processes are defined, over the relational descriptions or the numerical values.

The general imagery claim is that cognitive processes are defined at the level of the geometric primitives. Kosslyn claims, furthermore, that the primitives at the geometric level are pixel arrays:[3] "The syntax: (1) The symbols belong to two form classes: points and empty space. (2) The points can be arranged so tightly as to produce continuous variations or so sparsely as to be distinct (like the dots in a comic strip). (3) The rules for combining symbols require only that points be placed in spatial relation to one another" (1990, p. 86).

The third crucial claim associated with the imagery literature is about how an image refers to the imaged object. An "analog" relationship between pixels in the image and the object referred to is said to underwrite reference:

The primary characteristic of representations in this format is that every portion of the representation must correspond to a portion of the object such that the relative interportion distances on the object are preserved by the distances among the corresponding portions of the representation. (Kosslyn, 1981, p. 50)

The association between a representation and what it stands for is not arbitrary; rather, depictions "resemble" the represented object or objects. That is, (a) each part of the representation must correspond to a visible part of the object or objects, and (b) the represented "distances" among the parts of the rep-

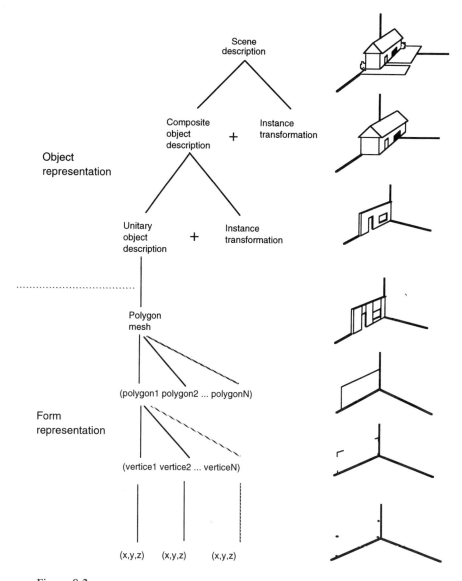

Figure 8.2
A typical hierarchically organized data structure used in geometric/spatial modeling (reproduced from Goel, 1988, with permission of Academic Press)

resentation must mirror the distances among the corresponding parts of the actual object (as they appear from a particular point of view). (Kosslyn, 1990, p. 86)

The three claims are logically independent. It is possible to accept them in any combination. The most substantive of the three claims—the only one addressed by the classical generation, retention, rotation, zooming, panning, and scanning experiments (Kosslyn, 1983, 1990; Shepard and Cooper, 1982)—is the second one, postulating a pixel array or some other type of geometric data structure. Furthermore, the experimental support of geometric data structures and processes and the emerging neuropsychological evidence lend credibility to the architectural claims.

However, it is not at all clear to me what the third claim—that resemblance underwrites reference—adds to the story. I have already commented on the resemblance relation in the previous chapter. To repeat, there is no denying the fact that, when I view a picture of an object, or imagine the object in my "mind's eye," I *experience* the picture or the image as looking like, or resembling, the object.[4] But from the fact that resemblance is a genuine psychological phenomenon, it does not follow that it is resemblance that is underwriting the reference. If anything, the experience of resemblance requires an explanation; it is not a construct that can be used *as* an explanation. In sum, the resemblance claim may serve to give voice to our subjective experience, but it is neither supported by any data, nor is the assumption necessary for interpreting the above-cited data. It serves more to confound than to illuminate the imagery claims.

This said, let me specify the relationship of my concerns to the imagery literature. I think my Goodmanian claims about the structure of symbol systems are neutral with respect to the imagery debate. Consider the following:

1. The symbol systems that possess, and those that lack, the CTM-properties do not break down along the lines of "linguistic" and "pictorial," as these are normally construed in the imagery literature. On my account, it is drafting systems (which are forms of "pictorial" or "diagrammatic" representations, as these terms are commonly used), not natural language, that share the properties of CTM-systems. The

subset of natural language used to write the specifications also approximates these properties. The symbol system furthest removed from these properties, that of sketching, is also a "pictorial" or "diagrammatic" system.

This reiterates an important point mentioned in the Preface: My use of the term *sketches*, in the title and throughout, is very general. It is not restricted to "drawings" of a certain type. It is meant to refer to any symbol system—whether it is "pictorial" or not—that is characterized by the properties in column 4 of table 8.1. Even more narrowly, my technical arguments concern only symbol systems as individuated by the CTM-properties.

2. The classification offered is mercifully independent of the notoriously difficult question of how reference is fixed (i.e., the convention vs. resemblance issue). The account does consider various modes of reference, such as denotation, exemplification, and expression.

3. The classification is, to a large degree, independent of the notation/format issue. Only the repleteness criterion touches on the physical properties of symbol tokens. All the other properties are predicated over the structure of symbol schemes and systems, not the structure of individual tokens.

4. The classification scheme does not reduce to the analog/digital controversy. Notice that only one of the eight criteria—density—has any relation to the analog/digital issue. The others are totally independent of it. Furthermore, there is a big difference between the work that 'analog' does in the imagery literature and the work 'density' does for us here. In the imagery debate, 'analog' predicates over the relation between the internal structure of the symbol/image and the internal structure of the referent (Kosslyn, 1981). In our appeal to 'density', it predicates over the ordering of symbols in a scheme and the ordering of reference classes.[5]

My argument thus far and the empirical results to be presented in chapter 9 do not speak to the question of whether we think in images or not.[6] The postulation of mental images is compatible with both CTM- and non–CTM-type symbol systems. What my final results will add to this literature is that, insofar as there are images, some will be notational, others non-notational. The former category will be accounted for by our current accounts of computational information processing; the latter will not. However, we still have a number of steps to take before such a conclusion is justified.

8.3   No Second-Class Citizens

I have argued that designers sometimes use symbol systems that are dense, ambiguous, and replete. I can imagine someone raised in the logical-analytical tradition sneering, with Lord Russell or with Tarski, as follows: "So what? The argument only shows that designers use weak, substandard, or defective symbol systems. They should educate and train themselves to use more powerful notational systems." Or they may even argue that when these designers are using such symbol systems, they are not engaged in bona fide problem-solving activities. They are just scratching marks on paper, analogous to the way dogs at play will scratch the ground.

Although such a position is not overtly defended in the cognitive science literature, it is present and implicitly underlies Fodor's (1975) criticisms of "pictorial" or "iconic" representations. On the surface, Fodor's objection to pictorial representations has to do with the inadequacy of the resemblance relation underlying pictorial reference. I have already commented on this above and am in complete agreement with Fodor. However, the form of Fodor's critique is telling. It raises the issues of nondisjointness and ambiguity and argues that these are undesirable properties for the language of thought:

For example, what would it be like to have a representational system in which the sentence 'John is fat' is replaced by a picture? Suppose that the picture that corresponds to 'John is fat' is a picture of John with a bulging tummy. But then, what picture are we going to assign to 'John is tall'? The same picture? If so, the representational system does not distinguish the thought that John is tall from the thought that John is fat. A different picture? But John will have to have some shape or other in whatever picture we choose, so what is to tell us that having the picture is having a thought about John's height rather than a thought about his shape? Similarly, a picture of John is a picture of John sitting or standing, or lying down, or it is indeterminate among the three. But then, what is to tell us whether having the picture is having the thought that John is tall, or having the thought that John is sitting, or having the thought that he is standing, or having the thought that he is lying down, or having the thought that one doesn't know whether John is sitting, standing, or lying down? (pp. 179–80)

Now, although the resemblance relation may be sufficient to make a symbol system nondisjoint and ambiguous, it is certainly not necessary, as we have seen. More generally, then, Fodor's argument is against the undesirability of nondisjoint and ambiguous symbol systems. It can hold for both "pictorial" and "nonpictorial" systems.[7] One could also introduce the issue of density and make it an argument against non-notational symbol systems.

As noted in chapter 1, this is the classical position stemming from the logical-analytical tradition and inherited by much of the cognitive science community. There is something to it. Certainly, not *all* our thoughts can be non-notational. This would be unbearable and not particularly conducive for survival. But it would be equally absurd to assert, and detrimental to survival, if all our thoughts were notational. In the balance of this chapter, I suggest that there are times when thoughts *need* to be intersecting, undifferentiated, and ambiguous. In the next chapter, I try to support the position further with empirical data. The general point is that non-notational symbol systems are not weak, substandard, or defective in any sense. They are extremely powerful and productive, and much of their power comes from the very fact that they are nondisjoint, ambiguous, dense, replete, and so on. They have an important role to play in human cognition, and they may lie at the root of human creativity.[8] Let us continue to develop our argument by returning to designers' use of symbol systems.

8.4   Different Symbol Systems Correlate with Different Cognitive Processes

We have noted that designers use several distinct symbol systems. We have also been able to identify some of the crucial properties of those systems and classify them accordingly. Now we need to note that they are used in a specific sequence. That is, different symbol systems correlate with different design phases and cognitive processes. Why should this be the case?

In chapter 5, I characterized design problem solving as involving four development phases—problem structuring, preliminary design, refinement, and detail specification—and noted that each phase differs with respect to the representations and cognitive processes associated with it.

The design problem space is depicted in figure 8.3. Problem spaces are generally depicted as triangles (Laird, Newell, and Rosenbloom, 1986a). The problem is mapped onto the single point at an apex, and the expanding area between the apex and the base metaphorically represents the expansion of the search space. In the case of design problem solving, the problem will have a number of interpretations and thus will not map onto a single point, but rather onto several points or alternatives (a1, a2, . . .). This mapping process is called problem structuring, and the primary symbol system involved is natural language. Once this mapping is completed, the designer then expands the problem space by actively generating and considering a number of alternative solutions (a1, a2, a3, a4, . . .). This process occurs during the preliminary design phase and is correlated with various forms of sketching. Finally, these several alternative solutions are quickly narrowed to one solution (a1), which is then developed at great length and detailed in the contract documents by some system of drafting. This constitutes the refinement and detailing phases and is depicted by the narrowing of the base of the geometric form in figure 8.3 to an apex.

Goodman's apparatus dovetails nicely with our account of design problem solving to give us some understanding of why different design

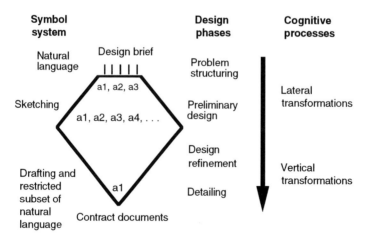

Figure 8.3
Different symbol systems correlate with different cognitive processes

documents fall into the categories they do. This, in turn, allows us to generate some interesting hypotheses about their cognitive role and their significance in the problem solving process. Taking into account both the earlier characterization of preliminary design—as a process of creative, ill-structured problem solving, in which generating and exploring alternatives is facilitated through a coarseness of detail, a low commitment to ideas, and a large number of lateral transformations—and the properties of the symbol system of sketching, one might propose an answer along the following lines:

1. The failure of the symbol system to be syntactically disjoint gives the marks a degree of coarseness by allowing marks to belong to many different characters. This is a necessary condition for remaining noncommittal about the character.

2. The failure of the symbol systems to be syntactically finitely differentiable (through density) gives the marks a degree of fine-grainedness by making every distinction count as a different character. This reduction in distance between characters is necessary to help transform one character into another.

3. The ambiguity of the symbol system insures that the extensions and/or contents of marks during the early phases of design are indeterminate. Ambiguity is important, because one does not want to crystallize ideas too early and freeze design development.

4. The failure of the symbol systems to be semantically disjoint means there will be overlap in the compliance classes. This overlap is needed to remain noncommittal about the exact referent of a character.

5. The failure (through density) of the symbol systems to satisfy semantic finite differentiability insures that the ordering of compliance classes will be dense. The dense ordering is necessary so as not to exclude possibilities.

It should also be clear why one must move in the direction of notational symbol systems as the design progresses. If the design is to be brought to closure, one needs to make, develop, and propagate commitments. The reason contract documents need to approximate a notational system should also be apparent. The process of constructing the artifact involves interpretation of the documents by many independent agents, and it is important that each arrives at the same conception. One also needs to be able to look at the constructed artifact and determine whether it is indeed the artifact specified by the contract documents.

The symbol systems used by designers not only denote spatial and nonspatial properties but also exemplify and express such properties as relative size, shape, location, elegance, formality, rigidity, and certainty. This generates another interesting hypothesis: Our perceptual system is set up to deal with these properties in the world at large. If our representations of the world can preserve these properties, we can deal with them directly rather than having to decode a purely denotational system and construct a mental model where they are reexemplified. Thus, having these properties exemplified relieves the cognitive system of overhead by providing the user with a representation in which these properties can be directly accessed and manipulated.

9

The Role of Sketching in Design Problem Solving

Language can become a screen that stands between the thinker and reality. That is the reason why true creativity starts where language ends.
—Arthur Koestler

9.1 Introduction

In the previous chapter, I claimed that non-notational symbol systems, that is, symbol systems lacking the CTM-properties, are not substandard or undesirable. On the contrary, they serve important cognitive functions. In this chapter, I describe a study carried out to explore the cognitive significance of a subset of these properties, specifically, syntactic density, semantic density, and ambiguity. The question under investigation is why should the symbol system of sketching be correlated with the preliminary phases of design problem solving? To repeat, the predictions are the following:

1. The dense ordering of symbols in the system of sketching gives the tokens a degree of fine-grainedness by making every distinction count as a different symbol. This reduction in distance between symbols helps insure that possibilities are not excluded and helps to transform one *symbol* into another.

2. Ambiguity of the symbol system of sketching insures that the referents and/or contents of symbols during the early phases of design are indeterminate. Ambiguity is important because one does not want to crystallize ideas too early and freeze design development.

3. The dense ordering of reference or content classes in the symbol system of sketching insures that possibilities are not excluded and helps to transform one *idea* into another.

The general claim is that lateral transformations need to occur during the preliminary phase of design problem solving and that the density and ambiguity of the symbol system of sketching facilitate these cognitive operations. A notational symbol system, such as drafting, which differs from sketching in being nondense and unambiguous, will hamper lateral transformations. Notice that these predictions have little, if anything, to do with the depictional or "pictorial" properties of sketches.

It is possible to test this claim by manipulating systems of drawing along the dimensions of density and ambiguity and seeing the impact on the design problem space in general and lateral transformations in particular. The prediction is that syntactic and semantic density will facilitate lateral transformations by allowing for densely ordered (finely individuated) symbols and referents and/or contents.[1] Furthermore, ambiguity will facilitate lateral transformations by allowing for multiple interpretations. This leads to the following hypothesis: (H) Symbol systems that are nondense and unambiguous will hamper the exploration and development of alternative solutions (i.e., lateral transformations) and force early crystallization of design development.

To test this hypothesis it is necessary to measure the density and ambiguity of symbol systems. Strictly speaking, density and ambiguity are binary criteria. Either they are satisfied or they are not. For any intensionally specified symbol system (i.e., one specified in terms of the syntactic and semantic "rules" of the system), if the rules are known, it is possible to determine whether it is or is not dense and/or ambiguous. We have already encountered arguments and illustrations to the effect that systems of sketching are, strictly and literally speaking, densely ordered (both syntactically and semantically) and ambiguous, whereas systems of drafting, strictly and literally speaking, are not. The reader is further referred to Elgin (1983) and Goodman (1976).

For empirical purposes, however, what is of interest to us is not so much the symbol system defined intensionally, but whether the system—as it is in fact used by our subjects during the experiment—differs with respect to syntactic and semantic density and ambiguity in the manner claimed? This calls for an extensional definition of symbol systems, in which a symbol system is defined not in terms of *possible* symbols and referents or contents that can be generated by the rules, but solely in terms of the *actual* symbols, referents, and contents generated by the subject during the experiment.

On such an extensional characterization, a symbol system can not, of course, be dense in the strict, technical sense. Given a finite number of symbols and referents or contents, no ordering of them will be dense. One can, however, use the notion of density in a quasi-technical sense and show that the symbols and referents or contents of one system are *more closely* (or "densely") ordered than that of another system, that is, relatively more dense. It is in this relative sense that the term 'density' is used in the balance of this chapter.

Similarly, in the case of ambiguity, our primary interest is not whether the rules constitutive of a symbol system allow for ambiguous symbols, but whether the system, as used by the subject during the experiment, contains ambiguous symbols. I will again use a graded criterion and speak of relative ambiguity, of one symbol system's being more ambiguous or less ambiguous than another.

Given these provisos, we can take two symbol systems and get empirical measures of their relative syntactic and semantic density and ambiguity. Given such measures, we can test the above hypothesis.

9.2   Experiment Design and Procedure

The experimental design required expert designers to engage in two one-hour problem-solving sessions while the external symbol systems they were allowed to use were manipulated along the syntactic and semantic dimensions identified above. In one condition, subjects were allowed to use the symbol system of sketching, while in the other case they were requested to use a symbol system with the syntactic and semantic properties of drafting systems. The goal of the manipulation was to enable a conclusion about the impact of the syntactic and semantic properties of sketching on the design problem space. As stated above, the expectation was that the absence of density and ambiguity in the second condition would hamper lateral transformations and freeze design development.

Subjects   Twelve subjects employed as professional designers by a multinational corporation volunteered to participate in the study. Although their professional experience varied from two to twenty years, each was deemed an expert, in virtue of being trained as a designer and successfully earning a living at it. They were accepted for the study on the basis of three criteria: (i) that they had received training in the traditional drawing tools and methods of their profession, (ii) that they regularly used a computational system for some part of their design and drawing activity, and (iii) that they were familiar with the MacDraw computer drawing package.

Six of the subjects were graphic designers; six were industrial designers. The basic difference between the two groups was that the graphic designers generally worked on tasks involving two-dimensional graphical/textual layout projects (such as corporate logos, posters, and brochures), whereas the industrial designers worked on three-dimensional projects (usually "product shells"). Accordingly, the tasks given the two groups varied along these dimensions.

Task Descriptions   There were three graphic-design tasks and two industrial-design tasks. The graphic tasks required the design of (i) a poster and/or technical report cover for the new cognitive science program at UC-Berkeley, (ii) a poster to promote the Shakespeare Festival at Stratford-on-Avon in Canada, and (iii) a poster to attract Canadian tourists to San Francisco. The industrial-design tasks required the design of (i) a desk timepiece to commemorate Earth Day, and (ii) a toy to amuse and educate a fifteen-month-old toddler. Each of these are open-ended, "real-world" problems. The actual problem statements given to the subjects are reproduced in appendix B.

The sequence of sessions was divided evenly between the twelve subjects. Six did the sketching session first, followed by the session on the nonsketching (drafting type) drawing system. Six did the session on the drafting-type system first, followed by the sketching session. In the case of three of the six subjects who did the sketching session first, there was a lapse of several weeks between the sketching sessions and the drafting sessions.

Instructions to Subjects   Subjects were given two sets of instructions. First, they were asked to "talk aloud" during the task and were encouraged to solicit additional information and/or clarification from the experimenter, who assumed the role of the client. The experimenter answered any questions that arose but did not initiate questions or conversation (apart from asking "what are you thinking now?" when the subject was silent for a prolonged period). Second, they were requested to generate several ideas and then to choose and develop one to completion. Due to the time constraints, they were not asked to come up with a complete specification. But their drawings were expected to be—and indeed were—detailed enough to communicate what the final product would be like.

Recording of Data   All sessions were recorded on two video cameras. One camera captured the general movements and gestures of the subject while the other was focused on the piece of paper or computer screen on which the subject was drawing and/or writing. The sessions that utilized a computer drawing package (see below) were recorded by MediaTracks, a piece of software that runs in the background and maintains a record of all screen activity, which can then be replayed.

Manipulation of Symbol Systems   The manipulation of symbol systems required finding a symbol system that differed from sketching only with respect to syntactic and semantic density and ambiguity. So, importantly, it needed to be a "drawing system" of some sort, as opposed to a "discursive language." The symbol system that came closest to meeting our needs was the system of drafting. It is, as has already been noted, a subset of the system of drawing, which differs from the system of sketching in just the right way.

In some pilot studies, an attempt was made to impose the discipline of drafting on the subjects during the preliminary design phase, when they would normally sketch freehand. They simply could not (or would not) follow the instructions. Therefore, the manipulation of symbol systems was effected through the manipulation of drawing tools and media.

Most natural symbol systems are complicated Intentional and social constructs given by precedent practice. Certainly, a logical distinction can be made between drawing tools and media, on the one hand, and symbol systems, on the other. In practice, however, this distinction can be blurred, especially in the case of computational interfaces. A computational interface not only provides a tool and a medium for drawing it also helps to reinforce a symbol system by easily facilitating certain marks and operations and discouraging or even disallowing others.

In one session, designers were allowed to use the tools, media, and symbol systems of their choice. They invariably chose to use paper and pencils and did a lot of sketching. In the second session, they were requested to use a computer interface, specifically a subset of the drawing package MacDraw (version 1.9.5; with the freehand tool turned off and the grid turned on), running on a Mac II with a large, two-page monitor.

MacDraw, or even computer interfaces in general, were not the focus of this experiment. MacDraw simply provided a drawing tool that encouraged subjects to make certain types of marks and prevented them from making others. In particular, it is not a sketching tool; it reinforces a restrictive subset of a drawing system, not unlike the subset found in the system of drafting. The major difference between the two is that in the case of drafting, the subset is specified by convention, whereas in MacDraw it is enforced by the tool. The sole utility of MacDraw for our purposes lies in the fact that the symbol system it helps to reinforce differs from the system of sketching along the dimensions of interest to us.

With the freehand tool disabled, MacDraw supports three closed-figure tools (ellipse, polygon, and rectangle with rounded corners), three straight-line tools, and one curved-line tool, all in four different line widths. Accuracy of line lengths, angles, and locations of the marks is limited by the grid to one-eighth inch. Within these constraints one can—indeed one must—make marks of only particular shapes and sizes and of the utmost precision and certainty. Despite these limitations, it is possible to build up surprisingly complex shapes and figures.

Given these constraints, the differentiation of two arbitrary shapes/marks is perceptually possible (for the human visual system), so there should be no problem in determining whether they belong to the same equivalence class. This satisfies our syntactic constraint. Determining whether the symbol system reinforced by MacDraw satisfies the two semantic constraints is more difficult. If the symbols are correlated with the corresponding geometric forms, then the unambiguity and semantic-nondensity criteria are met. If, however, the correlation is with mental contents or referents out in the world, then neither unambiguity nor nondensity can be guaranteed. One might think that a system that satisfies the syntactic properties will also satisfy the semantic properties, even though the two are logically independent—after all, how could differentiated symbols pick out densely ordered referents or contents? But natural language has solved this problem with combinatorial syntax and semantics and provides a persuasive counterexample. The semantic properties of a symbol system depend on the richness of the syntactic scheme and on how the subject chooses to carve up the world with it. But as already noted, we will obtain empirical measures of each property from the data.

There were a number of reasons for using MacDraw to reinforce the alternative symbol system to freehand sketching. The MacDraw system provides considerable drawing power while differing from the system of sketching along the relevant syntactic and semantic dimensions. It also preserves some of the basic spatial properties exemplified by the system of sketching.[2] Subjects were proficient at it,[3] and it was readily available. One concern about using a computational interface should be voiced. Paper and pencil and computational systems currently require very different physical actions to create marks. Dragging and clicking a mouse has a very different "feel" to it than drawing on paper with a lead pencil. I am assuming this is an inconsequential difference once a certain degree of competence has been acquired with a mouse (as each of our subjects had), or with a pencil for that matter.[4]

The hypotheses associated with the manipulation are as follows:[5]

Ha. The drawings in freehand sketching are more "densely" or closely ordered than the symbols or drawings in MacDraw.

Hb. The system of freehand sketching is more ambiguous than the system characterized by MacDraw.

Hc. The ideas/contents or referents associated with the drawings in freehand sketching are more "densely" or closely ordered than the ideas/contents or referents associated with symbols or drawings in MacDraw.

9.3   Informal Overview of Data

Before specifying the coding scheme and actually offering an analysis of the data, it may be a good idea to get an intuitive feel for the behavioral and design output differences across the two conditions. Figure 9.1 and figure 9.2 reproduce the output of two design sessions of two different subjects, one drawing freehand and the other using MacDraw. The freehand drawings (9.1) are from the cognitive science program poster task, while the MacDraw drawings (9.2) are from the Shakespeare Festival poster session.

Informally, and very briefly, the difference between the two cases is the following: In freehand sketching, when a new idea is generated, a number of variations of it quickly follow. The variations expand the problem space and are necessary for the reasons noted earlier. One actually gets the sense that the exploration and transformation of ideas is happening on the paper in front of one's eyes as the subject moves from sketch to sketch. Indeed, designers have very strong intuitions to this effect.

When a new idea is generated in MacDraw, its external representation (in MacDraw) seems to fixate and stifle further exploration. Most subsequent effort after the initial generation is devoted to either detailing and refining the same idea or generating the next idea. One gets the feeling that all the work is being done internally with a different type of symbol system and recorded after the fact, presumably because the external symbol system can not support such operations.

These observations are reinforced by some of the verbalizations of the subjects. Here are a few fragments to give the flavor of their utterances:

Something happens [in sketching] in the sloppy interaction when pen hits paper which is not happening here [in MacDraw]. You almost get committed to something before you know whether you like it or not [in MacDraw].

I have to decide beforehand what I want before I can draw it [in MacDraw].

It [MacDraw] is very frustrating . . . unless you have an idea of what you want before you even sit down.

Sketching is noncommittal. This [MacDraw] is forcing me to make a commitment.

I just sketch a shape and look at it and have something come out of it.

In sketching you can start drawing a line, and it will turn into something else. With this [MacDraw] you have to know what you are doing.

Subjects' comments were not confined to complaining about Mac-Draw. At a certain stage in the design process, they considered computational systems to be of value and even asked for them during the latter stages of their freehand sessions:

I really can't go any further. I would now move to the computer to clean this up and get the lines and types right.

At this point it would be nice to switch over to something like Adobe and to have access to all the typefaces and fonts and libraries of pictures.

I now present a coding scheme that tries to formally measure (i) the differences in the syntactic and semantic density and ambiguity of the systems of sketching and MacDraw, as used by the subjects during the experiment (hypotheses Ha, Hb, and Hc), and (ii) the impact of these differences on the design problem space (hypothesis H).

9.4   Coding Scheme

The protocols were first broken up into episodes, which are sequences of verbalizations united by a single subgoal. Subgoals can, of course, be individuated at different levels of granularity. They were individuated such that the resulting episodes corresponded to alternative solutions generated by the subjects. Episodes were then correlated with the sketches and drawings generated during the sessions. Furthermore, a one-to-one mapping was desired between drawings and alternative solutions. The first step in setting up this correlation was to discount any episodes/alternative solutions that did not result in marks on paper. The rationale for this was simply that the lack of marks on paper indicates a lack of commitment and, more importantly, it is after all these marks that are the object of study. The second step was to individuate these marks into drawings and sketches.

Figure 9.1
Output of a design session with freehand sketching, from the Cognitive Science
Program poster task

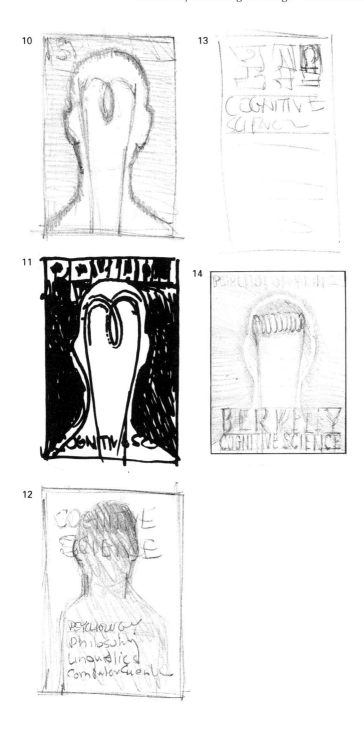

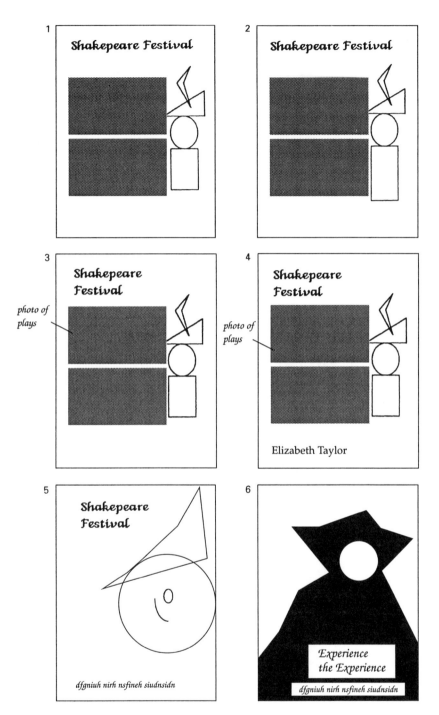

Figure 9.2
Output of a design session on MacDraw, from a Shakespeare Festival poster task

7

Stratford-on-Avon

Shakespeare

8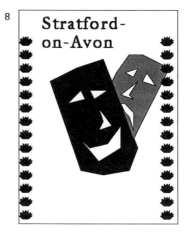

Stratford-on-Avon

9

Stratford-on-Avon

10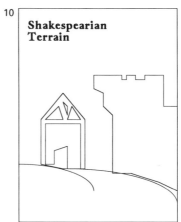

Shakespearian Terrain

11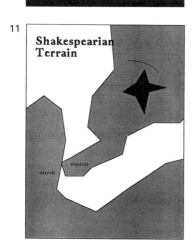

Shakespearian Terrain

detroit   windsor

12

A Canadian Comedy-Tragedy

The Stratford-on-Avon Shakespearian Festival

Individuating drawings and sketches was reasonably straightforward in the case of the freehand sessions. For the most part, subjects individuated the output by drawing rectangles around each separate drawing and even numbering them. (The numbering was done at the experimenter's request.) Most subjects also assigned a linguistic label to each drawing, which helped in the individuation process. This individuation of sketches resulted in a unique correspondence to alternative solutions.

Individuating the drawing output of the MacDraw sessions so that they uniquely corresponded to alternative solutions (or episodes) was more problematic. The difficulty resulted from the fact that the ability to cut, paste, delete, move, resize, translate, and so on, meant that changes were often made in place rather than resulting in a new drawing. So a single MacDraw drawing often corresponded to several episodes or alternative solutions.

The strategy used to overcome this difficulty was to individuate Mac-Draw drawing output temporally as well as spatially. A new drawing was considered to be instantiated whenever an existing drawing was changed in place by, for example, cut, paste, delete, move, resize, or translate commands. A clock was started when a drawing was started and stopped and restarted when the drawing was changed in place, completed, or abandoned. Any periods of drawing inactivity between the start and completion of drawings were counted as part of the episode. This temporal individuation did provide a unique mapping between alternative solutions and drawing output and resulted in a similar number of drawings or episodes across the two conditions, and the episodes turned out to have similar temporal duration (see table 9.2, in section 9.5).

No finer-grained breakdown of the protocol was undertaken. All subsequent coding and analysis was carried out at the episode, alternative-solution, or drawing level. This is appropriate because our hypothesized differences across the two conditions are stated at the level of alternative solutions, and the properties of symbol systems we are interested in are to be found at the level of complete drawings (actually in the relationships among drawings) rather than the internal structure of drawings.

Given this initial breakdown of the protocols, the drawings accompanying each episode were coded along three dimensions: (i) source type: where did the diagram originate? (ii) transformation type: how was it generated? and (iii) number of reinterpretations: did the drawings undergo any reinterpretations? The coding scheme is summarized in figure 9.3 and discussed below.

The *source-type* category is applied at both a syntactic level and a semantic level. So every drawing has a syntactic source and a semantic source. The syntactic source traces the origin of the drawing, whereas the semantic source traces the origin of the idea or content of the drawing. There is no a priori reason these two components should coincide, and often they did not. The two possibilities for a source are long-term memory (LTM) and previous solutions.

Categorizing a drawing as originating in LTM at the syntactic level is to say that the drawing is new. Categorizing a drawing as originating in LTM at the semantic level is to say that the idea or content of the drawing is new. In either case it is just another way of saying we do not know where the drawing or idea came from but that it is not related to previously generated drawings or ideas in any obvious way. The first drawing in every session is automatically classified as originating in

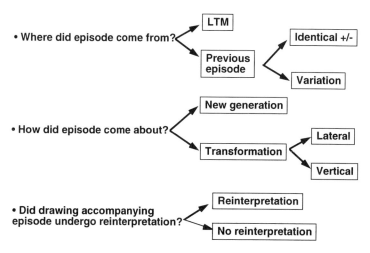

Figure 9.3
Outline of coding scheme for sketching study (see text)

LTM (at both the syntactic and the semantic levels), as are subsequent drawings that have no obvious relations to previous drawings. For example, drawings 1 and 5 in figure 9.1 are classified as originating in LTM at both the syntactic and semantic levels. Drawing 7 in figure 9.1 is classified as originating in LTM at the semantic level but not at the syntactic level. (It is syntactically related to previous drawings but received a new interpretation as a "light bulb.") In figure 9.2, drawings 1, 8, 10, and 11 are classified as originating in LTM at both the syntactic and the semantic levels. Drawing 6 (figure 9.2) is classified as originating in LTM at the syntactic level but not at the semantic level (it is the same idea as in the previous drawing, that of portraying a Shakespearean actor in period costume). The LTM category serves as a measure of "new generations" or new solutions.

Where a drawing is categorized as originating in one or more previous solutions, it means that it is related to one or more existing drawings (which correspond to previous solutions in a one-to-one manner) by the relation of variation, identical +/−, or identical.

A variation relation means that the current drawing is recognizably similar to earlier drawings.[6] At the syntactic level, this means that the marks constituting the drawing are closely related to, but distinct from, the marks constituting one or more previous drawings. A variation rating at the semantic level means that the idea or content of the drawing is similar (but not identical) to the ideas or contents of one or more previous drawings. For example, in figure 9.1, drawing 2 is considered a variation of drawing 1 at both the syntactic and the semantic levels. Drawing 7, however, is considered a variation of drawing 1 at the syntactic level but not at the semantic level, because it has received a totally new interpretation as a "light bulb." In figure 9.2, variations are much less frequent. A good example, however, is provided by drawing 12, which is considered a syntactic and semantic variation of drawing 8. The variation category serves as a measure of relative density by providing a measure of relative "closeness" or "similarity" between drawings generated in the two conditions.[7]

An identical +/− rating means that the drawing is identical to a previous drawing except for specifiable differences. At the syntactic level, this means that the marks constituting the drawing are identical to the marks constituting an earlier drawing except for a few specifiable details. At the semantic level, it means that the idea or content of the drawing is identical to the content of an earlier drawing except on one or two specific counts. Examples of this category are common in the MacDraw condition. For instance, in figure 9.2, drawing 2 is syntactically and semantically identical +/− to drawing 1, drawing 3 is syntactically and semantically identical +/− to drawing 2, and drawing 4 is syntactically and semantically identical +/− to drawing 4. Although this category can occur in the freehand case, it is not common.

The identical +/− category differs importantly from the variation category in that it involves refining or augmenting an existing drawing, not generating a different drawing. This reveals an important point about individuating and coding drawings: Individuation and coding is not based strictly on congruence and orientation of drawings. Congruence and orientation are used as guide lines along with a host of verbal semantic and contextual cues to determine sameness of drawing.

An identical rating means that the drawing is identical to a previous drawing. At the syntactic level, it signifies a type identity (in terms of congruence and orientation) between marks constituting the current drawing and marks constituting earlier drawings. At the semantic level, an identical rating signifies a type identity between the content of the current drawing and the content of earlier drawings. This category never occurred in the freehand case, though it could have (through tracing or photocopying drawings, for example). Interestingly, tracing was used frequently in the freehand sessions. However, it never resulted in an identical drawing, but always a variation of the old drawing. The identical category did occasionally occur in the MacDraw case.

The identical +/− and identical categories are not considered to be a measure of density, because they do not result in new drawings or ideas.

The *transformation-type* category is also applied at both the syntactic and semantic levels. Syntactic transformations are defined over the drawing, whereas semantic transformations are defined over the contents of drawings. Transformations are classified as either new generations or transformations of previous solutions.

New generations result in new drawings unrelated to previous drawings. At the syntactic level, a new generation means that the marks that constitute the drawing are unrelated in form to marks constituting earlier drawings. At the semantic level, it signifies that the content of the current drawing is unrelated to the content of earlier drawings. All (and only) syntactic and semantic source types that have their origin in LTM are classified as new generations. For example, drawings 1 and 5 in figure 9.1 are classified as new generations at both the syntactic and the semantic levels. Drawing 7 is classified as a new generation at the semantic level but not at the syntactic level. (It is syntactically related to previous drawings but has received a new interpretation as a "light bulb.") In figure 9.2, drawings 1, 8, 10, and 11 are classified as new generations at both the syntactic and the semantic levels. Drawing 6 is classified as a new generation at the syntactic level but not at the semantic level (it is the same idea as in the previous drawing, that of portraying a Shakespearean actor in period costume).

Current solutions or drawings are often transformations of previous solutions or drawings. Three such transformations are recognized: lateral transformations, vertical transformations, and duplication. The concepts of lateral and vertical transformations have already been introduced. To repeat, a lateral transformation modifies a drawing into another related, but distinctly different, drawing (as opposed to a more detailed version of the same drawing, a totally unrelated drawing, or an identical drawing). A vertical transformation reiterates and reinforces an existing drawing through explication and detailing. A duplication transformation results in movement from a drawing to a type-identical drawing. Syntactic transformations relate the form of the marks that constitute drawings, whereas semantic transformations relate the associated contents or ideas.

Lateral transformations were very common in the freehand sessions. To take just one example, the transformation from drawing 9 to drawing 10 in figure 9.1 is a lateral transformation at both the syntactic and the semantic levels. In MacDraw (figure 9.2), the best example of a lateral transformation is the transformation from drawing 8 to drawing 12. Vertical transformations, on the other hand, are more common in MacDraw. Good examples are the transformations from 1 to 2, 2 to 3, and 3 to 4, in figure 9.2. Duplicate transformations occurred only in MacDraw.

Finally, *reinterpretation* occurs where a subject assigns one meaning to a drawing and subsequently assigns a different meaning to the same drawing. For example, drawing 1 in figure 9.1 was a "silhouette figure going from dark to light." It was later reinterpreted as a "light bulb" (drawing 7) and as a "Berkeley student" (drawing 12). In figure 9.2, the "Shakespearean actor" in drawing 5 was reinterpreted as Shakespeare in drawing 7. Reinterpretation provides a measure of the relative ambiguity of the two symbol systems.

All the coding was done by the experimenter. Subsequently, three randomly chosen protocols were coded by a colleague experienced in coding protocols but with no detailed knowledge of the project or vested interest in the outcome of the results. The colleague was given both an oral and a written explanation of the coding scheme, and a few examples of each category were worked through jointly. The mean overall inter-rater agreement was 86.5 percent.

9.5   Results

In comparing the problem spaces across the two conditions, the first thing to note is that there are no statistically significant differences in the mean duration of episodes, the mean number of episodes per session, or the mean duration of sessions (table 9.1). This suggests that the subjects did not have a great deal of difficulty in using MacDraw. They were neither so frustrated as to shorten the sessions nor so handicapped as to be unable to generate episodes or drawings. There were, however, significant differences across the two conditions in the types of episodes and their accompanying transformations. These data are discussed below and summarized in table 9.2.

First of all, as hypothesized, the sketches or episodes in freehand drawing were much more densely ordered (i.e., more of them received a variation rating; see section 9.4) than the drawings or episodes in MacDraw. At the syntactic level, a mean of 10.8 (S = 4.8) sketches per session received a variation rating in freehand, whereas in MacDraw a

Table 9.1
Mean duration of sessions and episodes in minutes, and mean number of episodes and new solutions per session

	Freehand	MacDraw
Duration of sessions (min.)	57.5 (S = 11.5)	56.25 (S = 14.2)
Duration per episode (min.)	2.5 (S = 1.1)	2.8 (S = 0.6)
Number of episodes	16.3 (S = 6.9)	14.4 (S = 5.9)
Number of new solutions (syntactic level)	5.4 (S = 3.4)	4.4 (S = 1.8)
Number of new solutions (semantic level)	5.7 (S = 3.3)	4.6 (S = 1.8)

Note: S stands for standard deviation.

Table 9.2
Mean numbers of densely ordered episodes and reinterpreted episodes per session

	Freehand	MacDraw
Syntactic density	10.8 (S = 4.7)	2.4 (S = 3.1)
Semantic density	10.3 (S = 3.7)	4.3 (S = 3.6)
Ambiguity	2.9 (S = 3.3)	0.75 (S = 0.87)

Note: S stands for standard deviation.

mean of only 2.4 (S = 3.1) drawings per session received a variation rating. The difference is statistically significant (t (11) = 6.2, p = .0001, one-tail).

Second, also as hypothesized, a similar difference exists at the semantic level. In freehand sketching, a mean of 10.3 (S = 3.7) episodes per session was categorized as variation, whereas a mean of only 4.3 (S = 3.6) episodes per session were categorized as such in the MacDraw case. Although the gap narrows in the syntactic case, the difference is statistically significant (t (11) = 4.3, p = .0007, one-tail). The reason for this narrowing is discussed below.

Third, also as predicted, the freehand sketches are more ambiguous than the MacDraw drawings: A mean of 2.9 (S = 3.3) reinterpretations in the freehand sessions as compared to a mean of 0.75 (S = 0.87) in MacDraw. These figures are also significant (t (11) = 2.7, p = .01, one-tail).

These results allow us to reject the null hypotheses associated with hypotheses Ha, Hb, and Hc and suggest that the two symbol systems are indeed being used in the manner predicted. That is, the system of freehand sketching, as used by our subjects during the experiment, is more densely ordered and ambiguous than MacDraw. Now that we have reason to believe that our manipulation of symbol systems via tools and media has been successful, we can investigate whether this has the predicted impact on the design problem space.

The main hypothesis of interest, H, predicts that replacing sketching-type symbol systems with drafting-type symbol systems will hamper the exploration and development of alternative solutions (i.e., lateral trans-formations) and force early crystallization of the design. A comparison of the mean number of lateral transformations (both at the syntactic and the semantic levels) across the two conditions shows this indeed to be the case (table 9.3).

At the syntactic level, the freehand (sketching) condition resulted in a mean of 8.8 (S = 4.1) lateral transformations per session. This is significantly more (t (11) = 4.2, p = .0007, one-tail) than the mean of 3.0 (S = 2.8) found in the MacDraw (nonsketching) case. At the semantic level, the freehand (sketching) condition resulted in a mean of 8.1 (S = 3.2) lateral transformations. This is again significantly more (t (11) = 3.8, p = .0014, one-tail) than the mean of 3.5 (S = 3.0) found in the Mac-Draw (nonsketching) case.

Table 9.3
Mean numbers of lateral transformations per session

	Freehand	MacDraw
Syntactic lateral transformations	8.8 (S = 4.1)	3.0 (S = 2.8)
Semantic lateral transformations	8.1 (S = 3.2)	3.5 (S = 3.0)

Note: S stands for standard deviation.

9.6   Discussion and Conclusion

The data seem to provide the evidence needed to reject the null hypothesis associated with hypothesis H. The conclusion I wish to draw from these results is simply that dense and ambiguous symbol systems are not useless or inferior. They play a very important role in our cognitive processes, albeit a very different one from unambiguous, differentiated symbol systems. Before we actually accept this conclusion, several aspects of the experiment design and logic need to be discussed and some alternative interpretations of the results need to be considered.

9.6.1   Issues Concerning Logic and Design of Experiment

Use of Experts as Subjects   One issue that may give rise to concern is the use of expert designers as subjects, especially since we want our conclusions to be more generally applicable. Does not the use of experts confound the question of representations with issues of schooling, professional norms and practices, and maybe even unusual innate abilities? Such a concern, I think, is ill founded. First, all of us, design experts and novices alike, have learned our external systems of representation, and our use of these systems is embedded in social norms, conventions, and practices. There is simply no getting away from this. Symbol systems are parasitic on human intentionality and are generally given by precedent practices and exist and function in societal contexts.

Second, for reasons noted earlier, I made a conscious decision to restrict the investigation to design domains rather than look at a heterogeneous collection of ill-structured problems. Design is an activity we all engage in at times, with varying degrees of success. Restricting the experiments to expert designers increases homogeneity in the subject population and reduces noise.

Sorting out Factors   A more serious concern about the experiment design is that although we chose to examine the effect of three of the CTM-properties—syntactic and semantic density and ambiguity—we ended up with a one-factor design and are thus unable to say anything about the contribution of individual properties (e.g., whether all the effects come from one property or from the three properties equally) and the interaction among the properties. It would certainly be very desirable to design an experiment that does answer these additional questions. However, the fact I have not done so is not an oversight.

It has already been noted that syntactic density, semantic density, and ambiguity are, strictly speaking, binary properties. They are also logically independent properties; that is, they can, *theoretically,* be manipulated independently of one another.[8] Three independent binary properties should result in an eight-cell matrix, each cell containing different symbol systems, and enable a multifactor experiment design that would allow us to parcel out effects. The properties do result in an eight-cell matrix containing different symbol systems (including sketching and drafting), but the multifactor design required to answer the above questions may nonetheless not be *actually* possible. There is a deep reason for this paradoxical state of affairs.

Although it is possible to specify artificial symbol systems that would occupy each of the eight cells, in actuality, most of these cells are void of "naturally" occurring symbol systems. The symbol systems people actually use cluster in some subset of this space. Another way of saying this is that although each of the cells is occupied by logically possible symbol systems, they are not occupied by *psychologically* possible symbol systems. For example, consider a drawing system that is syntactically dense, semantically nondense, and ambiguous. Such a system would allow for a dense ordering of drawings, but the semantic realm would contain "gaps." Many drawings in this system will have no referent; many will be coextensive. Although this system results in waste or redundancy, it is a perfectly coherent conception. We can certainly *imagine* what such a system would be like. But it is not a naturally occurring system, and it is not clear how one would enforce the use of such a system. As another example, consider the matrix cell that contains the drawing systems that are syntactically and semantically dense but unambiguous. Again, this is a perfectly coherent conception. We can imagine what such a system would be like. In fact, on the surface, it would look very much like sketching, except the drawings would not be subject to different interpretations. But again it is not a naturally occurring system, and it is not clear in what circumstances one could get subjects to learn and use such a system. Even if we could, it would probably not be very meaningful to compare these systems with naturally occurring systems.

Why we can use only symbol systems that cluster in certain cells is a fascinating question requiring further exploration. I think it says something deep about the structure of human symbol systems and the cognitive machinery that processes them.

Despite the fact that there seems to be no obvious way to parcel out effects to individual factors, one can nonetheless draw useful conclusions from the study. I summarize these conclusions below after considering some alternative interpretations of the results.

9.6.2   Alternative Interpretations

Hypothesis H predicts that the manipulation will hamper cognitive processes involved in lateral transformations. The first difficulty is that *any* manipulation that results in a deviation from normal working conditions—whether it be an uncomfortable room temperature or being forced to draw with a seven-pound pencil—will hamper cognitive processes. So the differences that have been noted may have nothing to do with the theoretical reasons underlying the manipulation, but may simply result from the fact that one system of drawing (freehand sketching) was more familiar, or easier to use, than the other (MacDraw).

There are several reasons for rejecting this alternative hypothesis. First, as already noted, the manipulation does not affect the duration of sessions, the number of episodes generated per session, or the duration of these episodes (see table 9.1). Nor does it have any effect on the number of new alternative solutions generated per session. At the syntactic level, subjects generated a mean of 5.4 (S = 3.4) new alternatives per session for the freehand condition, as compared with a mean of 4.4 (S = 1.8) for the MacDraw condition. At the semantic level, the freehand condition resulted in 5.7 (S = 3.3) new episodes, whereas the MacDraw condition resulted in 4.6 (S = 1.8) episodes. Neither difference is significant. So it does not seem that freehand sketching is easier to use, or simply more familiar, than MacDraw. Second, it is interesting to note that subjects actually asked for the computational medium during the latter stages of their freehand design sessions.

A second alternative hypothesis that may account for the results is that the differences observed are a result of the protocol-analysis methodology rather than the manipulation. The claim here is that there are really no differences across the two conditions. What seems like a disruption of lateral transformations can be more simply accounted for as an unfortunate artifact of the methodology. If we assume that the system of *internal* representation is densely ordered and ambiguous, then there is a better match between it and the system of sketching than the system specified by MacDraw. This fact, combined with a well-accepted hypothesis about protocol analysis—that a more complete record of internal activity will result if there is a good match between the internal and external symbol systems than if there is not (Ericsson and Simon, 1984)—suggests that what is being interpreted as a disruption of certain cognitive processes is just a difference in the completeness of the records. That is, the freehand protocols are a more complete record of cognitive activity than the MacDraw protocols. If the two records were equally complete (or incomplete), no difference in the number or distribution of lateral and vertical transformations across the two conditions would be apparent.

I have much sympathy for this interpretation, and there is some evidence to support it. The discrepancies in the correspondence of the various syntactic and semantic measures noted above suggest that less of the cognitive burden is being off-loaded on the external symbol system in the MacDraw case than in the freehand case.

However, accepting this alternative interpretation does not jeopardize the conclusion I wish to draw from the study. In fact, it leads to the same conclusion I am approaching; it requires that the system of *internal* representation share the density and ambiguity properties of sketching. But an additional step is required before one can embrace this conclusion. Given the discussion in part I, I cannot freely assume that the language of thought fails the CTM-constraints. On the contrary, I must accept that the language of thought satisfies the CTM-constraints until I can demonstrate otherwise. In fact, given the logic of the situation, I must actually assume that it is the MacDraw protocols that provide a more complete record of internal cognitive activity and that the freehand protocols provide at best a sketchy and fragmented picture.

Thus I can not directly avail myself of this interpretation but must rely on an additional argument to reach it.

Therefore, at this point, I wish to draw only the following modest conclusion: freehand sketches—in virtue of being syntactically and/or semantically dense and/or ambiguous—play an important role in the creative, explorative, open-ended phase of problem solving. This role includes facilitating lateral transformations and preventing early fixation or crystallization via a dense ordering of syntactic and semantic elements and ambiguity of contents and/or referents. These functions are hampered by external representations that possess the CTM-properties. This is our fourth substantive conclusion.[9]

9.7   Conclusion to Part II

In part II, I have argued for making a real distinction between design and nondesign problem types, where design serves as an example of an ill-structured problem type and cryptarithmetic and the Moore-Anderson task serve as examples of well-structured problem types. Thus the more general claim is that the distinction also applies at the level of ill-structured and well-structured problems.

The distinction was shown to hold at both the task-environment and psychological levels. Certain cognitive processes were identified as occurring in the design problem space but not in the nondesign problem space. It was also noted that designers used a number of distinct external symbol systems as they traversed the design problem space and that these symbol systems lined up with different cognitive processes. In particular, the cognitive processes associated with the preliminary design phase correlated with symbol systems lacking the CTM-properties (i.e., sketching). It was argued that these were not substandard or inferior symbol systems, as implied by most of the work in cognitive science. On the contrary, it was suggested that they played an important role in certain types of open-ended, explorative cognitive processes. This prediction was tested by manipulating (along the CTM-properties dimension) the external symbol systems designers were allowed to use during design problem-solving sessions. The results indicated that cognitive processes were affected in a very selective and predictable manner.

This leads us to the conclusion that, although many well-structured problems may be explained by postulating a CTM-type external (and internal) symbol system, at least some ill-structured problems require postulating non–CTM-type *external* symbol systems. I wish to demonstrate next that this result has important implications for the system of *internal* representations, for the language of thought. In particular, I will argue that if one accepts the psychological reality and utility of external systems that lack the CTM-properties, one must also—other things being equal—accept a language of thought that, at times, fails the CTM-constraints. This will be the fifth and final step in our argument.

III
Implications, Directions, and Conclusions

Could he whose rules the rapid comet bind,
Describe or fix one movement of his mind?

—Pope

10

Implications for the Computational Theory of Mind

Its aspect gives the angels power,
Since none can solve Thee no Thy ways;
And all Thy works beyond us tower,
Sublime as on the first of days.

—Goethe (translation by G. M. Priest)

10.1 From External to Internal Symbol Systems

One crucial issue remains to be addressed in this third and final part of the argument. The results of part II have to do with *external* symbol systems. What, if anything, do these results have to do with the Computational Theory of Mind, which is, after all, a claim about the system of *internal* representations? Surely, to think that results based on manipulating external symbol systems map onto internal symbol systems is to exhibit an uncommon degree of naïveté, to say nothing of confusion.

True, the cognitive claim does require that before an external symbol system can be known and used, it be internally represented.[1] Thus external symbol systems like sketching must have *some* internal representation. But it explicitly *does not* require that the internal symbol system have the same properties as the external symbol system, only that the two be "informationally equivalent" or have the same "expressive power." If this is the claim—and there is considerable agreement that it is—then clearly there is no problem with the internal representation of external symbol systems that lack the CTM-properties. All that is required is a mechanism that maps the external symbol systems onto the internal symbol system. Where these symbol systems match up with respect to relevant properties (CTM-properties), it is a straightforward mapping. Where there is a mismatch, as when the external symbol system fails the CTM-properties, then this mechanism must do a little more work in converting the external non-CTM system into the internal CTM-system. There are two possible candidates for this mechanism, transducers and computational systems. The burden of this section is to demonstrate that neither mechanism is sufficient for the task and that to think otherwise is to misunderstand the nature of the problem involved in mapping non–CTM-type symbol systems onto CTM-type symbol systems.

Consider what is required for such mapping. First, we need a mechanism that can look at arbitrary marks and assign them to characters (i.e., sort them into equivalence classes). Any two distinct marks will share a number of properties and will differ in a number of others. Any partitioning into equivalence classes will have to specify which of these properties are *constitutive* of the equivalence class. Thus the mechanism would have to distinguish between the constitutive and the contingent properties of the marks. But this information is simply not contained in the marks. It is a function of the syntax or symbolic scheme in effect. Second, the mechanism would need to disambiguate the referent of the characters. Again, this simply cannot be done on the basis of any physical properties of the marks themselves. It is a function of the symbol system in effect.

Now consider what transducers are. In physical/engineering domains, transducers belong to a class of well-specified mechanisms that transform one type of energy into another. In cognitive science we are interested in "psychological transducers," which are an interface between the physical and the psychological domains. They are a magic box in which the world crawls in one end and symbols march out the other end. Here is Pylyshyn's design specification for a psychological transducer:

• The function carried out by a transducer is *primitive* and is itself *nonsymbolic*.[2] At least, the function is not described as carried out by means of symbol processing; it is part of the functional architecture.

• A transducer is, to a first approximation, a stimulus-bound component operating independently of the cognitive system. It is also *interrupt-* or *data*-driven by its environment.

• The behavior of a transducer is to be described as a *function* from physical events onto symbols:

(a) The domain of the function must be couched in the language of physics.

(b) The range of the function must be computationally available, discrete atomic symbols.

(c) A transducer can occur at any energy transfer locus where, in order to capture the regularities of the system, it is necessary to change descriptions from physical to symbolic. The only requirement is that the transformation from the input, described physically, to the ensuing token computational event, also described physically, follow from physical principles. (1984, pp. 153–54)

This specification contains five constraints on psychological transducers. First, notice that the input to a transducer can be any physical stimuli; it need not be restricted to the subset that satisfies the CTM-constraints. Thus one might think that non-CTM systems are bona fide input into such a mechanism. This is not quite the case, because the input must be specified in purely physical vocabulary. Qua undifferentiated stimuli, such input is acceptable, but qua representational scheme or system, it can not be allowed. The notion of a syntax (much less a semantics) can not enter into the description. It has already been noted above that the information regarding the constitutive and contingent properties of marks is not contained in the physical properties of the marks but in the scheme. Second, the output of the mechanism must satisfy the CTM-constraints (and by virtue of this will be amenable to a semantic description). Third, the transduction process itself must be nonsymbolic. That is, it must not be predicated over the CTM-properties of the input, even if the input happens to have these properties (which it need not have). Fourth, there must be no top-down knowledge component associated with the process. The only "information" available to the function is that contained in the physical properties of the input qua physical properties. Fifth, it has to be realizable as a physical process. The first and fourth constraints rule out transducers as candidate mechanisms for mapping non-CTM symbol systems onto CTM symbol systems.

More generally, transducers on this account map "nonsymbolic" stimuli onto "symbolic" data structures. I have already suggested that Pylyshyn's vocabulary of "symbolic" maps onto my vocabulary of "CTM symbol systems." Thereafter, it is tempting to think that his notion of "nonsymbolic" may correspond to my notion of "non-CTM symbol systems." This is, however, only partially true. For Pylyshyn, to be nonsymbolic is to fail the CTM-constraints, but to fail the CTM-constraints is to no longer be a representational system of any kind.[3] Qua representational systems, neither CTM-systems nor non-CTM systems can be inputs to psychological transducers.

The notion of a transducer can not, and was never intended to, do the work of mapping non–CTM-type symbol systems onto CTM-type symbol systems. Well, perhaps then this is a job for computational systems. But as we have already seen, our notions of computation presuppose the CTM-constraints. We do not know how to define computations over symbol systems that fail these constraints. Thus the task can not be relegated to a computational mechanism.

It should be clear that the problem here is not one of visual perception but one of *interpreting* symbol systems in the absence of any explicit rules and conventions. It is not a problem of how we perceive the various marks or tokens but how we sort them into equivalence classes in the absence of any agreement as to which properties are constitutive of the classes, and how we disambiguate the reference classes in the absence of any unique partitioning of the world by the symbol system in effect.

Here is another way of understanding the issue. Linguistic works are sorted into equivalence classes on the basis of their spelling (Elgin, 1983; Goodman, 1976); identity of spelling entails identity of the work or character. Paintings, however, are sorted into equivalence classes on the basis of their history of production (i.e., author, time, place, and means of production). It is the Mona Lisa if and only if it has the requisite history of production. The problem of mapping a non–CTM-type symbol system onto a CTM-type symbol systems is the general case of the problem of developing a symbol system that would, in a nontrivial way, free the identity conditions of paintings from their history of production. To be nontrivial, such a system would have to do justice to antecedent classification and project onto future instances in a way that conforms with precedent practice. As Goodman (1976) has pointed out, developing such a system would require nothing less than a real definition of what constitutes a painting.

The claim here is not that it is in principle impossible to transform non–CTM-type symbol systems into CTM-type symbol systems. Such transformations clearly are possible. A simple example is provided by analog and digital thermometers. Imagine a tube of mercury that is to be used as a thermometer. There are no marks on the face of the tube and every difference in the position of the mercury—no matter how small—is constitutive of a different character. In such a system, although there may be a fact of the matter as to what mark is being instantiated, there is no fact of the matter as to what character is being instantiated. Furthermore, if the level of mercury is correlated with room temperature, then there will also be no fact of the matter as to what temperature is being referred to. Such a system fails both the syntactic and the semantic effective differentiability criteria. How do we turn this into a digital thermometer or a system that is effectively differentiable?

As a start, we can graduate the tube into ten equal sections and mark them with horizontal lines. But this in itself is not enough. In addition to graduating the thermometer, we need to (i) agree that each division of the tube is a character, (ii) agree that each point or region in that division counts as the same character (i.e., is character-indifferent or syntactically equivalent), (iii) agree that the subdivisions are separated by a perceptible gap, which is not itself a character, and (iv) preserve these three properties in the individuation of room temperature.

These agreements make it possible to map an undifferentiated system onto an effectively differentiable system. Each step in the process constitutes a social agreement, which in this case is easily arrived at, relative to specific usage. Which divisions of the tube we would accept as character-indifferent would vary depending on whether the thermometer was to be used to measure the temperature in my backyard, in a medical procedure, or in a chemistry lab.

Other agreements are also at work here: that no two gradations map onto the same character, and that each character be correlated with a unique temperature. These two need not be made explicitly, because they were already assumed in the analog version of the thermometer. Like the first set, they are not arbitrary. Unlike the first set, they are not based on a social consensus, but rather a theory of temperature measurement.

Although the thermometer is a relatively simple case, it is instructive to understand why it is simple. Its simplicity arises from the facts that we can arrive at a social consensus relative to usage and that we actually have a theory of temperature measurement. Otherwise, no mapping would be possible. Where theories and consensus to establish identity conditions exist, the mapping can be accomplished in even very complex domains, such as the systems of Western music and, to some extent, dance (Goodman, 1976). However, where there are no theories or social consensus of identity conditions (independent of the history of production), as in the case of sketching, painting, sculpturing, and the like, no mappings are possible.

We may of course develop such theories and consensus, but it seems clear that whatever this mapping function turns out to be in the case of sketches and paintings, it will require full cognitive capabilities. But if this is the case, then the computational theory of mind is precommitted to explaining it as a computational function.[4] Given our present notions of computation and its role in cognitive explanations, we can not even get started explaining this mapping function as a computational process. The conclusion would seem to be that we can neither explain the mapping from the non–CTM-type system of sketching onto a CTM-type "language of thought" nor leave it unexplained without begging the crucial question. Given that we are in the business of explaining cognitive functions, if the mapping is a cognitive function, we are obligated to explain it. We cannot leave it to " 'sensory encoding' neurophysiologists, biophysicists, and engineers" (Pylyshyn, 1984, p. 148).

It would seem that, given the results regarding the cognitive role of external symbol systems from part II, and in the absence of any mechanism to perform the mapping, we need to consider the possibility that some subset of the "language of thought" lacks the CTM-properties and is able to directly represent non-CTM symbol systems like sketching. This is the fifth and final substantive claim of the monograph and concludes my main argument. However, we are not quite through yet. There are a number of reasons to worry about the Computational Theory of Mind, quite independent of my argument about the structure of symbol systems. Let us examine several of these worries before turning to connectionism and identifying some of the issues and problems that need to be confronted.

10.2 Additional Concerns about the Computational Theory of Mind

Several serious problems with the Computational Theory of Mind, independent of my concerns, are highlighted by the analysis in part I.

First, recall that although the RTM-constraints account recognizes the semantic content of mental states at time t_i and t_j and causally implicates that content in the evolution of the system from t_i to t_j, it does not entail that the mediating processes also be semantic. But the RTM'-constraints commit us, by virtue of constraint C2'(i), not only to the semantic content (interpretability) of instantaneous descriptions at time t_i and t_j but also to the semantic content (interpretability) of the mediating instantaneous descriptions. We have experiential evidence of the semantic content of some mental states. But there is no corresponding evidence that the cognitive processes that mediate between such states are also representational. Hence we are forced to argue that these processes are unconscious. (In all fairness, it should be noted that we currently have little choice but to make the assumption that these processes are semantic, because, as noted above, at the moment we can not even imagine what type of nonsemantic predicate we could apply to a process that mediates between two semantic states.)

Second, we must claim that CTM-properties are a necessary condition on cognitive systems. This of course does not mean that one has to equate mental phenomena with CTM-properties, but it does mean that there can be no minds without CTM-properties. This seems highly implausible.

Third, nothing in the RTM-constraints requires a stronger relationship than supervenience between the physical and mental states. Supervenience is not sufficient, however, to satisfy the RTM'-constraints. As we have seen, a much stronger relationship is required. This seems to violate some rather strongly held intuitions. Incidentally, it also suggests that computational functionalism—the doctrine that computational states can be realized in *any* physical system—may not be as coherent a story as is widely thought.

The fourth and perhaps the most troubling difficulty is the following: We end up appealing to a CTM-system to explain the cognitive system's ability to process information. But the reason we needed a CTM-system to begin with was that we were satisfied with a computational account of content and reference that is substantially different from that of human mental states. The difficulty of course is that, from the fact that we need CTM-properties to satisfy the RTM'-constraints, nothing logically follows about the RTM-constraints.

One type of response the reader may be tempted to entertain is the following: "Doesn't all this just go to show the inadequacy of the 'classical' symbolic computation story and give us all the more reason to embrace connectionism? As if more reasons were needed." Surely the "classical" story is passé and obsolete. What is the point of beating a dead horse? In response, I claim that there is currently no connectionist theory of mind. In fact, there are no well-developed intuitions to form the basis of such a theory. We may ultimately get an alternative account, but presently there is more smoke than fire. The classical story is the only horse we have. Let us try to save it—even if we kill it in the attempt!

10.3   Connectionism: Where Is the Theory?

Connectionists are very adamant about the fact that they are not doing clumsy, old-fashioned symbol manipulation. They do, however, claim to be doing information processing. The problem is that, although connectionists make a commitment to the notion of information processing, they have failed to elucidate and ground their claims in any set of intuitions that do justice to the term (like the ITM- or RTM- and RTM'-constraints try to do for the "classical" story).

Furthermore, there is not one but several conceptually distinct research efforts being carried on under the general heading of connectionism. They can be categorized in terms of their inspirational source and theoretical vocabulary. There are three main sources: performance psychology, physics, and biology. The corresponding categories of research are parallel distributed processing (PDP), physical dynamical systems modeling, and neuronal modeling.

Much of the work associated with the PDP group is concerned with modeling some real-time performance aspects of cognition (McClelland and Rumelhart, 1986b, chapter 1; Rumelhart and McClelland, 1986, part 4). The models are viewed as architectural variants of physical symbol systems and hence information processing systems of some kind. The basic strategy is to pick some performance properties of cognitive systems (e.g., typing, letter recognition, word recognition) and to show that the PDP architecture can accommodate the task more accurately and naturally than the physical symbol systems architecture. The participants are anxious to insist that they are not "merely" exploring different implementations of physical symbol systems but are making substantive theoretical claims, quite different from those associated with physical symbol systems (see, for example, the exchange between Broadbent [1985] and Rumelhart and McClelland [1985], and chapter 4 in Rumelhart and McClelland [1986]). To evaluate and do justice to this controversy would take us too far afield. It is an internal disagreement not particularly relevant to our metatheoretical concerns. I merely note it to set it aside.

The physics-inspired models (Hinton and Sejnowski, 1986; Smolensky, 1986, 1988; Tank and Hopfield, 1987) offer a more radical picture. On this account, the network (and the cognitive system) is viewed as a continuous physical dynamical system, evolving through time like any other physical dynamical system, and engaged in "subsymbolic" or "numerical" computations (Smolensky, 1988) rather than symbolic computations. There are a number of outstanding questions as to the cognitive significance of these models, but what I want to emphasize here is that they want to hang on to the notion of information processing while abandoning the notion of symbol manipulation in favor of continuous numerical computations.

This latter point must also be made in connection with the biologically or neurologically inspired models. Although these researchers take neurophysiology very seriously—despite their disparaging remarks about classical AI and connectionist networks that only "look sideways to biology" (Reeke and Edelman, 1988)—they are also committed to the notion of information processing, albeit with slightly different computational architectures.

Thus the notion of information processing is a common theme running through these three endeavors. Yet each group claims to be offering a different account from the others and a radically different account from the computational information processing story associated with physical symbol systems and the language of thought, and further claims that this difference is of considerable theoretical importance to cognitive science.

The difficulty in accessing these claims is in understanding what connectionists mean by information processing. What are their intuitions about information processing? What facts about the dynamics of these systems makes them instances of information processing systems. We saw that the classical story appeals to some intuitions derived from folk psychology and captured in the ITM- or RTM-constraints, and that dynamical systems need to satisfy the RTM'-constraints to be instances of computational information processing systems. It is not clear whether connectionists would accept the ITM- or RTM-constraints on cognitive information processing as interesting or relevant. It is very doubtful that they would explicitly accept the RTM'-constraints on computational information processing. However, given the relationship between the RTM'-constraints and interpretability of symbol systems, the enormous amount of effort currently being devoted to interpreting the hidden nodes in multilayered networks can be viewed as an unwitting search for an analysis under which the network satisfies the RTM'-constraints.

In terms of our discussion, what is interesting to note is that it is not necessary (or even desirable) to satisfy the RTM'-constraints. Ideally what one wants to do is satisfy the RTM-constraints. This option is open to connectionists so long as they come up with a nonderivative account of reference and content that does justice to human mental states.

If, however, they want to stay with the current (interpretation-dependent) computational notions of reference and content, then there seem to be few nonvacuous alternatives to the RTM′-constraints. Without the ability to assign specific values to specific physical states and recover them (constraint C1′) it is not clear how one could even get started on the road to information processing. And without constraint C2′, one would have no basis for implicating representational content. One would just have a black box with a certain input and output, and this strictly behavioral story would be subject to the charge of vacuousness (see chapter 3, and Searle [1990b]).

Another option for connectionists is to give up the notion of information processing altogether. The difficulty here is in knowing what to replace it with. That is, in the absence of an appeal to mental contents, what fact about these dynamical systems makes them instances or models of cognitive systems? One hackneyed proposal is the appeal to complexity (Smolensky, 1988):

> A necessary condition for a dynamical system to be *cognitive* is that, under a wide variety of environmental conditions, it maintains a large number of goal conditions. The greater the repertoire of goals and variety of tolerable environmental conditions, the greater the cognitive capacity of the system. The issue of complexity is crucial here. A river (or a thermostat) only fails to be a cognitive dynamical system because it cannot satisfy a *large* range of goals under a *wide* range of conditions. Complexity is largely what distinguishes the dynamical systems studied in the subsymbolic paradigm from those traditionally studied in physics. (p. 15)

There are several puzzling aspects here. First, notice that this account does not do away with the appeal to mental states (goals) and hence mental contents; in fact, it freely attributes them to rivers and thermostats! But this apparently is not sufficient to render a system cognitive. What is crucial is the *number* of such states that can be attributed to the system. Second, attributions are cheap. If goals and mental contents are simply for the attribution, then the number of goals a river or a thermostat has depends on how I choose to individuate them. Thus a river could as easily qualify as a cognitive agent as you and I could. Perhaps most puzzling of all is that connectionist dynamical systems which can not account for a single mental state in a nonvacuous way are thought to explain the attribution of *many* such states.

It seems to me that the two options that hold the greatest promise of rapid transformation and advancement of the field are to motivate a notion of cognitive information processing independent of the RTM-constraints or, if one is going to accept the RTM-constraints, to find a mapping from them onto a new set, RTM″, that does not require a commitment to CTM-systems.

10.4 Summary and Conclusions

I have argued the thesis that cognitive science is committed to mental representations with the CTM-properties, but that there are many genuine cognitive tasks that require the postulation of mental representations lacking the CTM-properties. The strategy used to establish the thesis was, first, to demonstrate that the CTM-properties are indeed necessary for the computational story; second, to show that some genuine cognitive domains require the postulation of external symbol systems that fail the CTM-constraints; third, to demonstrate that if we grant a cognitive role to external symbol systems that fail the CTM-constraints, then we must accept that the internal representation of these symbol systems also fail to satisfy the CTM-properties.

In arguing for this thesis, I made and substantiated the following major claims:

1. The system of internal representation postulated by the Computational Theory Method must necessarily satisfy the CTM-constraints.

2. There are significant differences in the task environments of (at least some) ill-structured and well-structured problems.

3. There are significant differences in the cognitive processes found in the problem spaces of (at least some) ill-structured and well-structured problems.

4. External symbol systems lacking the CTM-properties are required to facilitate some of the cognitive operations found in ill-structured problem spaces.

5. A commitment to the psychological reality of non–CTM-type external symbol systems entails, all other things being equal, a commitment to non–CTM-type mental representations.

The general conclusion to be drawn from the work is largely a negative one: How we currently cash out the notion of mental representations via the computational information processing story is inadequate to do justice to the full range of human symbolic activity.

The Computational Theory of Mind was of course never meant to account for all *mental* processes, but it is meant to account for most *cognitive* processes (i.e., processes defined over mental representations). The results of the two empirical studies, to say nothing of common sense, along with the arguments in part III question this claim. They suggest that for many genuine cognitive functions, we need to assume mental representations that fail the CTM-properties. This is of course at odds with the Computational Theory of Mind.

Furthermore, the Computational Theory of Mind cannot be made compatible with these results in a nontrivial way. Any such attempt would have to either dismiss the problem-solving tasks studied as being noncognitive and involving only noncognitive mechanisms, or truncate these domains from the explanatory scope of cognitive science. Neither is a viable option. Given, on the one hand, that cognitive processes are those processes defined over mental representations and, on the other hand, the description of the design problem space, I take it no one is prepared to argue that what we are dealing with are noncognitive processes. Similarly, given that most real-world problems are of the ill-structured variety, I take it no one is prepared to do away with this domain and restrict cognitive science to the study of well-structured puzzle problems.

This conclusion however, should not be taken to imply the general inadequacy of computationalism. It speaks only to the inadequacy—or lack of coverage—of the Computational Theory of Mind as explicated in part I. Recall the structure of that story (figure 10.1). The phenomenon to be explained by computationalism was cognitive information processing, as specified by the RTM-constraints. There was, however, no direct mapping between computationalism and cognitive information processing because of the very different notions of semantic content and semantic causation that underlie the two. The RTM-constraints were then mapped onto the RTM'-constraints that can be satisfied or explained by certain mechanisms meeting the CTM-constraints. This very different phenomenon was explained by computationalism, and the explanation was extended to the original cognitive phenomenon by (to be blunt) hand waving. This realization suggests several directions of research that may alleviate some of the difficulties.

At least three plausible research projects need to be pursued. Each is nontrivial. First, we can manipulate the RTM-constraints on cogni-

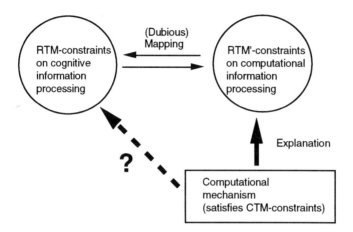

Figure 10.1
Structure of Computational Theory of Mind explanation

tive information processing. That is, we can argue that the notions of semantic content and semantic causation underlying the RTM-constraints do not really do justice to the human case and need to be reformulated. If we follow this route, we get a substantially different game, and all current commitments and arguments would have to be reformulated accordingly. I take it that some recent work by Cussins (1990) to broaden our notion of semantic content by introducing "non-conceptual content" is an attempt in this direction.

Second, we can come up with an account of computation in which the notions of semantic content and causation are not so cheap, but actually do justice to the human phenomenon. This would give us a computational account independent of the CTM-properties; again, the conflict noted here would not arise. This is Brian Smith's (1996, forthcoming) intellectual project. I think we will need to make progress on both of these fronts to vindicate some sort of computational theory of mind.

Lastly, we could keep the RTM-constraints in their current form and find an alternative (noncomputational) mechanism to satisfy them directly (without mapping them onto the RTM'-constraints). Such a mechanism would free us from the CTM-constraints, and the conflict noted here would not arise. On this last scenario, it is not clear what would be left of cognitive science as we understand it.

Appendix A
Methodological Details of Study 1: Structure of Design Problem Spaces

Subjects

One of the design protocols was produced by a subject performing the architecture task (subject S-A). Subject S-A was a Ph.D. student in the Department of Architecture at the University of California, Berkeley, who volunteered to participate in the study. He had six years of professional experience but had never worked on a problem similar to the given task. The second protocol was produced by subject S-M, while solving the mechanical engineering task. Subject S-M, a Ph.D. student in the Department of Mechanical Engineering at Stanford University volunteered to participate in the study. He had three years of professional experience, including designing bank teller machines for a firm in Italy. The third protocol was collected from subject S-I on an instructional design task. Subject S-I, a professional instructional designer working for a large multinational corporation who also volunteered to participate in the study, had over ten years of experience in designing technical training material for operating and servicing office machinery and systems.

Task Descriptions

Architecture　The architecture task was to design an automated post office (where postal tellers were replaced by automated postal teller machines) for a site on the UC-Berkeley campus. Subject S-A was given two documents: an outline of the experiment procedures and a design brief, which motivated the need for the post office and specified the client's needs and requirements.

Mechanical engineering   The mechanical-engineering task was to design an automated postal teller machine for the above post office. Subject S-M was given three sets of documents: the experimental procedures, the design brief, and the post office design generated by the architect.

Instructional design   The instructional design task was to design a self-contained instructional package to teach secretaries how to use the Viewpoint text-editing software running on Xerox Star. Subject S-I was given three documents: the experimental procedures, the design brief, and the Viewpoint reference manual. The experimental instructions and design briefs for each of the tasks are reproduced at the end of this Appendix.

Protocol-Coding Procedures

The verbal protocols were transcribed and cross-referenced with the written and drawn documents (henceforth referred to as marks on paper). The transcribed protocols were divided into utterances or statements, and each statement was coded at three levels: a statement level, a module level, and a design-phase level. This subsection specifies the criteria for individuating statements and provides an overview of the coding scheme.

Individuating Statements

The intuition behind dividing the protocol into statements was that each statement should convey or capture a single thought, expression, or idea. There are at least two ways of doing this. One is to individuate by content cues, so that whenever there is a shift in topic or in the point being made about the topic, a new statement is instantiated. A second way is to look for noncontent cues, such as pauses, end of phrases and sentences, and making and breaking contact between pen and paper. Both of these were examined, and the one that provided the finer-grained individuation was used. This resulted in a mean temporal duration of eight seconds per statement. The mean number of words per statement was fifteen.

Coding Scheme

A complex trilevel coding scheme is applied to each statement made by the subjects (figure A.1). The first- or design-phase-level code serves to aggregate statements and to divide the protocol into three important high-level categories: experimental-task statements, monitoring or metacognitive statements, and design-development statements. Monitoring and design-development statements are further divided into several subcategories. The second- or module-level code serves to aggregate statements into what are generally called episodes. The third- or statement-level code does not aggregate statements but locally attaches operator, content, mode-of-output, and source-of-knowledge labels to them. A general discussion of the key components, illustrated with examples, is offered below.

Design-Phase Level The design-phase level (see figure A.2) identifies the statement type as experimental task, monitoring (monitor), design development (design-development), or miscellaneous, defined as follows:

Experimental task statements have to do with the experimental design and setup. Example: "Do you want me to read the brief also?"

Monitor statements are used to take stock, further, review, or comment on the problem-solving process itself. Most of these correspond to what in the literature have been called metacognitive statements (Schoenfeld, 1985). Example: "I wonder why I did this rather than. . . ." We identify and code for four different types of monitoring statements:

• Design-operator statements are those in which an operation is explicitly mentioned. Example: "Let me see if I can organize this."

• Design-methodology statements are about "normal" procedure or practice—vis a vis the design process—in a particular situation, whether carried out or not. Example: "Normally at this point I would build a 3-D mockup."

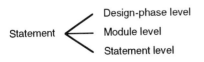

Figure A.1
A three-level coding scheme

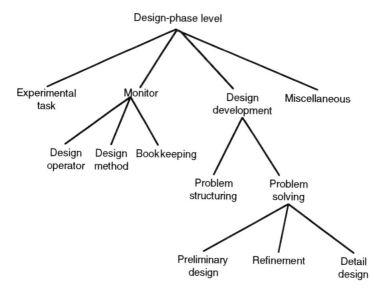

Figure A.2
Coding scheme: design-phase level

• Bookkeeping statements have to do with the organization of the external work space. Example: "This third sheet I call 'function,' 'functional organization.' "

Design-development statements advance the state of the design/artifact. They are categorized into four categories:

• Problem-structuring: A collection of statements that serve to solicit or generate information to structure the problem. Example: "And then you are giving me the complete freedom of choosing any automation system or equipment."

• Preliminary-design: A collection of statements that result in the initial generation and exploration of some aspect of the design. They are accompanied by fast, fluid drawings. Example: "I think a flat roof is appropriate here."

• Refine: A collection of statements that serve to elaborate and further the commitment to a previously generated design idea or element. They are accompanied by transformations or variations of existing drawings. Example: "The roof should not be too high. . . ."

• Detail: A collection of statements that serve to detail, and give the final form to, some aspect of the design. They are accompanied by crisp, straight-lined, dimensioned drawings, using a hard pencil or a pen. They often entail the use of precision drawing instruments, which were not available to our subjects. Example: "The dimensions of the roof are. . . ."

Miscellaneous statements do not fall into any of the other three categories.

The design-development categories are quite common in the literature. They are relative to the time and resources available to the designer, but even within short sessions it is possible to trace the development of the design and segment it into these phases.

Each design-development category is further differentiated into the following aspects of design-development subcategories: people, purpose, behavior, function, structure, and resource. As with the design-development categories, these subcategories are quite standard in the design literature. The ones employed here are adopted from Wade (1977). Briefly, the intuition behind them is that artifacts are designed to perform certain functions, which are calculated to support certain behaviors, which help in the realization of certain goals/purposes held by people/users (see figure A.3). This categorization provides a chain linking users to artifacts and recognizes that each intermittent step needs to be considered. I have added "resources" (e.g., time, money, and workforce) as a sixth category. It should be noted that these are not disjunctive categories. A single statement can fall into more than one category.

• People statements deal with the users of the artifact. Example: "We will be training twelve secretaries."
• Purpose statements deal with the motives, intentions, and goals of the users. Example: "Why do they want to learn Viewpoint?"
• Behavior statements specify the behavior the artifact is supposed to encourage and support. Example: "The secretaries should be proficient with Viewpoint after twelve hours of instruction."
• Function statements have to do with the desired, potential, or actual functionality of the artifact. Example: "This paging scheme should keep them from getting lost."
• Structure statements have to do with the desired, potential, or actual form of the artifact. Example: "I will divide the course up into six sections."

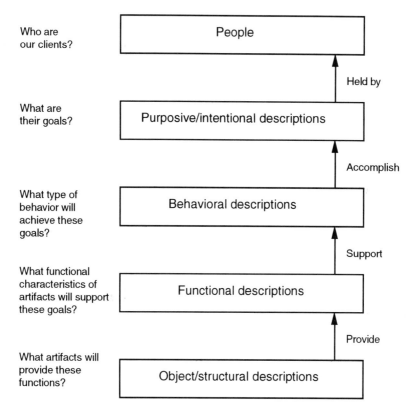

Figure A.3
Aspects of design development

- Resource statements consider resources, such as time, money, and people. Example: "So you need delivery in thirty-seven days."
- Miscellaneous statements do not fit into any of the other categories.

Module Level   The second- or module-level code has only two fields, a module label and the content of the module (figure A.4). A module label is an arbitrary name or number assigned to a module. The module content is a list or label specifying the content of the module, e.g., 'seating', 'handicap access to building'.

Modules are a subset of episodes. Episodes are generally taken to be a sequence of closely related statements united by a single problem-

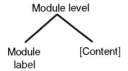

Figure A.4
Coding scheme: module level

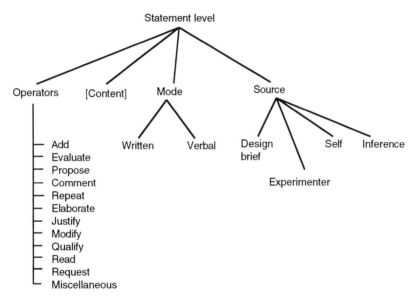

Figure A.5
Coding scheme: statement level

solving goal. Modules are episodes that focus on some component of the artifact being designed. Unlike the design-phase level, the module level is content-specific and thus dependent on particular tasks and subjects.

Statement Level The third- or statement-level code has four independent fields: the operator applied, the mode of the output, the source of knowledge used, and the content to which it is applied.

Operators A labeling of statements by the function they serve in the problem space. Although no theoretical commitment is made to any specific set, the eleven noted below (and in figure A.5) are adequate for current purposes:

• Add: The basic operation of putting something into the problem space with some degree of commitment.

• Propose: Indicates that an idea is being entertained but is not yet committed to the problem space.

• Evaluate: Means that the statement is an explicit evaluation of a previous statement or design component in the problem space.

• Comment: By and large, the report of an activity rather than the execution of it. They generally occur with monitoring statements. Often they involve the subject's explaining the action just taken or making some remarks that, while not directly related to the subject's progress, are nonetheless illuminating.

• Modify: A statement that deletes or alters an existing idea or element that is already a part of the problem space. It is sometimes difficult to distinguish between "add" and "modify"; between an old idea's being modified and a new one's being added.

• Elaborate: Expands an existent idea or element.

• Justify: Offers a rationale for adding to, modifying, or elaborating on ideas or elements in the problem space.

• Read: Any time the subject reads from the experimental task instructions, design brief, or any other documents supplied with the task.

• Qualify: A statement used to hedge or further qualify the previous statement.

• Request: Statements used to ask questions of, or make suggestions to, the experimenter.

• Repeat: The application of the same operator to the same content again. Although any operator can be repeated, usually only add, modify, and elaborate operations actually are repeated.

• Miscellaneous: Any statement that can not be coded with one of the other operators.

Mode of output   A statement's mode of output is encoded as either verbal or written. That is, each statement is encoded as being generated either verbally or as a mark on paper. Hand and facial gestures are not encoded.

• Verbal: Statements that are uttered only verbally, with no accompanying mark on paper.

• Written: Statements accompanied by marks on paper. These statements may or may not have an associated verbalization.

Source of knowledge   Each statement is also encoded for the source of knowledge for the statement. The four categories used are the experimenter, the design brief, self (retrieved from long-term memory), and (deductive) inference from the information existent in the problem space.

• Experimenter: This is information either given to the subject by the experimenter or actively solicited by the subject from the experimenter.
• Design brief: This is information the subject has gotten directly from the design brief and any accompanying documents.
• Self: This is information the subject either generates or retrieves from long-term memory.
• Inference: This is information the subject infers (in the strong deductive sense) from the information existent in the problem space.

Content   A paraphrase of the content of the statement.

Although this is a rather complex coding scheme, it serves to categorize statements at several different levels and in several different orthogonal ways, each of which illuminates the design problem space.

General Instructions to Subjects

Thank you for helping us with our study of design. Very generally, we are interested in learning what designers do and how they do it. Therefore, during the next two to three hours, we are going to ask you to propose a solution to the problem in the accompanying design brief.

As you can see, the design session will be taped on a video recorder. The tapes provide us with a trace of your design activity and allow us to engage in an in-depth analysis later.

For the recordings to be of maximal benefit to us, we are going to ask you to talk aloud as you proceed with the task. By this we do not mean that you should explain what you are thinking. Rather, you should just try to vocalize the fragments of thoughts and ideas that you might be attending to at the time. We would like to get a continuous stream of such vocalizations from you.

It is not easy (or even normal) to attend to a complex task and ver-
balize at the same time. Therefore, you will undoubtedly lapse into periods of silence. This is to be expected. During such periods, we will
prompt you to speak. This is a routine part of our experimental
methodology.

Due to practical considerations, we have decided to limit the session
to approximately three hours. Given this severe time constraint, your
design is not expected to be complete in every respect. However, it is
our intention that you address the problem as fully as possible within
the constraints (i.e., try to consider as many aspects of the problem as
you would normally).

Also, the enclosed design brief is rather sparse. It is intended that you
converse with the experimenter to iron out any difficulties and shortcomings.

Please begin.

Design Brief: Architecture

As you may know, there is a conspicuous lack of postal service on the
UC-Berkeley campus. There are, of course, stamp-dispensing machines
in the basement of the ASUC building, but they are quite inadequate for
most needs. Although the reasons for the lack of a campus post office
are shrouded in bureaucratic red tape (something having to do with the
union affiliations of UC-Berkeley and postal employees), an agreement
has been reached that will allow unlimited postal service on campus—
as long as it is automated. It is your job to design such a facility.

You must design both the transaction interface and the structure to
house it. There are few constraints on the transaction interface. You
may use any medium, or combination thereof, that will facilitate functioning. The company that will install the computerized equipment
claims they have the technology to implement almost any specified system. The constraints of the structure are also few and quite general. Basically, the structure must meet the local building-code requirements
and be realizable within budget. When completed, the postal station
should enhance and contribute to the overall campus design and life.

You will also need to know the following:

• Services: Should include, but not necessarily be restricted to, purchasing stamps, registering letters, weighing letters and parcels, and purchasing postage for the letters and parcels.

• Users: Users are expected to be substantially UC-Berkeley students. (Most faculty needs are taken care of by the university.)

• Service capacity: The utility is expected to service five hundred people per day, over a period of ten hours. Particularly heavy use is expected between the hours of noon and 2:00 PM.

• Budget: $250,000 has been budgeted for the structure. The automation equipment is being donated and installed by the computer/robotics firm.

• Equipment: The equipment will be designed to meet your specification for a user-transaction interface. It is expected to occupy 6,250 cubic feet and will be installed by the computer firm.

• Site: See attached plan.

Design Brief: Mechanical Engineering

As you may know, there is a conspicuous lack of postal service on the UC-Berkeley campus. There are, of course, stamp-dispensing machines in the basement of the ASUC building, but they are quite inadequate for most needs. Although the reasons for the lack of a campus post office are shrouded in bureaucratic red tape (something having to do with the union affiliations of UC-Berkeley and postal employees), an agreement has been reached that will allow unlimited postal service on campus—as long as it is automated.

A site has been chosen and an architect has been hired to design the facility. You are a member of the architect's design team, and it is your job to design the automated postal teller machine (APTM).

The structure will be located in front of Wurster Hall, surrounded by Barrows Hall, the sports field, and the music hall. You have at your disposal the architect's design brief and the resulting preliminary design sketches. You will note that, although the architect has pretty well articulated the site plan and building form, he has not developed the APTM. This is your job.

In developing your design, you are generally required to adhere to the architect's overall design scheme. But if you are unable to do the job within these constraints, we may negotiate specific changes in the building structure.

Design Brief: Instructional Design

The Acme Umbrella Co. is automating its administrative facilities. One important subgoal of this initiative is replacing typewriters with word-processing stations.

Acme has decided that Viewpoint running on Xerox Star is the right system for its text-editing needs. However, they have severe reservations about the instructional material it comes with. Acme would like to hire you as a freelance instructional designer to remedy this situation.

The Acme project manager in charge of automation is concerned that the manuals accompanying Viewpoint are not the best way for their secretaries to learn the system. All of these secretaries are familiar with electronic word processing, but the Viewpoint environment will be very different to them.

They would like you to design an innovative package tailored to their specific needs:

• Acme would like up to six hours of stand-alone instruction, preferably divided into one-hour slots. Furthermore, you can assume that the student has access to a workstation running Viewpoint.

• Each student is to sit for one lesson a day over two weeks. At the end of the period, each is expected to be a competent user of Viewpoint.

• During the next three hours, organize all the lessons and design in detail as much of the first hour as possible. Your design should (1) enable the client to extrapolate what the complete package will look like, (2) convince the client it will meet the company's instructional objectives, and (3) take full advantage of the expressive potential of the medium.

Appendix B

Methodological Details of Study 2: The Role of Sketching in Design Problem Solving

Design Brief 1: Poster for Cognitive Science Program at UC-Berkeley

The University of California, Berkeley, has just approved an undergraduate program in cognitive science and requires a poster to publicize it.

Cognitive science is an interdisciplinary field at the intersection of computer science, psychology, linguistics, and philosophy. Perhaps the single unifying theme is that human intelligence (or cognition) is a kind of computation; that is, it can be studied as a computational process.

Things to Take into Consideration

1. The program boasts a highly distinguished and interdisciplinary faculty.

2. Berkeley is noted for the particular approach it takes to the subject matter. The Berkeley approach is one of developing frameworks that, although they do not attempt to explain everything, do catalog the intricacies of specific aspects of cognition. (Other universities have proposed all-encompassing frameworks that claim to account for much of cognition, but often at the expense of distorting the subject matter.)

3. Some of the important results to come from the Berkeley group include work on categorization, natural language, and the "limits of computation."

4. Currently the program is a place where members of the four participating disciplines can collaborate to some extent. However, what we envision and hope to encourage is the emergence of a cohesive, interdisciplinary group from the interaction of these independent disciplines.

5. The artwork developed will be used on both promotional material and technical reports.

6. The audience for the poster will be undergraduate and graduate students and the general academic community.

7. To keep production costs down, we would like to avoid color.

Design Brief 2: Poster for the City of San Francisco

Since the 1989 earthquake, the city of San Francisco has experienced a decline in the number of tourists from Canada. As one step in reversing this trend, we would like to commission a promotional poster to be displayed in the offices of Canadian travel agencies.

To insure that our poster will stand out in the crowd of travel posters, we want to avoid photographs of the city, and perhaps even avoid color. We want a piece of artwork that captures and expresses the essence of the city at some abstract level. One possible theme for the poster is "the city on the bay." You are welcome to suggest others.

Things to Take into Consideration

1. A recent poll has revealed that the number one concern of Canadians traveling abroad to the United States is the fear of violence.

2. Most Canadians come to the Bay Area to do "city things" rather than "outdoor things" (which they can do at home). We should capitalize on this by emphasizing the distinctive aspects of San Francisco as a city.

3. The Bay Area has recently received some negative publicity in the Canadian press to the effect that the area is too expensive, too crowded, and suffers from smog.

4. Our major competitor for Canadian tourists (on the West Coast) is Los Angeles.

Design Brief 3: Poster for the Shakespeare Festival

One of the finest Shakespeare festivals in North America is held annually at Stratford-on-Avon in Ontario, Canada. A new piece of artwork is commissioned each year to publicize the event. We would like you to propose a design for the 1991 season.

Things to Take into Consideration

1. Stratford is a quiet, little rural town of about thirty thousand people in the middle of southern Ontario's tobacco-growing region (see enclosed map). It has been hosting the festival for thirty-two years. Festival-related activity is undoubtedly the town's largest generator of revenue. The activities are distributed over three theaters and large areas of lawns, gardens, ponds, and riverbanks.

2. The festival season lasts from mid-May to mid-October. Stratford is very pretty in the spring and fall (very green and lots of flowers). It is under snow and ice from November to April.

3. The production is supported by the Arts Council of Canada and is able to attract producers and actors of the highest caliber.

4. The festival attracts a large number of people from about a five-hundred-mile radius (including New York City, Chicago, Buffalo, Detroit, Pittsburgh, Montreal, and Toronto). High school students from all over Ontario are bused to the festival from mid-May to June and from September to mid-October.

5. Over the years the repertoire has expanded to include several Shakespearean and nonShakespearean works. For the 1991 season, the major productions will be *Hamlet, The Taming of the Shrew, Julius Caesar,* Christopher Fry's *The Lady Is not for Burning,* and readings of Oscar Wilde's *Fairy Tales.* Several chamber-music concerts are also planned.

6. The artwork is used on full-size posters, program and schedule pamphlets, and ticket covers.

Design Brief 4: Timepiece to Commemorate Earth Day

The Benjamin Mint has decided to issue a desktop timepiece to commemorate Earth Day. You are invited to propose a design for such a piece, using the following specifications:

maximum volume: 12″ by 12″
materials: your choice
construction method: your choice
cost per unit: approximately $500
target audience: corporate offices

Design Brief 5: Toy for a Toddler

I have a fifteen-month-old delinquent son. Christmas is fast approaching, so I feel obligated to give him a toy of some sort. However, I am not thrilled with the assorted junk peddled by our various commercial establishments. I would like you to design a toy with which he can interact to amuse, entertain, and educate himself.

He is a typical toddler. He waddles and runs about the house and occasionally falls. He can climb on furniture and roll off on his head. He likes to remove pots and pans from the kitchen cupboards and scatter them about the house. He is quite proficient at destroying books and newspapers, and takes great delight and interest in small, moving animals. There are indications that he understands some simple commands. He is very active and mischievous and, of course, does not like to be disciplined.

I would like the toy to address some of the skills he will be developing over the next six to twelve months.

Notes

Chapter 1

1. For most of the monograph, my discussion of cognitive science is restricted to what has come to be known as the "classical" story. I will remark on connectionism in the concluding chapter.

2. My use of the term *language of thought* in this introductory chapter is meant to be rather generic, simply a term for mental representations. Fodor's use is more specialized, as we will see in chapter 2.

3. The ill-structured and well-structured distinction is formally introduced in chapter 4. However, the reader will be able to grasp the gist of the distinction from the surrounding discussion.

4. A more sophisticated definition of 'discursive' is offered in chapter 7.

5. This is, of course, true only in the vocabulary of chess, narrowly defined. In the larger context, a pawn also belongs to the class of chess pieces, the class of material objects, etc. But this is consistent with the point being made here.

6. The reader will recognize this as a form of the Whorfian Hypothesis (Whorf, 1956). However, the properties of languages that I am interested in are radically different from those that preoccupied Whorf.

7. 'Problem space' is a technical term in Newell and Simon's (1972) information processing theory. It is a computational modeling space that is supposed to be psychologically real. It is introduced in chapter 4.

8. I use the terminology of 'symbol system' and 'representational system' interchangeably.

9. This is, of course, not to suggest that 'is a father of' is a representational relation, only that it shares the properties of being a two-place, asymmetric relation.

10. There are three similar-sounding terms that are easily confused here: 'intention', 'intension', and 'Intentional'. 'Intentional' with a capital 'I' refers to the property of certain mental states that allows them to refer to states of affairs beyond themselves. 'Intension' with an 's' is a logical property of certain

sentences that makes them referentially opaque. 'Intention' with a small 'i' (and sometimes a 'd' as in 'intending') is just one of many Intentional states, which unfortunately happens to be spelled the same way. Following Searle (1983), I will capitalize the 'I' in 'Intentional' when referring to the semantic properties of mental states, to avoid confusion.

11. See Cummins (1989) for an alternate view.

12. This is not to suggest that these are equivalent characterizations.

13. An important exception is the work of Jerry Fodor. As we will see in the next chapter, Fodor's claims about the structure of the language of thought encompass $S(r)$.

14. This particular terminology is borrowed from Elgin (1983).

15. To appreciate some of the problems inherent here, consider a road map of California. What are the symbols? There are, of course, the linguistic labels, but what about the red line that represents Interstate 5? What about the spatial relation between the dot representing Berkeley and the one representing Stanford? What about the blue pigment that specifies areas of water? The situation is not clarified by referring to the system of mapmaking. What the difficulties suggest is that the notion of a symbol may not, in the long run, be the most appropriate concept on which to build a general theory of representation.

16. The term 'compliance' is borrowed from Goodman (1976). However, my proposed usage is quite different from his.

17. The latter is, of course, also true of internal symbol systems.

Chapter 2

1. July 4, 1993, pp. C1 and C3.

2. The first three are noted by McGinn (1989).

3. Cummins (1989) suggests using this terminology to differentiate this view from another, to be introduced shortly.

4. See Searle (1990a, 1992) for a critique.

5. Throughout the monograph, I am going to be making a number of claims about computation and computational information processing. These claims make some presuppositions about what computation is. This however, is an open question. Furthermore, it is a question to be settled by the computer science community, not by cognitive scientists. Hence, my claims about computations should not be interpreted as being about computation-in-the-large, whatever this may turn out to be, but rather about the notion of computation employed by the "classical" cognitive science community (Fodor and Pylyshyn, 1988; Newell, 1980, 1990; Pylyshyn, 1984).

6. Strictly speaking, this is true only of simple formal systems. Gödel's famous theorem showed that in a formal system powerful enough to represent arith-

metic, one can not have both completeness and consistency. That is, if one tries to generate all the theorems of arithmetic, one will also generate inconsistent theorems (i.e., truth will not be preserved). If one wants to generate only consistent theorems, the system must remain incomplete.

7. Computation is first and foremost a *process,* that is, a sequence of time-ordered states, consisting of an initial state, intermediate states, and a final state. Each state in the sequence is often called an instantaneous description (Wegner, 1968). Each instantaneous description has several levels of descriptions and/or realizations, starting from the hardware level and ascending to various virtual-machine levels. At the hardware level—which is the level I am mostly concerned about—they minimally consist of the contents of memory locations and various CPU (central processing unit) registers, including the instruction register, the program-counter register, the memory-address register, the memory-data register, and various general-purpose registers.

8. See Smith (forthcoming) for arguments to the contrary.

9. For arguments, see Fodor (1981c, 1987) and Searle (1980, 1984, 1990c, 1992). Fodor (1985) also offers a nice discussion of the playing field of mental-representation theories, identifying the major players and positions.

10. To simplify the exposition, I will assume that reference, insofar as it is "explained" by computational systems, is restricted to other computational states and hardwired devices. This is justified on the grounds that no one has developed a coherent version of the external reference story for computational systems. If and when such a story is developed, to the extent that it would be an extension of the internal reference story, my remarks could be extended to include it.

Chapter 3

1. See Schiffer (1991) for the argument that although this conclusion is plausible, it does not follow as a point of logic.

2. Fodor and Pylyshyn do not say enough about the semantic domain to determine whether semantic finite differentiation (CTM6) is also required.

3. I think it is simply too abstract a notion for our purposes. It propagates a harmful distinction between the notion of computation and the physical environment in which it is realized. Although such Platonic conceptions may be appropriate for mathematics, they are detrimental for cognitive science. We need a theory that will allow us to talk about computation as a set of processes embedded in the physical world (Smith, 1996, forthcoming).

4. I believe that Chomsky's vocabulary of "cognizing" and "rule following" maps onto the notion of computational information processing in a straightforward way.

5. Kirk Ludwig in conversation.

6. There actually are devices built into the system whose function is to sustain this mapping.

Chapter 4

1. Connectionist models need not be restricted to these foundational constraints. We will take up this issue in the last chapter.

2. It is rather puzzling that the goal should be part of the task environment rather than the agent. In any event, goals are assumed but not explained in information processing theory.

3. A brief discussion and literature review is offered in Goel and Pirolli (1989).

4. Many of these features of design problems have been previously noted by designers. See, for example, the papers in Cross (1984). However, they have not been fully appreciated by the cognitive science community and, with the exception of Goel and Pirolli (1989), have not been brought together and used to constrain design problem spaces.

5. The distinction between constitutive and regulative rules is adopted from Searle (1969).

Chapter 5

1. The transition network formalism is preferable to the flowchart/algorithm formalisms, because, although transition networks represent decision points, they do not specify how the decision was made. They are what Winograd (1983) calls "nondeterministic schemas" for algorithms. We currently have no way of extracting decision procedures from the data, so it is best to be silent about them.

2. This is compatible with a widely held view among designers that design is an attempt at global optimization with finite resources.

Chapter 6

1. In cryptarithmetic and the Moore-Anderson task, the subjects also seemed to be manipulating models, or at least marks on paper. However, there is an important difference between the two situations. In the design case, the marks are representational in the sense that there is a distinction and a complex semantical relation between the marks and the entities in the world for which they stand. In the nondesign cases, the marks were not representational. There was no such distinction or relation. They were simply syntactic objects.

Chapter 7

1. Two important questions that have escaped his attention are the issue of how reference is fixed and the issue of intrinsic vs. derived Intentionality.

2. One can speak of either possessing properties or instantiating labels, depending on one's metaphysics. Although the two are not necessarily equivalent (Elgin, 1983; Goodman, 1976), little hangs on the distinction for our limited purposes. I will employ both vocabularies.

3. Section 7.2.1 and parts of section 7.2.2 are adopted from Goel (1991) and reproduced here with the permission of Kluwer Academic Publishers.

4. The dual of ambiguity is redundancy. It occurs where several inscriptions (which are not true copies of each other) have the same compliance class. It is generally considered harmless.

5. A number of writers have tried to differentiate symbols on the basis of their internal properties (e.g., Langer, 1942). When cognitive scientists refer to "pictorial" and "propositional" representations as being "analog" or "continuous," and "discrete," they generally take these to be predicates on the internal structure of symbols or the reference relation. It is not clear what sense can be made of this view. This position is critiqued by Haugeland (1991).

6. See section 9.6.1 for examples.

7. Goodman differentiates density from continuity. The difference between the two is the difference between rational numbers and real numbers. Density on its own—irrespective of continuity—is sufficient to destroy finite differentiation.

Chapter 8

1. My use of the term 'icon' is quite different from that sometimes found in the cognitive science literature, where iconic representations are said to resemble what they refer to and are contrasted with propositional representations. Icons on contract drawings do not resemble what they refer to.

2. As a further illustration of the apparatus at work, let us see what it would say about the representations in the Larkin and Simon (1987) pulley example. The two original figures Larkin and Simon start with were reproduced as figures 6.15a and 6.15b. Figure 6.15a is the "sentential" representation and 6.15b is the "diagrammatic" representation. Given the symbol systems they belong to, we can make the following observations. First, neither representation is nonnotational (nor dense, nor replete). Second, both representations are either notational systems or discursive languages. I do not know enough about the symbol system in effect to say which. In either case, on the notationality criteria, the types of diagrams being looked at have more in common with systems of postal ZIP Codes or the predicate calculus than with sketches. Third, they

exemplify very different labels or properties. In particular, the diagram exemplifies certain spatial properties, such as relative shape, size, and location. Fourth, they have different character sets. Fifth, they have different syntactic and semantic rules of combination.

So, on the Goodman account there are a number of interesting distinctions to be made between the two representations, which could result in cognitive differences. The Larkin and Simon analysis is not capable of capturing any of these. The fact that their analysis does not say anything about the difference in exemplified properties is, in particular, a serious shortcoming.

3. The choice of geometric primitives has well-known computational consequences (Requicha, 1980).

4. There are, however, some interesting differences, as has been pointed out in the imagery literature.

5. Strictly speaking, density is not the same as continuity.

6. Personally, I have no doubt that we have images and that there are cognitive processes defined over them (i.e., they are not just epiphenomenal). Both the first-person experience and the experimental data are overwhelming.

7. It is trivial to devise a discursive language with intersecting syntactic expressions.

8. Currently I am still discussing the properties of *external* symbol systems used by designers. Fodor's claim is, of course, about the structure of *internal* symbol systems. It is naive to think that there will be a transparent mapping between the two. This issue is taken up explicitly in chapter 10. For the moment I am content to restrict my remarks to external symbol systems.

Chapter 9

1. In the coding scheme I will use the notion of contents or ideas rather than referents.

2. Although it does preserve the gross spatial properties (e.g., shape, size, and location), it does not preserve the more subtle properties, or most of the expressive properties of the system of sketching. At least one subject complained about this.

3. The subjects all used sophisticated computational drawing systems as part of their jobs. These systems, for the most part, were a superset of MacDraw.

4. Another possibility considered was to contrast MacDraw with a computational paint program like MacPaint. It was discarded because the available programs were not up to the task. They fell short of sketching in terms of the properties of interest. In particular, they did not allow for spontaneous variability of line widths and pixel intensity.

5. The reader is reminded that the terms 'density' and 'ambiguity' are being used in a relative, nonstandard way, as per the discussion above.

6. I use the term 'variation' in a very different manner than Goodman (Goodman and Elgin, 1988).

7. For example, consider two symbol systems, *SS1* and *SS2*. In *SS1* characters consist of equivalence classes of line lengths that, when measured in feet, correspond to the integers. So we have lengths of 1′, 2′, 3′, etc. In *SS2* characters consist of equivalence classes of line lengths that, when measured in feet, correspond to the rational numbers. So we have lengths of 1′, 2′, 3′, . . . ; but also lengths of 1.5′, 2.5′, 3.5′, . . . and 1.25′, 2.25′, 3.25′, . . . and 1.125′, 2.125′, 3.125′, . . . and so on. Lines of lengths 1.125′ and 1.25′ are no more identical than are lines of length 1′ and 2′; neither pair belongs to the same equivalence class. However, line lengths of 1.125′ and 1.25′ are much more "similar," are "closer to each other"—with respect to length—than are lines of 1′ and 2′. Thus the notions of "similarity" or "closeness" seem to be an integral (necessary?) part of density.

8. See Goodman (1976) for a demonstration.

9. It would be desirable to call upon other experimental literature to support my conclusion, but I do not know of any works that explore the properties of symbol systems that I am concerned with here. Some reviewers have directed me to the perceptual and spatial reasoning literature. There is a large literature concerned with depictional, spatial, and perceptual aspects of drawings to which I have already referred in chapter 8. But as I have indicated, the issues of interest to me regarding design and sketching have no special connection to perception and spatial reasoning. My choice of a spatial domain, and the fact that sketches are "pictorial" or depictional, are irrelevant to my argument. (It may turn out that certain perceptual and spatial reasoning processes require symbol systems lacking the CTM-properties, but this is an empirical question that, to my knowledge, has yet to be addressed.)

A more promising literature to relate to would be studies of cognition in the arts. Such studies are almost nonexistent. I tried very hard to make contact with Rudolf Arnheim's (1969, 1977) various works on the psychology of art and architecture. In the end I had to abandon the effort because (i) Arnheim thinks that everything of importance in understanding a work of art is in the perceptual processes, and (ii) there is no straightforward way to map Arnheim's vocabulary onto computational information processing vocabulary.

Chapter 10

1. This is a trivial consequence of a representational theory of mind.

2. "Symbolic" for Pylyshyn, I take it, is the part of the physical world that satisfies the CTM-constraints. "Nonsymbolic" would then be the part of the world that fails the CTM-constraints. (This is not quite right. It will be qualified in the text shortly.)

3. Given the RTM'-constraints on computational information processing, this is a perfectly coherent position.

On my account, a system can fail the CTM-constraints and still be a bona fide representational system. The CTM-constraints are constitutive of a certain type of representational system but not of the notion of representation itself.

4. If cognition is, in general, a computational process, then the explanation of this particular cognitive process can not be relegated to a mysterious noncomputational process.

References

Akin, O. 1986a. A Formalism for Problem Restructuring and Resolution in Design. *Environment and Planning B: Planning and Design* 13:223–32.

Akin, O. 1986b. *Psychology of Architectural Design.* London: Pion Limited.

Albarn, K., and J. M. Smith. 1977. *Diagram: The Instrument of Thought.* London: Thames and Hudson.

Alexander, C. 1964. *Notes on the Synthesis of Form.* Cambridge, Mass.: Harvard University Press.

Alexander, C. 1965. A City Is not a Tree. *Architectural Forum* 122 (April-May): 58–62.

Anderson, J. R. 1983. *The Architecture of Cognition.* Cambridge, Mass.: Harvard University Press.

Anderson, J. R. 1986. Knowledge Compilation: The General Learning Mechanism. In *Machine Learning.* Vol. 2, ed. R. S. Michalski, J. G. Carbonell, and T. M. Mitchell. Los Altos, Calif.: Morgan Kaufmann.

Anderson, J. R. 1990. Analysis of Student Performance with the LISP Tutor. In *Diagnostic Monitoring of Skill and Knowledge Acquisition,* ed. N. Frederiksen, R. Glaser, A. Lesgold, and M. Shaffo. Hillsdale, N.J.: Lawrence Erlbaum.

Anderson, J. R., and G. H. Bower. 1973. *Human Associative Memory.* Washington, D.C.: V. H. Winston and Sons.

Anderson, J. R., R. Farrell, and R. Sauers. 1984. Learning to Program in LISP. *Cognitive Science* 8:87–129.

Anderson, J. R., and R. Thompson. 1989. Use of Analogy in a Production System Architecture. In *Similarity and Analogical Reasoning,* ed. S. Vosniadou and A. Ortony. Cambridge: Cambridge University Press.

Anzai, Y., and H. A. Simon. 1979. The Theory of Learning by Doing. *Psychological Review* 86 (2):124–40.

Arnheim, R. 1969. *Visual Thinking.* Berkeley, Calif.: University of California Press.

Arnheim, R. 1977. *The Dynamics of Architectural Form.* Berkeley, Calif.: University of California Press.

Austin, J. L. 1962. *How to Do Things with Words,* 2d ed. Cambridge, Mass.: Harvard University Press.

Baddeley, A. 1992. Working Memory. *Science* 255:556–559.

Biederman, I. 1987. Recognition-by-Components: A Theory of Human Image Understanding. *Psychological Review* 94 (2):115–147.

Block, N., ed. 1981. *Imagery.* Cambridge, Mass.: MIT Press.

Braine, M. D. S. 1978. On the Relation between the Natural Logic of Reasoning and Standard Logic. *Psychological Review* 85 (1):1–21.

Brentano, F. 1874/1970. The Distinction between Mental and Physical Phenomena. In *Introduction to the Philosophy of Mind,* ed. H. Morick. Glenview, Ill.: Scott, Foresman.

Broadbent, D. 1985. A Question of Levels: Comment on McClelland and Rumelhart. *Journal of Experimental Psychology, General* 114 (2):189–92.

Brown, D. C., and B. Chandrasekaran. 1989. *Design Problem Solving.* San Mateo, Calif.: Morgan Kaufmann.

Carbonell, J. G. 1983. Learning by Analogy: Formulating and Generalizing Plans from Past Experience. In *Machine Learning: An Artificial Intelligence Approach,* ed. J. G. Carbonell, R. S. Michalski, and T. M. Mitchell. Palo Alto, Calif.: Tioga Press.

Carbonell, J. G. 1986. Derivational Analogy: A Theory of Reconstructive Problem Solving and Expertise Acquisition. In *Machine Learning.* Vol. 2, ed. R. S. Michalski, J. G. Carbonell, and T. M. Mitchell. Los Altos, Calif.: Morgan Kaufmann.

Chomsky, N. 1957. *Syntactic Structures.* The Hague: Mouton.

Chomsky, N. 1965. *Aspects of the Theory of Syntax.* Cambridge, Mass.: MIT Press.

Chomsky, N. 1980. Rules and Representations. *Behavioral and Brain Sciences* 3:1–61.

Chomsky, N. 1981. *Lectures on Government and Binding: The Pisa Lectures.* Dordrecht, Holland: Foris Publications.

Churchland, P. M. 1984. *Matter and Consciousness: A Contemporary Introduction to the Philosophy of Mind.* Cambridge, Mass.: MIT Press.

Churchland, P. S. 1986. *Neurophilosophy.* Cambridge, Mass.: MIT Press.

Clement, J. 1982. Analogy Generation in Scientific Problem Solving. In *Proceedings of the Fourth Annual Conference of the Cognitive Science Society* 137–40. Hillsdale, N.J.: Lawrence Erlbaum.

Collins, A. M., and M. R. Quillian. 1969. Retrieval Time from Semantic Memory. *Journal of Verbal Learning and Verbal Behavior* 8:240–47.

Craik, F. I. M., and R. S. Lockhart. 1972. Levels of Processing: A Framework for Memory Research. *Journal of Verbal Learning and Verbal Behavior* 11: 671–84.

Cross, N., ed. 1984. *Developments in Design Methodology.* New York: John Wiley and Sons.

Crowe, N., and P. Laseau. 1984. *Visual Notes for Architects and Designers.* New York: Van Nostrand Reinhold.

Cummins, R. 1989. *Meaning and Mental Representation.* Cambridge, Mass.: MIT Press.

Cussins, A. 1990. The Connectionist Construction of Concepts. In *The Philosophy of Artificial Intelligence*, ed. M. A. Boden. Oxford: Oxford University Press.

Dennett, D. C. 1978. *Brainstorms: Philosophical Essays on Mind and Psychology.* Cambridge, Mass.: MIT Press.

Dennett, D. C. 1981. The Nature of Images and the Introspective Trap. In *Readings in Philosophy of Psychology.* Vol. 2, ed. N. Block. London: Methuen.

Dennett, D. C. 1987. *The Intentional Stance.* Cambridge, Mass.: MIT Press.

Devitt, M. 1991. Why Fodor Can't Have It Both Ways. In *Meaning in Mind: Fodor and His Critics,* ed. B. Loewer and G. Rey. Cambridge, Mass.: Basil Blackwell.

Dietrich, E. 1990. Computationalism. *Social Epistemology* 4 (2):135–54.

Dietrich, E., ed. 1994. *Thinking Computers and Virtual Persons: Essays on the Intentionality of Machines.* New York: Academic Press.

diSessa, A. A. 1988. Knowledge in Pieces. In *Constructivism in the Computer Age,* ed. G. Forman and P. Pufall, 1–24. Hillsdale, N.J.: Lawrence Erlbaum.

diSessa, A. A. 1993. Toward an Epistemology of Physics. *Cognition and Instruction* 10 (2-3):105–225.

Eastman, C. M. 1969. On the Analysis of Intuitive Design Processes. In *Emerging Techniques in Environmental Design and Planning,* ed. G. Moore. Cambridge, Mass.: MIT Press.

Elgin, C. Z. 1983. *With Reference to Reference.* Indianapolis, Ind.: Hackett.

Ericsson, K. A., and H. A. Simon. 1984. *Protocol Analysis: Verbal Reports as Data.* Cambridge, Mass.: MIT Press.

Ernst, G. W., and A. Newell. 1969. *GPS: A Case Study in Generality and Problem Solving.* New York: Academic Press.

Evans, J., ed. 1983. *Thinking and Reasoning: Psychological Approaches.* London: Routledge and Kegan Paul.

Farah, M. J. 1984. The Neuropsychology of Mental Image Generation: Converging Evidence from Brain-Damaged and Normal Subjects. In *Spatial Cognition: Brain Bases and Development,* ed. J. Stiles-Davis and V. Bellugi. Chicago: University of Chicago Press.

Farah, M. J. 1989. The Neuropsychology of Mental Imagery. In *Handbook of Neuropsychology.* Vol. 2, ed. F. Boller and J. Grafman. Oxford: Elsevier Science Publishers.

Feigenbaum, E. A., and H. A. Simon. 1984. EPAM-like Models of Recognition and Learning. *Cognitive Science* 8:305–36.

Finke, R. A., and S. Pinker. 1982. Spontaneous Imagery Scanning in Mental Extrapolation. *Journal of Experimental Psychology: Human Learning and Memory* 8:142–47.

Finke, R. A., S. Pinker, and M. J. Farah. 1989. Reinterpreting Visual Patterns in Mental Imagery. *Cognitive Science* 13:51–78.

Finke, R. A., and R. N. Shepard. 1986. Visual Functions of Mental Imagery. In *Handbook of Perception and Human Performance,* ed. K. R. Boff, L. Kaufman, and J. P. Thomas. New York: John and Sons.

Flegg, H. G. 1974. *From Geometry to Topology.* London: English Universities Press.

Flemming, U., R. Coyne, T. Glavin, and M. Rychener. 1988. A Generative Expert System for the Design of Building Layouts—Version2. *Artificial Intelligence in Engineering* 3:445–64.

Fodor, J. A. 1975. *The Language of Thought.* Cambridge, Mass.: Harvard University Press.

Fodor, J. A. 1978. Propositional Attitudes. *Monist* 61 (4):501–23.

Fodor, J. A. 1981a. Computation and Reduction. In *Representations: Philosophical Essays on the Foundations of Cognitive Science.* Cambridge, Mass.: MIT Press.

Fodor, J. A. 1981b. Methodological Solipsism Considered as a Research Strategy for Cognitive Psychology. In *Mind Design,* ed. J. Haugeland. Cambridge, Mass.: MIT Press.

Fodor, J. A. 1981c. Three Cheers for Propositional Attitudes. In *Representations: Philosophical Essays on the Foundations of Cognitive Science.* Cambridge, Mass.: MIT Press.

Fodor, J. A. 1983. *The Modularity of Mind: An Essay on Faculty Psychology.* Cambridge, Mass.: MIT Press.

Fodor, J. A. 1985. Fodor's Guide to Mental Representation: The Intelligent Auntie's Vade-Mecum. *Mind* 94:76–100.

Fodor, J. A. 1987. *Psychosemantics: The Problem of Meaning in the Philosophy of Mind.* Cambridge, Mass.: MIT Press.

Fodor, J. A. 1991. Replies. In *Meaning in Mind: Fodor and His Critics,* ed. B. Loewer and G. Rey. Oxford: Blackwell.

Fodor, J. A., and B. P. McLaughlin. 1990. Connectionism and the Problem of Systematicity: Why Smolensky's Solution Doesn't Work. *Cognition* 35:183–204.

Fodor, J. A., and Z. W. Pylyshyn. 1988. Connectionism and Cognitive Architecture: A Critical Analysis. *Cognition* 28:3–71.

Freud, S. 1933/1965. *New Introductory Lectures on Psycho-Analysis.* New York: Norton.

Funt, B. V. 1983. Analogical Modes of Reasoning and Process Modeling. *Computer* (October): 99–104.

Gardner, H. 1982. *Art, Mind, and Brain: A Cognitive Approach to Creativity.* New York: Basic Books.

Gardner, H. 1983. *Frames of Mind: The Theory of Multiple Intelligences.* New York: Basic Books.

Gentner, D., and A. Stevens, eds. 1983. *Mental Models.* Hillsdale, N.J.: Lawrence Erlbaum.

Ginsburg, H. P., N. E. Kossan, R. Schwartz, and D. Swanson. 1983. Protocol Methods in Research on Mathematical Thinking. In *The Development of Mathematical Thinking,* ed. H. P. Ginsburg. New York: Academic Press.

Glasgow, J., and D. Papadias. 1992. Computational Imagery. *Cognitive Science* 16 (3):355–94.

Goel, V. 1991. Notationality and the Information Processing Mind. *Minds and Machines* 1 (2):129–65.

Goel, V. 1992a. "Ill-Structured Representations" for Ill-Structured Problems. In *Proceedings of the Fourteenth Annual Conference of the Cognitive Science Society.* Bloomington, Ind.: Lawrence Erlbaum.

Goel, V. 1992b. Are Computational Explanations Vacuous? In *Proceedings of the Fourteenth Annual Conference of the Cognitive Science Society.* Bloomington, Ind.: Lawrence Erlbaum.

Goel, V. 1992c. Comparison of Well-Structured and Ill-Structured Task Environments and Problem Spaces. In *Proceedings of the Fourteenth Annual Conference of the Cognitive Science Society.* Bloomington, Ind.: Lawrence Erlbaum.

Goel, V. 1994. A Comparison of Design and Nondesign Problem Spaces. *Artificial Intelligence in Engineering* 9:53–72.

Goel, V., and J. Grafman. 1993. Modularity and the Possibility of a Cognitive Neuroscience of Central Systems. In *Proceedings of the Fifteenth Annual Conference of the Cognitive Science Society.* Boulder, Colo.: Lawrence Erlbaum.

Goel, V., and P. Pirolli. 1989. Motivating the Notion of Generic Design within Information Processing Theory: The Design Problem Space. *AI Magazine* 10 (1):18–36.

Goel, V., and P. Pirolli. 1992. The Structure of Design Problem Spaces. *Cognitive Science* 16 (3):395–429.

Goldschmidt, G. 1991. The Dialectics of Sketching. *Creativity Research Journal* 4 (2):123–43.

Goldschmidt, G. In press. Visual Design Thinking: The Vis Kids of Architecture. *Design Studies.*

Goodman, N. 1976. *Languages of Art: An Approach to a Theory of Symbols.* 2d ed. Indianapolis, Ind.: Hackett.

Goodman, N. 1978. *Ways of Worldmaking*. Hassocks, Sussex: Harvester Press.

Goodman, N., and C. Z. Elgin. 1988. *Reconceptions in Philosophy*. Indianapolis, Ind.: Hackett.

Guindon, R., H. Krasner, and B. Curtis. 1987. Cognitive Processes in Software Design: Activities in Early, Upstream Design. In *Interact '87: Proceedings of the Second IFIP Conference on Human-Computer Interaction* 383–88. Amsterdam: North-Holland.

Hamacher, V. C., Z. G. Vranesic, and S. G. Zaky. 1978. *Computer Organization*. New York: McGraw-Hill.

Haugeland, J. 1981. Semantic Engines: An Introduction to Mind Design. In *Mind Design,* ed. J. Haugeland. Cambridge, Mass.: MIT Press.

Haugeland, J. 1991. Representational Genera. In *Philosophy and Connectionist Theory,* ed. W. Ramsey, D. Rumelhart, and S. Stich. Hillsdale, N.J.: Lawrence Erlbaum.

Hayes, J. R., and H. A. Simon. 1974. Understanding Written Problem Instructions. In *Knowledge and Cognition,* ed. L. W. Gregg. Hillsdale, N.J.: Lawrence Erlbaum.

Heller, J. I., and H. N. Hungate. 1985. Implications for Mathematics Instruction of Research on Scientific Problem Solving. In *Teaching and Learning Mathematical Problem Solving: Multiple Research Perspectives,* ed. E. A. Silver. Hillsdale, N.J.: Lawrence Erlbaum.

Hinton, G. E., and T. J. Sejnowski. 1986. Learning and Relearning in Boltzmann Machines. In *Parallel Distributed Processing: Explorations in the Microstructure of Cognition*. Vol. 1, Foundations, ed. D. E. Rumelhart and J. L. McClelland. Cambridge, Mass.: MIT Press.

Jackendoff, R. 1983. *Semantics and Cognition*. Cambridge, Mass.: MIT Press.

Jackendoff, R. 1988. Conceptual Semantics. In *Meaning and Mental Representations,* ed. U. Eco, M. Santambrogio, and P. Violi. Indianapolis: Indiana University Press.

Jeffries, R., A. A. Turner, P. G. Polson, and M. E. Atwood. 1981. The Processes Involved in Designing Software. In *Cognitive Skills and Their Acquisition,* ed. J. R. Anderson. Hillsdale, N.J.: Lawrence Erlbaum.

Johnson-Laird, P. N. 1983. *Mental Models: Towards a Cognitive Science of Language, Inference, and Consciousness*. Cambridge, Mass.: Harvard University Press.

Kant, E. 1985. Understanding and Automating Algorithm Design. *IEEE Transactions on Software Engineering* 11:1361–74.

Kant, E., and A. Newell. 1984. Problem Solving Techniques for the Design of Algorithms. *Information Processing and Management* 20 (1–2):97–118.

Kirsh, D. 1990. When Is Information Explicitly Represented? In *Information, Thought, and Content,* ed. P. Hansen. Vancouver: University of British Columbia Press.

Koestler, A. 1975. *The Act of Creation.* London: Pan Books.

Kolers, P. A., and S. J. Brown. 1984. Commentary: On Pictures, Words, and Their Mental Representation. *Journal of Verbal Learning and Verbal Behavior* 23:105–113.

Kolers, P. A., and W. E. Smythe. 1984. Symbol Manipulation: Alternatives to the Computational View of Mind. *Journal of Verbal Learning and Verbal Behavior* 23:289–314.

Kolodner, J. L., ed. 1993. *Case-Based Reasoning.* San Mateo, Calif.: Morgan Kaufman.

Kosslyn, S. M. 1980. *Image and Mind.* Cambridge, Mass.: Harvard University Press.

Kosslyn, S. M. 1981. The Medium and the Message in Mental Imagery: A Theory. *Psychological Review* 88 (1):46–66.

Kosslyn, S. M. 1983. *Ghosts in the Mind's Machine: Creating and Using Images in the Brain.* New York: W. W. Norton & Company.

Kosslyn, S. M. 1990. Mental Imagery. In *Visual Cognition and Action,* ed. D. N. Osherson, S. M. Kosslyn, and J. M. Hollerbach. Cambridge, Mass.: MIT Press.

Kosslyn, S. M., N. M. Alpert, W. L. Thompson, V. Maljkovic, S. B. Weise, C. F. Chabris, S.E. Hamilton, S. L. Rauch, and F. S. Buonanno. 1993. Visual Mental Imagery Activates Topographically Organized Visual Cortex: PET Investigations. *Journal of Cognitive Neuroscience* 5 (3):263–87.

Kosslyn, S. M., S. Pinker, G. E. Smith, and S. P. Shwartz. 1981. On the Demystification of Mental Imagery. In *Imagery,* ed. N. Block. Cambridge, Mass.: MIT Press.

Kosslyn, S. M., and J. R. Pomerantz. 1981. Imagery, Propositions, and the Form of Internal Representations. In *Readings in Philosophy of Psychology.* Vol. 2, ed. N. Block. Cambridge, Mass.: Harvard University Press.

Kosslyn, S. M., and S. P. Shwartz. 1977. A Simulation of Visual Imagery. *Cognitive Science* 1:265–95.

Kosslyn, S. M., and S. P. Shwartz. 1978. Visual Images as Spatial Representations in Active Memory. In *Computer Vision Systems,* ed. A. R. Hanson and E. M. Riseman. New York: Academic Press.

Kroll, J. F., and M. C. Potter. 1984. Recognizing Words, Pictures, and Concepts: A Comparison of Lexical, Object, and Reality Decisions. *Journal of Verbal Learning and Verbal Behavior* 23:39–66.

Kulkarni, D., and H. A. Simon. 1986. *The Processes of Scientific Discovery: The Strategy of Experimentation.* Tech. report no. CMU-CS-86-111. Dept. of Computer Science, Carnegie-Mellon University.

Laird, J. E., and A. Newell. 1983. *Universal Weak Method.* Tech. report no. CMU-CS-83-141. Dept. of Computer Science, Carnegie-Mellon University.

Laird, J. E., A. Newell, and P. S. Rosenbloom. 1986a. *Soar: An Architecture for General Intelligence*. Tech. Report No. CMU-CS-86-171. Dept. of Computer Science, Carnegie-Mellon University.

Laird, J. E., P. S. Rosenbloom, and A. Newell. 1986b. Chunking in Soar: The Anatomy of a General Learning Mechanism. *Machine Learning* 1:11–46.

Lakoff, G. 1987. *Women, Fire, and Dangerous Things: What Categories Reveal about the Mind*. Chicago: University of Chicago Press.

Lakoff, G. 1993. Grounded Concepts without Symbols. In *Proceedings of the Fifteenth Annual Conference of the Cognitive Science Society* 161–64. Boulder, Colo.: Lawrence Erlbaum.

Langer, S. K. 1942. *Philosophy in a New Key: A Study in the Symbolism of Reason, Rite, and Art*. New York: Mentor Books.

Langley, P. 1979. Rediscovering Physics with BACON.3. In *Proceedings of the Sixth International Joint Conference on Artificial Intelligence* 505–7. Los Altos, Calif.: Kaufman.

Larkin, J. 1981. Cognition of Learning Physics. *American Journal of Physics* 49 (6):534–41.

Larkin, J. H. 1985. Understanding, Problem Representations, and Skill in Physics. In *Thinking and Learning Skills*. Vol. 2, Research and Open Questions, ed. S. F. Chipman, J. W. Segal, and R. Glaser. Hillsdale, N.J.: Lawrence Erlbaum.

Larkin, J. H., and H. A. Simon. 1981. Learning through Growth of Skill in Mental Modeling. In *Proceedings of the Third Annual Conference of the Cognitive Science Society* 1–15. Berkeley, Calif.: Lawrence Erlbaum.

Larkin, J. H., and H. A. Simon. 1987. Why a Diagram Is (Sometimes) Worth Ten Thousand Words. *Cognitive Science* 11:65–99.

Laseau, P. 1989. *Graphic Thinking for Architects and Designers*. New York: Van Nostrand Reinhold.

Leibniz, G. W. V. 1684/1965. *Monadology and Other Philosophical Essays*. Trans. P. Schrecker and A. M. Schrecker. New York: Bobbs-Merrill.

Lindsay, R. K. 1988. Images and Inference. *Cognition* 29:229–50.

Marr, D. 1979. Representing and Computing Visual Information. In *Artificial Intelligence: An MIT Perspective*. Vol. 2, ed. P. H. Winston and R. H. Brown. Cambridge, Mass.: MIT Press.

Marr, D. 1982. *Vision: A Computational Investigation into the Human Representation and Processing of Visual Information*. San Francisco: W. H. Freeman.

Mayer, R. E. 1985. Implications of Cognitive Psychology for Instruction in Mathematical Problem Solving. In *Teaching and Learning Mathematical Problem Solving: Multiple Research Perspectives*, ed. E. A. Silver. Hillsdale, N.J.: Lawrence Erlbaum.

McCarthy, J. 1960. Recursive Functions of Symbolic Expressions and Their Computations by Machines. *Communications of the ACT* 7:184–95.

McClelland, J. L., and D. E. Rumelhart. 1986a. A Distributed Model of Human Learning and Memory. In *Parallel Distributed Processing*. Vol. 2, ed. D. E. Rumelhart and J. L. McClelland, 170–215. Cambridge, Mass.: MIT Press.

McClelland, J. L., and D. E. Rumelhart, eds. 1986b. *Parallel Distributed Processing: Explorations in the Microstructures of Cognition*. Vol. 2, Psychological and Biological Models. Cambridge, Mass.: MIT Press.

McGinn, C. 1989. *Mental Content*. Oxford: Basil Blackwell.

Medawar, P. 1974. A Geometric Model of Reduction and Emergence. In *Studies in the Philosophy of Biology*, ed. F. J. Ayala and T. Dobzhansky. Berkeley, Calif.: University of California Press.

Metz, K. E. 1985. The Development of Children's Problem Solving in a Gears Task: A Problem Space Perspective. *Cognitive Science* 9:431–71.

Metzler, J., and R. N. Shepard. 1974. Mental Images and Their Transformations. In *Theories in Cognitive Psychology: The Loyola Symposium*, ed. R. Solso. Hillsdale, N.J.: Lawrence Erlbaum.

Miller, A. J. 1985. Design—A Prototype Expert System for Design Oriented Problem Solving. *The Australian Computer Journal* 17 (1):20–26.

Miller, G. A., E. Galanter, and K. H. Pribram. 1960. *Plans and The Structure of Behavior*. New York: Holt, Rinehart and Winston.

Mittal, S., C. L. Dym, and M. Morjaria. 1986. Pride: An Expert System for the Design of Paper Handling Systems. *Computer* 19 (7):102–14.

Newell, A. 1969. Heuristic Programming: Ill-Structured Problems. In *Progress in Operations Research*. Vol. 3, ed. J. Aronofsky, 360–414. New York: John Wiley and Sons.

Newell, A. 1980. Physical Symbol Systems. *Cognitive Science* 4:135–83.

Newell, A. 1990. *Unified Theories of Cognition*. Cambridge: Mass.: Harvard University Press.

Newell, A., J. C. Shaw, and H. A. Simon. 1957. Empirical Explorations of the Logic Theory Machine. In *Proceedings of the Western Joint Computer Conference* 11:218–30.

Newell, A., and H. A. Simon. 1956. The Logic Theory Machine—A Complex Information Processing System. *IRE Transactions on Information Theory* IT-2 (3):61–79.

Newell, A., and H. A. Simon. 1972. *Human Problem Solving*. Englewood Cliffs, N.J.: Prentice-Hall.

Newell, A., and H. A. Simon. 1981. Computer Science as Empirical Inquiry: Symbols and Search. In *Mind Design*, ed. J. Haugeland. Cambridge, Mass.: MIT Press.

Olson, D. R., and E. Bialystok. 1983. *Spatial Cognition: The Structure and Development of Mental Representations of Spatial Relations*. Hillsdale, N.J.: Lawrence Erlbaum.

Paivio, A. 1977. Images, Propositions, and Knowledge. In *Images, Perception, and Knowledge*, ed. J. M. Nicholas. Dordrecht, Holland: D. Reidel.

Paivio, A. 1986. *Mental Representations: A Dual Coding Approach*. New York: Oxford University Press.

Palmer, S. E. 1978. Foundational Aspects of Cognitive Representation. In *Cognition and Categorization*, ed. E. Rosch and B. Lloyd. Hillsdale, N.J.: Lawrence Erlbaum.

Pentland, A. 1987. From Naive Physics to Naive Physics. *Computational Intelligence* 3:204–5.

Perkins, D. 1981. *The Mind's Best Work*. Cambridge, Mass.: Harvard University Press.

Perkins, D., and B. Leondar, eds. 1977. *The Arts and Cognition*. Baltimore: Johns Hopkins University Press.

Pirolli, P. 1986. Model and Tutor for Recursion. *Human-Computer Interaction* 2 (4):269–358.

Polanyi, M. 1966. *The Tacit Dimension*. London: Routledge and Kegan Paul.

Posner, M. I. 1989. Structures and Function of Selective Attention. In *Clinical Neuropsychology and Brain Function: Research, Measurement and Practice*, ed. T. Boll and B. Bryant. Washington, D.C.: American Psychological Association.

Potter, M. C. 1976. Short-Term Conceptual Memory for Pictures. *Journal of Experimental Psychology: Human Learning and Memory* 2 (5): 509–22.

Potter, M. C., K.-F. So, B. Eckardt, and L. B. Feldman. 1984. Lexical and Conceptual Representation in Beginning and Proficient Bilinguals. *Journal of Verbal Learning and Verbal Behavior* 23:23–38.

Pylyshyn, Z. W. 1984. *Computation and Cognition: Toward a Foundation for Cognitive Science*. Cambridge, Mass.: MIT Press.

Reeke, G. N., and G. M. Edelman. 1988. Real Brains and Artificial Intelligence. *Daedalus* 117 (1):143–73.

Reitman, W. R. 1964. Heuristic Decision Procedures, Open Constraints, and the Structure of Ill-Defined Problems. In *Human Judgements and Optimality*, ed. M. W. Shelly and G. L. Bryan. New York: John Wiley and Sons.

Reitman, W. R. 1965. *Cognition and Thought: An Information-Processing Approach*. New York: John Wiley and Sons.

Requicha, A. A. G. 1980. Representations for Rigid Solids: Theory, Methods, and Systems. *ACM Computing Surveys* 12 (4):437–64.

Rittel, H. W. J., and M. M. Webber. 1974. Dilemmas in a General Theory of Planning. *DMG-DRS Journal* 8 (1):31–39.

Rollins, M. 1989. *Mental Imagery: On the Limits of Cognitive Science*. New Haven and London: Yale University Press.

Rosch, E. 1978. Principles of Categorization. In *Cognition and Categorization*, ed. E. Rosch and B. Lloyd. Hillsdale, N.J.: Lawrence Erlbaum.

Rosenbloom, P. S., and A. Newell. 1986. The Chunking of Goal Hierarchies: A Generalized Model of Practice. In *Machine Learning*. Vol. 2, ed. R. S. Michalski, J. G. Carbonell, and T. M. Mitchell. Los Altos, Calif.: Morgan Kaufmann.

Rumelhart, D. E., and J. L. McClelland. 1985. Levels Indeed! A Response to Broadbent. *Journal of Experimental Psychology: General* 114 (2):193–97.

Rumelhart, D. E., and J. L. McClelland, eds. 1986. *Parallel Distributed Processing*. Vol. 1, Foundations. Cambridge, Mass.: MIT Press.

Schank, R. C. 1972. Conceptual Dependency: A Theory of Natural Language Understanding. *Cognitive Psychology* 3 (4):552–631.

Schiffer, S. 1991. Does Mentalese Have a Compositional Semantics. In *Meaning in Mind: Fodor and His Critics,* ed. B. Loewer and G. Rey. Cambridge, Mass.: Basil Blackwell.

Schoenfeld, A. H. 1985. *Mathematical Problem Solving*. New York: Academic Press.

Searle, J. R. 1969. *Speech Acts: An Essay in the Philosophy of Language*. Cambridge: Cambridge University Press.

Searle, J. R. 1980. Minds, Brains and Programs. *The Behavioral and Brain Sciences* 3:417–57.

Searle, J. R. 1983. *Intentionality: An Essay in the Philosophy of Mind*. Cambridge: Cambridge University Press.

Searle, J. R. 1984. *Minds, Brains and Science*. Cambridge, Mass.: Harvard University Press.

Searle, J. R. 1990a. Consciousness, Explanatory Inversion, and Cognitive Science. *Behavioral and Brain Sciences* 13 (4):585–642.

Searle, J. R. 1990b. Is the Brain a Digital Computer? In *Sixty-fourth Annual Pacific Division Meeting for the American Philosophical Association* (March 30, 1990). Los Angeles, 21–37.

Searle, J. R. 1990c. Is the Brain's Mind a Computer Program? *Scientific American* 262 (1):26–31.

Searle, J. R. 1992. *Rediscovering the Mind*. Cambridge, Mass.: MIT Press.

Shepard, R. N. (1975). Form, Formation and Transformation of Internal Representations. In *Information Processing and Cognition: The Loyola Symposium,* ed. R. L. Solso. Hillsdale, N.J.: Lawrence Erlbaum.

Shepard, R. N. 1982. Perceptual and Analogical Bases of Cognition. In *Perspectives on Mental Representation,* ed. J. Mehler, E. C. T. Walter, and M. Garrett. Hillsdale, N.J.: Lawrence Erlbaum.

Shepard, R. N., and L. A. Cooper. 1982. *Mental Images and Their Transformations*. Cambridge, Mass.: MIT Press.

Shepard, R. N., and J. Metzler. 1971. Mental Rotation of Three-Dimensional Objects. *Science* 171:701–3.

Shwartz, S. P., and S. M. Kosslyn. 1982. A Computer Simulation Approach to Studying Mental Imagery. In *Perspectives on Mental Representation*, ed. J. Mehler, E. C. T. Walker, and M. Garrett. Hillsdale, N.J.: Lawrence Erlbaum.

Simon, H. A. 1956. Rational Choice and the Structure of the Environment. *Psychological Review* 63:129–38.

Simon, H. A. 1962. The Architecture of Complexity. *Proceedings of the American Philosophical Society* 106:467–82.

Simon, H. A. 1967. The Logic of Heuristic Decision Making. In *The Logic of Decision and Action*, ed. N. Rescher, 1–20. Pittsburgh: University of Pittsburgh Press.

Simon, H. A. 1973a. The Organization of Complex Systems. In *Hierarchy Theory*, ed. H. H. Pattee. New York: G. Braziler.

Simon, H. A. 1973b. The Structure of Ill-Structured Problems. *Artificial Intelligence* 4:181–201.

Simon, H. A. 1975. The Functional Equivalence of Problem Solving Skills. *Cognitive Psychology* 7:268–88.

Simon, H. A. 1977. How Complex Are Complex Systems? *Proceedings of the 1976 Biennial Meeting of the Philosophy of Science Association* 2:507–22.

Simon, H. A. 1978. On the Forms of Mental Representation. In *Perception and Cognition: Issues in the Foundation of Psychology*, ed. C. W. Savage. Minneapolis: University of Minnesota Press.

Simon, H. A. 1981. *The Sciences of the Artificial*. 2d ed. Cambridge, Mass.: MIT Press.

Simon, H. A. 1983. Search and Reasoning in Problem Solving. *Artificial Intelligence* 21:7–29.

Simon, H. A., and A. Newell. 1958. Heuristic Problem Solving: The Next Advance in Operations Research. *Operations Research* 6 (1):1–10.

Simon, H. A., and P. A. Simon. 1962. Trial and Error Search in Solving Difficult Problems: Evidence from the Game of Chess. *Behavioral Science* 7 (4):425–29.

Skinner, B. F. 1953. *Science and Human Behavior*. New York: Macmillan.

Smith, B. C. 1996. *On the Origin of Objects*. Cambridge, Mass.: MIT Press. Forthcoming.

Smith, B. C. Forthcoming. *The Middle Distance: An Essay on Computation and Intentionality*. Cambridge, Mass.: MIT Press.

Smith, N. R., and M. B. Franklin, eds. 1979. *Symbolic Functioning in Childhood*. Hillsdale, N.J.: Lawrence Erlbaum.

Smolensky, P. 1986. Information Processing in Dynamical Systems: Foundations of Harmony Theory. In *Parallel Distributed Processing: Explorations in the Microstructures of Cognition*. Vol. 1, Foundations, ed. D. E. Rumelhart and J. L. McClelland. Cambridge, Mass.: MIT Press.

Smolensky, P. 1987a. The Constituent Structure of Connectionist Mental States: A Reply to Fodor and Pylyshyn. *The Southern Journal of Philosophy* 26:137–53.

Smolensky, P. 1987b. *On Variable Binding and the Representation of Symbolic Structures in Connectionist Systems*. Tech. report no. CU-CS-355-87. Dept. of Computer Science, University of Colorado, Boulder.

Smolensky, P. 1988. On the Proper Treatment of Connectionism. *Behavioral and Brain Sciences* 11:1–74.

Smythe, W. E. 1984. Psychology and the Traditions of Symbolization. In *Cognitive Processes in the Perception of Art*, ed. W. R. Crozier and A. J. Chapman. Amsterdam (North-Holland): Elsevier Science Publishers.

Snodgrass, J. G. 1980. Towards a Model for Picture and Word Processing. In *Processing of Visible Language 2*, ed. P. A. Kolers, M. E. Wrolstad, and H. Bouma. New York: Plenum Press.

Snodgrass, J. G. 1984. Concepts and Their Surface Representations. *Journal of Verbal Learning and Verbal Behavior* 23:3–22.

Snodgrass, J. G., and M. Vanderwart. 1980. A Standardized Set of 260 Pictures: Norms for Name Agreement, Image Agreement, Familiarity, and Visual Complexity. *Journal of Experimental Psychology: Human Learning and Memory* 6 (2):174–215.

Stefik, M. 1981. Planning with Constraints (Molgen: Part 1). *Artificial Intelligence* 16:111–40.

Stich, S. 1983. *From Folk Psychology to Cognitive Science: The Case against Beliefs*. Cambridge, Mass.: MIT Press.

Talmy, L. 1983. How Language Structures Space. In *Spatial Orientation: Theory, Research and Application*, ed. H. L. Pick and L. P. Acredolo. New York: Plenum Press.

Talmy, L. 1988. The Relation of Grammar to Cognition. In *Topics in Cognitive Linguistics*, ed. B. Rudzka-Ostyn. Amsterdam: John Benjamins.

Tank, D. W., and J. J. Hopfield. 1987. Collective Computation in Neuronlike Circuits. *Scientific American* 257 (6):104–14.

Tolman, E. C. 1932. *Purposive Behavior in Animals and Men*. New York: Appleton-Century-Crofts.

Treisman, A. 1988. Features and Objects: The Fourteenth Bartlett Lecture. *Quarterly Journal of Experimental Psychology* 40A:201–37.

Tulving, E., and W. Donaldson, eds. 1972. *Organization of Memory*. New York: Academic Press.

Tversky, A., and D. Kahneman. 1974. Judgment under Uncertainty: Heuristics and Biases. *Science* 185:1124–31.

Tversky, A., and D. Kahneman. 1981. The Framing of Decisions and the Psychology of Choice. *Science* 211:453–58.

Tye, M. 1984. The Debate about Mental Imagery. *The Journal of Philosophy* 81 (11):678–91.

Ullman, D. G., T. G. Dietterich, and L. A. Stauffer. 1988. *A Model of the Mechanical Design Process Based on Empirical Data.* Tech. report no. DPRG-88-1. Dept. of Mechanical Engineering, Oregon State University.

Ullman, D. G., L. A. Stauffer, and T. G. Dietterich. 1987. Preliminary Results of an Experimental Study of the Mechanical Design Process. In *NSF Workshop on Design Theory and Methodology.* Oakland, Calif.: National Science Foundation.

Vanderwart, M. 1984. Priming by Pictures in Lexical Decision. *Journal of Verbal Learning and Verbal Behavior* 23:67–83.

Vosniadou, S., and A. Ortony, eds. 1989. *Similarity and Analogical Reasoning.* Cambridge: Cambridge University Press.

Wade, J. W. 1977. *Architecture, Problems and Purposes: Architectural Design as a Basic Problem-Solving Process.* New York: John Wiley and Sons.

Wapner, W., and H. Gardner. 1981. Profiles of Symbol-Reading Skills in Organic Patients. *Brain and Language* 12:303–12.

Warrington, E. K. 1982. Neuropsychological Studies of Object Recognition. *Philosophical Transaction of the Royal Society London B* 298:15–33.

Wegner, P. 1968. *Programming Languages, Information Structures, and Machine Organization.* New York: McGraw-Hill.

Whorf, L. B. 1956. *Language, Thought and Reality.* Cambridge, Mass.: MIT Press.

Winograd, T. 1973. A Procedural Model of Language Understanding. In *Computer Models of Thought and Language,* ed. R. C. Schank and K. M. Colby. San Francisco: W. H. Freeman.

Winograd, T. 1983. *Language as a Cognitive Process.* Vol. 1, Syntax. Reading, Mass.: Addison-Wesley.

Index